A Century of Celluloid Dolls

by Shirley Buchholz

All photographs unless otherwise credited are by John Axe

OPPOSITE PAGE: Close-up of rare celluloid lady of fashion. See *Illustration 4* for description.

Printed in the United States of America

ISBN: 0-87588-200-0

Table of Contents

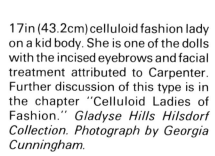

18in (45.7cm) rare celluloid lady of fashion. See *Illustration 4* for description.

17in (43.2cm) celluloid fashion lady on a kid body. She is one of the dolls with the incised eyebrows and facial treatment attributed to Carpenter. Further discussion of this type is in the chapter "Celluloid Ladies of Fashion." *Gladyse Hills Hilsdorf Collection. Photograph by Georgia Cunningham.*

The 13in (33cm) two-faced doll has celluloid faces and a cloth and wood combination for the body. The head swivels around so the doll has a choice of expressions. A rare item. Her companion is an all-original Käthe Kruse celluloid head on a cloth body that is marked on the foot. Another of this type is seen in *Illustration 341. Gladyse Hills Hilsdorf Collection. Photograph by Georgia Cunningham.*

11in (27.9cm) rare Topsy-Turvy Twins. One face is laughing and the other is crying. Cloth bodies; each twin has a set of arms with celluloid hands. *Gladyse Hills Hilsdorf Collection. Photograph by Georgia Cunningham.*

Acknowledgments

There are many people to thank for sharing their dolls, their time and their talents to make this book possible. Among them are: Juanita Acklin; Betsey, Ray and Carolyn Baker; Robert Beckett; Margaret Benike; Pauline Bonnett; Irene and Steve Brown; Rosemarye Bunting; Penny Caswell; Janet and John Clendenien; the Colemans; Georgia Cunningham; Lois Fida; Betty Grimes; Marion Holt; Sara Kocher; Katherine Malcomb; Richard Merrill; Ursula Mertz; Becky Moncrief; Lillian Mosley; Raymond J. Mouly; Mary Piper; Jennie Polley; Maurine Popp; Jean Pritchard; A. Christian Revi; Faye and Jim Rodolfos; Anili Scavini; Patricia and John Schoonmaker; Yolanda Simonelli; Mary Skolfield; Marjorie Smith; Mary Lu Thompson; Z. Frances Walker; Ruth Whittier; Judith Whorton; Margaret Wirgau; Edward and Berdine Wyffels; and Evelyn Yalsch.

Others I am indebted to are: Hobby House Press, Inc.; The Margaret Woodbury Strong Museum; Museum of American Architecture and Decorative Arts; PPG Industries; and Ralph's Antique Doll Museum.

I especially want to thank a dear friend, John Axe, and my daughter, Jane, for the many hours they spent photographing the dolls; another special friend, Joyce Kintner, for drawing all of the trademarks; my editor, Donna H. Felger, for her patience; my friend and publisher, Gary Ruddell, for his never-failing good humor; and my husband, Ed, for all of his assistance with the manuscript. I am grateful to them all, more than they know.

Dedication

To Ed, who never complains when I drop everything to work and play in the world of dolls.

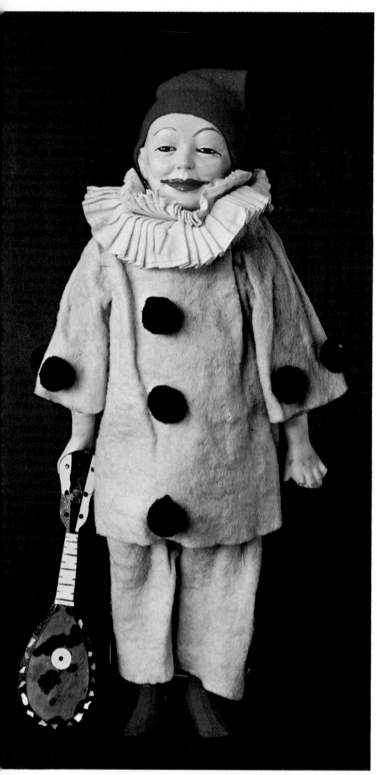

A group of celluloid toys. The large ram is a rattle. It is 5¾in (14.7cm) across. It is marked with the American Indian head trademark shown in *Illustration 23*. The 3in (7.6cm) box holds a tiny china doll, a sponge, a celluloid soap dish and mirror and a little powder puff with a celluloid handle. The 2½in (6.4cm) celluloid plate of cake is marked with the trademark in *Illustration 270*. The doll's accessories, mirrors, combs and tray are unmarked. *Photograph by Jane Buchholz.*

Celluloid character animals. See *Illustration 283* for description. *Photograph by Jane Buchholz.*

Pierrot. See *Illustration 117* for description. *Photograph by Jane Buchholz.*

ABOVE: Japanese walking doll and "Bonzo." See *Illustration 319* and *283* for descriptions. *Photograph by Jane Buchholz.*

ABOVE RIGHT: All-celluloid scout with removable hat. He is described in *Illustration 245*.

BELOW RIGHT: Two Japanese dolls with molded clothes. The colonial man is described in *Illustration 243*. The little boy with a banjo is 6in (15.2cm). He is unmarked, but the red brows denote Japanese. *Photograph by Jane Buchholz.*

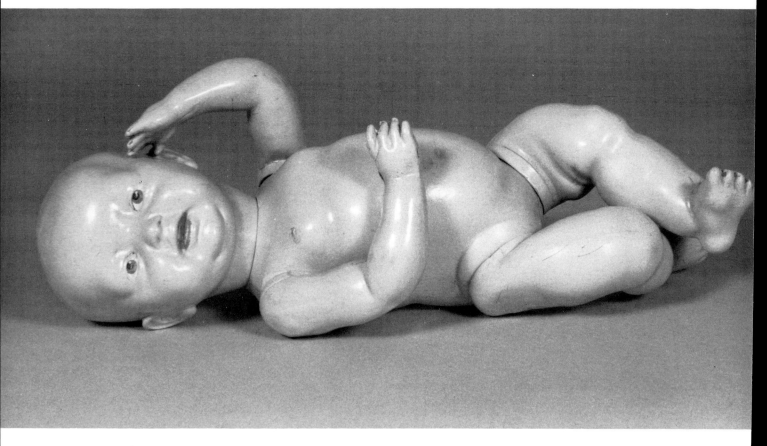

10½in (26.7cm) Parsons-Jackson baby of strong Biskoline, jointed at the neck, shoulders and hips. These dolls have an exaggerated ball on the body and the socket is on the limb. The mouth is open/closed and the eyes are painted blue. The head is marked with a stork and the body is marked with the complete trademark.

Introduction

When someone asked the mountain climber why he had struggled so long to get to the top of the mountain, his reply was, "Because it was there." I can say that about this little book. It has bothered me for a long time that there are so few lines written about celluloid dolls and comparatively few photographs of them in the books we have at our disposal; that sometime in the future collectors might ask, "What were they like?" and have no answer.

Celluloid dolls are part of the history of our hobby and as such should be given a bit of recognition. They are fragile and are disappearing at an alarming rate, possibly because they have not been held in great esteem by those who may have found them packed among possessions in an attic. If they had not been packed away with care, their discovery by a later generation usually resulted in their being tossed away, for often all that remained was a squashed doll or a tissue paper full of shards.

It is human nature, though, to preserve something we have loved or something for which we have spent a good deal of money, so examples of many of the types still remain. I have gathered some of them here for you to see and to learn about, if you wish. There are lovely ones to enjoy and funny ones to laugh at. I do not ask that you love them or that you buy them for your collections. Just be aware of them. Think of all the hugs they have received and of all the kisses that have been planted on those little cheeks. Give them their place in our world of dolls.

There is not a great deal of documentation available about celluloid dolls, and I am not sure that it is even necessary. Dolls should be collected and enjoyed for what they are, not for the labels they wear.

Over the years romantic stories have sprung up about some dolls, sometimes the result of a casual observation made by a person considered an expert at the time. Repetition has given credibility to many a dealer's sales pitch, and fond recollections about "Grandmother's Doll" have innocently blurred fact. What information finds its way into print is usually considered to be gospel simply because it is the printed word. As the man in the song said, "It ain't necessarily so." Authors make honest mistakes, typesetters err, sources are sometimes overly enthusiastic; what is originally written often receives slightly different interpretation each time it is repeated -- all these are the hazards of ever putting anything on paper. Let's face it; what is written will not and should not diminish or exalt a doll. It should stand on its own merit, not on a label.

This book is presented to you with the idea that those who are interested in celluloid dolls may have the available information at hand, with the hope that those who are not interested in them may become aware of them in a different way, and with the feeling of relief that comes when the climber reaches the top of that mountain.

Shirley H. Buchholz

A little Dutch boy and his dog. See *Illustration 161* for description. *Photograph by Jane Buchholz.*

A French doll dressed in an oriental costume. See *Illustration 178* for description. *Photograph by Jane Buchholz.*

A little German girl from the World War II era. See *Illustration 324* for description. *Photograph by Jane Buchholz.*

The taller 20in (50.8cm) girl is all-celluloid, jointed at hip and shoulder. She has molded blonde hair and blue glass eyes. Her clothes are all original. Mark: "(crowned mermaid)//51½." Her little friend is made of heavy celluloid, jointed at neck, hip and shoulder. He is 16in (40.6cm) tall and is marked with the symbol of König-Wernicke, "K W//W//29/9 inside a circle." *Gladyse Hills Hilsdorf Collection. Photograph by Georgia Cunningham.*

The Madame Hendren boy is described in *Illustration 130.* The 19in (48.3cm) little girl with him is an unusual doll with her molded blonde snail braids and glass eyes. She is on an Amberg Victory Doll body. Mark: "(turtle in diamond)//45." *Gladyse Hills Hilsdorf Collection. Photograph by Georgia Cunningham.*

The illustrations in this book are grouped for reference by type. Naturally, some dolls fall into more than one category, so the most outstanding characteristic is used for the primary grouping. A doll with molded clothes would be found under that heading rather than "All-Celluloid With Straight Legs," for instance, but a *Kewpie* with molded clothes would be located under *"Kewpies"* (Tinies and *Kewpie*-Types).

This is only the author's method of categorizing the dolls for this book. It should not be considered an authority for any other purpose, such as entering dolls in competition. That is each individual's responsibility.

Within each group an attempt has been made to present the dolls according to mark or manufacturer, and to keep those of certain countries together. It is not possible in all cases, of course.

Some readers may wonder why anyone would bother to include the little "cheapies" in a book. In most cases they are ugly and of poor quality, but these, too, are the things children played with. They are part of the story of celluloid dolls. They were considered toys of the moment, not "good toys." They were cheap and disposable, discarded without much feeling when they broke or when a child tired of them.

It was thus in the cases of so many "everyday" items of the past. Today we have record of many quality possessions for they were carefully preserved. Among the rarities in the world of antiques are those everyday articles that no one really thought much of as they tossed them out.

As the total number of dolls in the world increases, the number of celluloid dolls is decreasing as they are discarded by non-collectors or as accidents befall them. They will one day, many believe, be quite rare. Fine examples, just as with any other antique, will always be in demand and command better prices than dolls of lesser quality.

A Little Bit of History

It probably would be safe to assume that of the total number of dolls manufactured since the middle of the 19th century, celluloid dolls were a very small percentage. Another seemingly safe assumption would be that an even smaller percentage survived because, although they were advertised as unbreakable, celluloid dolls proved to be quite fragile. This may be one of the reasons that they have not previously found favor with many collectors.

Indeed, in the early doll books of the 1940s they are scarcely mentioned, and by the 1960s Clara Fawcett in her book, *Dolls, A New Guide For Collectors,* devotes only two pages of type, one photograph and some line drawings to the subject. She ends her chapter with an observation that old and unusual celluloid dolls are worth collecting, but are secondary collectors' items. It was no doubt a valid reflection of the thinking of that period, but today's collectors are looking at celluloid with a different eye. They see that just as bisque, for example, has on the one hand dolls of exquisite beauty and quality and on the other hand some perfectly miserable examples, so does celluloid.

A comparison of prices in old catalogs will show that the cost of early celluloid dolls was equal to or more than that of comparable bisque dolls.

Celluloid, originally a patented name, is now a generic term. Just as the word "Kleenex" has come to mean a facial tissue, so has "celluloid" become to doll collectors the accepted word that describes a doll made of a certain type of material. Celluloid is in reality an early plastic.

Late in the 19th century the introduction of synthetic and semisynthetic plastic materials had considerable economic and social impact on the daily lives of people. Prior to this time, common articles such as combs and toothbrushes were only available to most people in crude wooden form. The skill and labor required to make them from bone or ivory made the cost almost prohibitive, but then, as legend has it, an accident in a laboratory provided an important contribution.

Cellulose nitrate had first been prepared by Braconnot in 1832, but the man who developed the preferred method of manufacturing it was a scientist, C. F. Schoenbein. While working in his laboratory one day in 1845, he spilled a flask of nitric and sulphuric acids on the floor and wiped it up with his wife's cotton apron which he then hung to dry in front of a fire. The resulting explosion made it quite clear to Mr. Schoenbein that he had just invented guncotton.[1]

The military world greeted his invention with enthusiasm for it did not cause the dense smoke that gunpowder did. Now the generals could SEE whom they slaughtered!

Fortunately, there were other more peaceful interests in nitrated cellulose. A French scientist, Louis Menard, developed collodian,[2] a transparent film used as a dressing for cuts and wounds and on photographic plates, but the first use for everyday objects was achieved by Alexander Parkes, an Englishman.

---

1. A highly explosive cellulose nitrate made by digesting clean cotton in a mixture of one part nitric acid and three parts sulfuric acid.
2. A soluble guncotton dissolved in a mixture of ether and alcohol.

A native of Birmingham, England, Parkes was a very busy man. Not only did he hold 80 patents, he was also the father of 20 children. In 1856 Parkes attempted to waterproof woven fabrics by treating them with cellulose nitrate, but his major discovery was that the addition of castor oil and camphor to nitrated cellulose would soften it at a reasonably low temperature and it could be molded. He very modestly named it "Parkesine" and in the Great Exhibition at the Crystal Palace in 1862, he won a medal for excellence of product.

Commercially Parkesine was a failure, but it was the beginning of the plastics industry.

The next step in the development of celluloid came in America as a direct result of a worldwide shortage of ivory. Phelan and Callendar, manufacturers of billiard balls, offered a prize of $10,000.00 (a handsome sum in those days) to anyone who could invent a substitute for ivory billiard balls.

John Wesley Hyatt, Jr., of Albany, New York, experimented with Parkesine in an effort to win the prize, which he did not. But he did establish the Albany Billiard Ball Company which used a mixture of gum shellac and pulp to make balls which were coated with nitrocellulose. This was an interesting combination chemically. Hyatt later reported receiving a letter from a saloon keeper in Colorado. It seems that occasionally the violent contact of the balls would result in a small explosion. The proprietor did not really object to the noise, but to the fact that instantly every man in the room pulled a gun!

That prompted Hyatt to investigate the properties of nitrocellulose in more detail and he finally solved the manufacturing problems. He was the first to work with nitrocellulose and camphor in a plastic mass. He called his invention "celluloid" and Letters of Patent No. 91,341 were issued to John W. Hyatt, Jr., of Albany, New York, and Isaiah S. Hyatt of Rockford, Illinois, (his brother) on June 15, 1869. Celluloid was the first successful synthetic plastic.[3] Many items that previously had been fashioned by hand could now be mass produced. Items such as combs, knife handles, tooth-brushes, thimbles and the like were manufactured faster and cheaper and so were available to more people.

Manufacturing products from pyroxylin plastics[4] involved three basic procedures: compression molding, injection molding and extrusion. Hyatt patented all three. A type of blow molding was first used to manu-facture toys from celluloid. Two sheets of celluloid were clamped together between the two halves of a mold. These sheets were heated and air or steam pressure was introduced between them. Thus, they were blown out to make contact with the mold surfaces. When they were cooled and set, they could be removed from the mold.

---

3. To be scientifically accurate, it was not a true synthetic, but rather, a chemically modified natural polymer.
4. Pyroxylin: a nitrocellulose compound containing fewer nitro groups than guncotton.

KID BODY DOLLS WITH LIGHT AND DARK HAIR

HIP JOINTED,

With Shoulder and Elbow Joints, Bisque Forearms, Bisque Head, Moving Eyes, Dimpled Cheeks, Character Face, Sewed Mohair Wig, Shoes and Stockings.

C63641—19 inches in length; 1-12 dozen in box.......Dozen 27.00
C63644—21 inches in length; 1-12 dozen in box.......Dozen 30.00
C63648—22½ inches in length; 1-12 dozen in box ....Dozen 39.00

C63641 to C63648

FULL JOINTED,

Jointed Hip, Knees, Elbows and Shoulders, Celtid Forearms and Legs, Celtid Heads, Moving Eyes with Eyelashes, Parted Mohair Wig, Shoes and Stockings.

C63940—15½ inches in length; 1-12 dozen in box....Dozen 27.00
C63942—19 inches in length; 1-12 dozen in box.......Dozen 36.00
C63944—23½ inches in length; 1-12 dozen in box....Dozen 48.00

C63940 to C63944

HIP AND KNEE JOINTED.

Cork Stuffed, Celtid Head, Moving Eyes, Mohair Wig, Side Parted, Shoes and Stockings.

C64006—17 inches in length; 1-12 dozen in box......Dozen 17.00
C64007—19 inches in length; 1-12 dozen in box......Dozen 24.00
C64008—23 inches in length; 1-12 dozen in box......Dozen 36.00

C64006 to C64008

HIP AND KNEE JOINTED.

Cork Stuffed.

Extra Stout Bodies with Celtid Heads, Arms and Legs, Moving Eyes, Eyelashes, Absolutely Unbreakable.

Hip and knee, shoulder and elbow joints, rivet jointed; finest dull finish celtid heads; finest sewed angora wigs, side parted with ribbon bow; openwork socks, sateen shoes.

C64013 to C64020

	Length, inches	Dozen in box	Dozen
C64013.	17	1/12	39.00
C64014.	18½	1/12	48.00
C64016.	21½	1/12	66.00
C64018.	24½	1/12	84.00
C64020.	27	1/12	120.00

FINEST FULL HIP, KNEE AND ARM JOINTED,

Cork Stuffed,

Extra Stout Dolls, Moving Eyes with Eyelashes, Finest Sewed Wigs. Full kid legs; rivet jointed, bisque arms; finest bisque heads; finest side parted full sewed angora wigs, with ribbon bow; fine molded hands; openwork stockings, assorted; sateen shoes.

C64050 to C64055

	Length, inches	Dozen in box	Dozen
C64050.	18	1/12	30.00
C64051.	19	1/12	36.00
C64052.	21	1/12	48.00
C64053.	23½	1/12	60.00
C64054.	25	1/12	78.00
C64055.	28	1/12	90.00

Illustration 1. *1914 Marshall Field & Company Doll Catalog* reprinted by Hobby House Press, Inc.

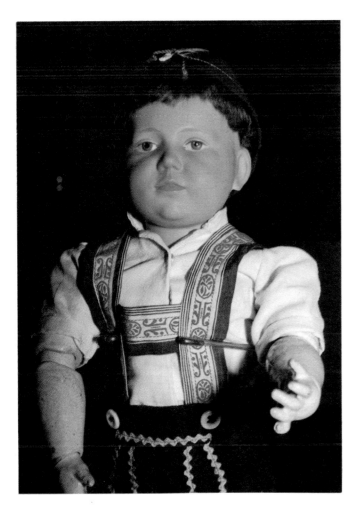

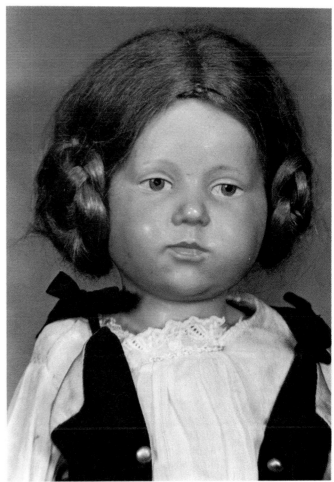

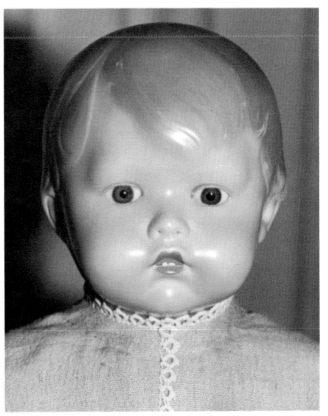

ABOVE: K★R 301, "Peter." See *Illustration 141* for description.

ABOVE RIGHT: K★R 301, "Marie." See *Illustration 142* for description. *Photograph by Steve Brown.*

BELOW RIGHT: *Baby Bo-Kaye* designed by Joseph Kallus. See *Illustration 128* for description. *Photograph by Beverly Port.*

OPPOSITE PAGE: A K★R all-celluloid girl and an Irwin baby. See *Illustration 92* for description. *Photograph by Jane Buchholz.*

W. B. Carpenter filed application for a patent for a "method of coloring the eyebrows, etc. of celluloid dolls" May 28, 1880. He was granted Patent No. 235,933 December 28, 1880. It was a method of incising the celluloid and working color into it. The patent may be found in the section "Patents." Hyatt's patent and the 1881 Lefferts and Carpenter patent No. 237,559 concerning a celluloid doll may also be found there.

According to Beverly Ann Metzger in her article in *The Antique Trader,* April, 23, 1980, in addition to Hyatt's Celluloid Manufacturing Company, there were two other major companies located in the East in the 1870s. They were The Celluloid Novelty Company and The Celluloid Fancy Goods Company. They made numerous articles of jewelry and items such as key rings, games, thimbles and the like.

In 1891 Hyatt's company absorbed their competitors and reorganized as The Celluloid Company. In 1918 it became known as The American Cellulose and Chemical Company. Hyatt died in 1920 and in 1927 his company became known as The Celanese Corporation of America. It is now known as The Celanese Corporation.

The Arlington Company in New Jersey manufactured celluloid products called "Pyrolin." DuPont purchased the company in 1915 and continued to produce pyroxylin plastics under that name until shortly after World War II.

For over 50 years celluloid was a major industry in America. One of the essential ingredients was camphor. The Japanese had a monopoly on the world's supply of camphor and from 1868 to 1907 the price rose from 7½¢ to 76½¢ per pound and peaked at $4.00 per pound in 1918. Camphor trees were not able to be grown commercially in this country, so expensive methods of producing synthetic camphor were developed. As soon as factories for production were built, the wily Japanese dropped prices and many companies went bankrupt. However, it did lead to other synthetic plasticizers and the birth of what is considered the true plastics industry.

Because there is little documentation, it would be difficult to say definitely when the first celluloid dolls and toys were made, but we do know that the Hyatts were making celluloid in 1869.

Mary Hillier in her article "Don't Despise Those Celluloid Dolls" in *Doll Reader* (October/November 1980) relates that the famous Rheinische Gummi und Celluloid Fabrik Co. of Mannheim, Neckarau, Bavaria, was founded in 1873 by the Hessian merchants Lenel, Bensinger and Company to manufacture rubber goods and that Fritz Jander instituted production of celluloid for them about 1880. A disastrous fire, one of the hazards of making celluloid, destroyed the main factory building in 1885 and in the ensuing reconstruction, the manufacture of dolls was added when the owners realized the commercial possibilities of the material for artistic molding.

Their trademark was the tortoise or, in German "Schildkröte." It denoted the long life and durability of the product. It was first registered in 1889 without the diamond frame. In 1899 they used the tortoise (turtle) in

W. B. CARPENTER
Method of Coloring the Eyebrows, &c., of Celluloid Dolls.

No. 235,933.   Patented Dec. 28, 1880.

M. C. LEFFERTS & W. B. CARPENTER.
Celluloid Doll.

No. 237,559.   Patented Feb. 8, 1881.

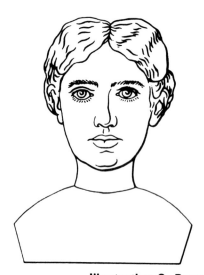
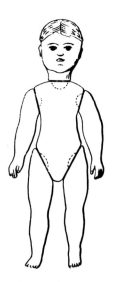

Illustration 2. Patent drawings for the Carpenter and Lefferts and Carpenter patents concerning celluloid dolls. These were the first patents we have knowledge of for celluloid dolls in the United States. *Photograph by Juanita Acklin.*

a diamond frame as a trademark and registered it for dolls of pyrolylin compounds. That year they also obtained a German patent for molded doll heads and in 1905 another for a method of inserting glass eyes in celluloid heads.

The Rheinische Gummi und Celluloid Fabrik Co. continued to make dolls of celluloid and registered their turtle trademark in France and Great Britain in 1914 and in the United States in 1915. Collectors will probably find more dolls with the turtle mark than any other.

Rheinische Gummi also made dolls for other companies. Dolls have been found with the marks of firms such as Kestner and Kämmer & Rheinhardt in conjunction with the turtle.

The front of a broken shoulder plate was found to have "US Pat. No. 1,645,275" stamped with blue ink. The back is marked: "GERMANY// (turtle in diamond frame//12."

The application for this patent was filed September 29, 1926, and it was granted to Albert Beyler of Mannheim-Neckarau, Germany, October 11, 1927. It was a patent for the manufacture of "dolls and parts thereof from cellulose derivatives" and was assigned to Rheinische Gummi und Celluloid Fabrik Co. of Mannheim.

Beyler explained that the porcelain industry as well as the celluloid industry had been seeking methods of making more realistic looking dolls' heads and limbs. They tried various methods such as painting the inside or outside of transparent celluloid or by dipping or lacquering white celluloid and finally adopted the method of adding the flesh color to the celluloid mass.

Beyler's invention was to use a background of cream-white color with a greenish tinge ("the ashen-greenish appearance of the flesh of a corpse of the white race") and to spray blood red coloring over it, thus producing "a relatively dull....cream-like and rosy skin of the white....race." This was probably the product Mary Hillier referred to in *Doll Reader* as MIBLU -- the initials standing for Milch and Blut, (milk and blood) referring to the rosy complexions typical of the German child. In some cases this material took on a bluish tinge as it aged.

Although Rheinische Gummi was one of the largest firms, the manufacture of this new product was not confined to one area or one type of product. At the International Exhibition in Paris, France, in 1878 a medal was awarded to the Compagnie Francaise du Celluloid who supplied the makers of cinematographic film.

A French patent (No. 182616) was granted in 1887 to Valmore Boitel for the manufacture of celluloid heads. He claimed that until then they had been made of wood, papier-mâché, rubber or bisque.

The Paris firm, Petitcolin, was founded in 1902 and had factories at Oyannaux. By 1914 they had factories at Lilas, Seine, Étain and Meuse. They also had a shop in Paris. They specialized in baby dolls but were suppliers of the girl dolls that were used for costuming in regional dress. Among their customers were Madam Le Minor of Pont L'Abbé (Finistère) and Martel.

Illustration 3. Trademarks of the Rheinische Gummi und Celluloid Fabrik Co. The components of these two marks may be found in various forms. "Schutz-Marke" is the German word for "trademark."

Madam Le Minor was considered one of France's most famous doll makers, but to be accurate, she only costumed them. She designed and created costumes for dolls in provincial dress that were elaborate and luxurious. They represented the clothing worn by the French in the various sections of Brittany. She was in business in the 1930s, and by the 1950s had earned enough respect to have her little creations called works of art by those interested in dolls.

Dolls in regional dress have always been popular in France as souvenirs. This is probably because the clothing is so unique and colorful. With the exception of the dolls made by Jumeau, almost all the dolls used in this manner were made of celluloid.

The Nobel dolls, products of Société Nobel Francaise whose trademark was the initials SNF in a diamond, were used for regional costuming by Les Fetiches Nicois, located in Nice, France, and also by Martel. The SNF trademark was registered in 1939 and again in 1960.

One of the largest producers of celluloid in France was Société Industrielle du Celluloid, headed by the manufacturers Neumann and Marx whose initials appear in the trademark, the winged dragon or "wyvern." They used the tradename "Sicoid" and "Sicoine."

In the book *All Dolls are Collectible* by Genevieve Angione and Judith Whorton there is a photograph of a "late celluloid" doll that they term "probably the last doll made by Jumeau." It has sleep eyes with synthetic eyelashes, one-stroke brows and a bright red mouth. They say that the quality is poor and the best thing about the head is the name "Jumeau" embossed on the back of it.

ABOVE LEFT: A lovely French costume doll by Le Minor. See *Illustration 175* for description.

ABOVE RIGHT: Celluloid head on a cloth body and dressed in a Swedish costume. See *Illustration 153* for description. *Photograph by Jane Buchholz.*

BELOW LEFT: A pair of all-celluloid dolls in Tyrolian costume. See *Illustration 150* for description. *Photograph by Jane Buchholz.*

OPPOSITE PAGE: A beautiful Kestner baby. See *Illustration 32* for description. *Photograph by Jane Buchholz.*

The period around the turn of the century found many firms experimenting with celluloid. It was a natural selection of material for dolls and toys since it was washable and did not shatter as the bisque and china did; nor did it flake and peel like composition. Toys for the bath were especially popular.

By the second decade there is record of celluloid dolls also being made in Poland (P. R. Zast), in Hungary (Ignac Rédo), in Holland, Japan, the United States and probably most of the other industrial nations.

The properties that made celluloid desirable for toys were balanced by those that were not. It proved to be fragile, fading and flammable. Heavier weight celluloid would crack and shatter under force and the items made of thinner celluloid were quite squashable. If left in bright sunlight, it bleached and became brittle. Too much heat would cause it to soften or warp. At 100 degrees centigrade it would decompose. Nevertheless, it was popular for 50 years and then, like other threatened species, evolved into another form to survive -- the one we generically term "plastics."

By its very composition, what we call celluloid may be many things depending on a multitude of processes. Unfortunately, the manufacturers were not terribly interested in what collectors of the future might want to call their products and simply proceeded to innovate in the interest of gross sales and net profits.

Meaningful production of celluloid dolls spans a period of about 60 years. They were made by a variety of manufacturers in as many countries and most are marked in some manner as to country of origin. Many have trademarks, some of which have been identified.

The very earliest celluloid dolls resembled ivory or the pale bisque they were copying. Searching for a more lifelike appearance led to tinting the material with flesh tones. The dolls were heavier and of a glossier celluloid and the color tends to be a yellowish-tan, although this could be the result of aging. Later dolls are comparatively lightweight, some with a matte finish and generally better flesh tones

Celluloid dolls very often have painted eyes, but some of the better quality dolls have glass eyes that can be stationary, sleep or even flirting. Kämmer & Reinhardt used flirting eyes in their dolls of the 1920s. Difficulty in obtaining glass eyes from Germany in the days of the World War I led to the development of celluloid eyes.

These dolls may have either molded hair or wigs. Larger play dolls of better quality can be found with mohair or human hair wigs while the little dime store variety usually have molded hair, as do the dolls from Japan. The French used mohair wigs on many of their small dolls in provincial costume as well as on their larger models.

Celluloid dolls are jointed in as many ways as other types. Some of the dolls with celluloid heads on other type bodies have knee and elbow joints.

Most of the dolls were strung with elastic by knotting the ends and pushing the knots through holes or slits in the limbs. A note of caution to the reader: Celluloid dolls are very fragile and once broken are very difficult if not impossible to repair. They may be restrung with patience, care and a light touch. Do not try to pull the old knot out, but cut the elastic close to the limb and gently push it in. A small hemostat is an invaluable tool. Make a knot large enough to stay caught and gently work it into the hole or slit with the hemostat. Thread it through the body (here is where the patience comes in) and carefully pull it taut enough to hold the limbs in place. Clamp the elastic with a hemostat and tie another knot. Cut the remaining elastic free, leaving a tail which you will thread into the hole and, with another hemostat, work that knot into the other limb.

Celluloid dolls were most popular during the decade before World War I and through the 1920s. As the newer composition dolls made their appearance and as technology of the 1930s produced safer, more durable plastics, manufacture of these fragile playthings declined.

Dolls became heavier, stronger and not as flammable (one of celluloid's big drawbacks). The new methods of molding gave designers the ability to build into dolls durability and more efficient methods of stringing.

Other than small souvenir-type dolls, celluloid as we think of it had almost disappeared.

What we shall look at in this book are the dolls we call celluloid and the transition dolls that carry us over into what we think of as "plastic" dolls. We are not attempting to define celluloid or categorize it for any purpose. We simply want to make collectors more aware and appreciative of these fragile little members of the doll world.

Celluloid Ladies of Fashion

Because they are so rare, many doll collectors do not realize that the fashion type dolls with celluloid heads exist. Much speculation, but little documentation surrounds them. In the *Doll Collectors Manual 1956-1957* there is an excerpt from a letter from Mrs. F. M. Kasch of Chicago, Illinois, to Mrs. Richard Merrill, dated September 8, 1955. It concerns these dolls. Mrs. Kasch wrote: "You possess a doll like ours, the celluloid one. I am glad to know it is French as Janet Johl immediately said, but inasmuch as it came to us from an Eastern firm, we did not know. But I am convinced now that it is French as the firm imported shoe-horns and button-hooks from France. They had one dozen dolls made but found them too expensive and so gave them to some special customers and my father was one of them. Our doll is seventy-six years old, that much I know as my sister was not over nine years of age and would now be eighty-five."

A little calculation would date the Kasch doll about 1879, just about the time that William Carpenter would have been working on his idea for his method of "coloring eyebrows etc. of celluloid dolls." He applied for his patent May 28, 1880.

All of the swivel-head lady dolls we have pictures of seem to be finished in this manner. It is obvious that they bear a great resemblance to the so-called French Fashions of the period. The heads have open crowns with cork pates and are attached to the shoulder plates in the same manner as the bisque models. The heads have been found on both leather bodies and cloth bodies with leather arms. Who can say how they originally started out? Whether they were made in France or by an American firm remains a mystery, but surely if Mr. Carpenter developed his process and went to the trouble to patent it, the Celluloid Novelty Company planned to use it. It is not customary for an industry to patent a process they are not ready to use for someone else may make a slight change and use it first. It would have been a simple matter to make a mold from an available head. It was done all the time.

At the risk of incurring the wrath of collectors who think that it has to be French to be good, I would like to speculate. What do we know that is fact and not fantasy?

Fact: The Kasch doll is the only one we presently have record of that had remained in the same family. (Hopefully, we will learn of others.)

Fact: The doll "came from an Eastern firm."

Fact: They did not know "what it is" until Janet Johl told them it was French.

Fact: In 1955 Mrs. Kasch's sister would have been 85 years old.

Fact: The dolls closely resemble the bisque dolls of the day.

Fact: They are found on different types of bodies.

Illustration 4. 18in (45.7cm) A rare lady of fashion with a swivel head of celluloid that has the incised and colored brows and lashes described in the Carpenter patent. The shoulder plate, which had not been exposed to light over the years, is a warm flesh color. The head has darkened only slightly to the shade of old ivory. She has blown glass eyes with threaded gray-blue irises and black pupils and her brown human hair wig is attached to a cork pate. Some of her facial painting is gone, but there are still red dots at the nostrils and the corners of her eyes. A bit of paint remains on her lips, but cheek color has either faded or been washed away. None of this detracts, however, from her serene, smiling expression. She has been redressed in a costume made for another doll in the 1950s.

Illustration 5. A close-up of the doll in *Illustration 4* that shows the incised and colored celluloid around the eyes.

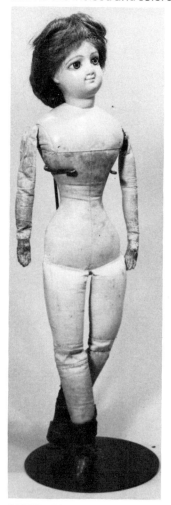

LEFT: Illustration 6. The fashion doll, undressed, showing her original cloth body with kid arms. She wears what seem to be original brown leather slippers without heels that tie around the ankle and red lace stockings.

RIGHT: Illustration 7. Back view of the undressed fashion doll showing body construction and her lovely old wig.

Fact: In the 1870s there were three major celluloid manufacturing firms located in the East.

Fact: W. B. Carpenter applied for a patent concerning finishing celluloid dolls' heads in May 1880, and the patent was granted December 28, 1880. It was assigned to "himself and to the Celluloid Novelty Company of New York, New York."

Fact: Lefferts and Carpenter applied for a patent concerning the manufacture of a celluloid doll January 7, 1881. It was granted February 8, 1881, and assigned to the Celluloid Manufacturing Company of New York, New York.

Fact: In the years 1880 and 1881 there were at least two major firms in the New York area that were interested enough in the manufacture of celluloid dolls to take out patents.

Fact: It was customary in the 1880s for department stores, doll hospitals, toy shops and wholesale toy dealers to carry as a regular line of stock all kinds of doll heads and bodies so that they could be purchased separately and assembled in the manner the buyer chose, or a broken part could be replaced.

Fact: Celluloid was a fragile material.

Fact: The largest firm making celluloid in Germany did not commence to make dolls until after 1885.

Fact: Most of the French firms that made celluloid dolls came into being around the turn of the century. Boitel patent for heads 1887.

Fact: Manufacturers of dolls and toys were in business to make money.

Fact: Manufacturers of celluloid were in business to make money.

Fact: In the heyday of the French lady dolls, the European factories were turning out bisque heads by the thousands every week, much of the output destined for the American market.

Fact: If there is a hot item on the market, everyone wants a piece of the action.

Fact: In the early 1880s lady dolls were hot items in the toy market.

Theory: The product known as celluloid was very new. Articles had only been made from it for about ten years. The manufacturers, ever searching for new applications for a new product and thus making more money for their businesses, decided to try their hands at making dolls. Now comes the fantasy. The setting is the office of a well-known celluloid firm in the late 1870s. Two members of the firm are having a discussion.

Marsh: "What else can we make out of this stuff, Bill? We need to expand."

OPPOSITE PAGE: Illustration 8. This 19in (48.3cm) early French Fashion-type celluloid lady has the typical swivel head and kid body of the lady dolls of the period. The head is heavy ivory-colored celluloid that has been finished in a manner like that described in the Carpenter patent. Her incised brows and lashes and luminous blue glass eyes are outstanding features. She has her original wig of blonde mohair. This fine example of this type doll is from the collection of the Madeline Merrill and is described in *Handbooks of Collectible Dolls,* copyright 1977. Used by permission. *Photograph by Richard Merrill.*

Illustration 9. The doll from the Merrill collection after she had been recostumed by her owner. *Handbooks of Collectible Dolls,* copyright 1977. *Photograph by Richard Merrill.*

Bill: "I'll look into it. What's moving on the market?"

Marsh: "Toys. They're always good. There are always kids and they need toys."

Bill: "What about dolls? Every little girl in this country needs lots of dolls."

Marsh: "We make combs and brushes. How are we going to make a doll? Where do we get the molds. I don't want to invest a lot of money in having a design made until I know it will work!"

Bill: "Leave it to me. I know a little doll shop nearby. I'll run down and get a few heads and see if we can make a decent mold. Let's just stick to the heads. They make bodies that have arms and everything. No need to go to that extent; we can probably buy them fairly cheap from the supplier."

Marsh: "Good thinking, Bill. Get to it and keep in touch."

Several weeks later: The factory mold maker has completed the experimental molds and a few heads have been produced. Bill does not like the general appearance of the item and devises a new method for applying the color and the brows and lashes. More expensive. He orders a short production run. The dolls

look great. A quick order goes to the wholesale supplier of doll bodies. He has to hire a few more people to assemble the dolls. Another meeting.

Marsh: "Well, Bill, I see you have those doll heads on the line."

Bill: "Yep."

Marsh: "How do you think they'll move?"

Bill: "I don't know. We lost a lot in assembly."

Marsh: "What's the bottom line?"

Bill: "Marsh, we just can't make them as cheaply as they ship them in from Europe. By the time we get the eyes and wigs for the darn things and put them on bodies, they cost about twice what I can buy the model for! Maybe it wasn't such a hot idea. Do you think we can sell the rights to the technology?"

Marsh: "Okay, okay, so we sell the rights, but what are we going to do with the rest of the dolls? They are too expensive to move retail!"

Bill: "Let's send them as gifts to some of our customers and tell them they are a limited edition from France. That gets 'em every time."

Fade. Curtain.

There is no doubt that these lady dolls are rare. Although legend persists that they numbered about a dozen, the fact that the author knows the whereabouts of at least eleven of them would negate that claim. It would mean that 92% of the production of dolls made over 100 years ago had survived intact. Hardly likely. The exact number would, of course, be interesting to document. It probably was a small number as production of dolls goes and an exceedingly small percentage of the thousands of dolls that were made in that Golden Age of Dolls.

Illustration 10. This 17in (43.2cm) fashion lady wears her original pink gown and straw hat. She has blue glass eyes and a brown mohair wig. The pale ivory-colored head is on a kid body with individually wired fingers. Cost must have been the reason for the small number of these lovely dolls reaching the market. It could not have been lack of appeal, for they are every bit as beautiful as the bisque dolls they copied. Their appearance was probably more warm and lifelike. *Marion Holt Collection. Photograph by Frances Walker.*

Illustration 11. This 15in (38.1cm) charmer in her original taffeta and velvet costume has blue glass eyes and a brown mohair wig. The modeling of the ears seems to be different from the Merrill doll and they are pierced-in to hold the seemingly original earrings. It is possible that the ears were pierced after the doll was made, when she was originally costumed or even later. The hands of her kid body have fingers indicated by stitching instead of the individually wired fingers of the other dolls shown. This is merely a point of information, not a vital statistic. Heads were attached to bodies at hand by the assembler who may have been a commercial producer or a mother or doll repair shop. Collectors must always be aware that somewhere in a doll's past the body or head may have been changed. Sometimes it is obvious; sometimes it is not. Sometimes it is important (when you are getting the "all original" sales pitch); sometimes it is not, (when you love the doll, regardless, and simply do not feel it is important). *Courtesy of the Margaret Woodbury Strong Museum.*

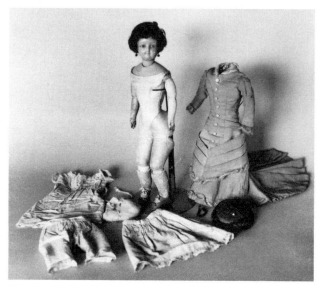

Illustration 13. The doll in *Illustration 12* shown undressed with her clothing. *Courtesy of the Museum of American Architecture and Decorative Arts, Houston, Texas. Photograph by Becky Moncrief.*

Illustration 12. 15in (38.1cm). This fashion doll was discovered in the collection of Theo Redwood Blank whose dolls were given to a museum in Houston, Texas. The familiar head with its cork pate is on a cork-stuffed kid body. The light auburn wig is human hair, dressed with two upswept braids and bangs. Her clothing consists of a blue faille dress, shift, petticoat, drawers and a separate bustle that buttons around the waist. Her natural straw hat is trimmed with black net and blue velvet ribbon and her stockings are lace and the shoes made of blue leather. Her necklace and earrings (which are pegged in with wood) are made from tiny coral beads. The fact that this doll's clothing is all original and appears to be made for her would lead us to believe that the kid body is original to the doll. This is not always the case. *Courtesy of the Museum of American Architecture and Decorative Arts, Houston, Texas. Photograph by Becky Moncrief.*

The dolls in *Illustrations 14* and *15* are in private collections and were photographed by one of the owners. Other fine examples may be seen in the color section.

Illustration 14. 15in (38.1cm). She, too, has her original brown mohair wig, blue glass eyes and kid body with individually wired fingers. She has been recostumed in deep rose silk taffeta.

Illustration 15. This is a 13in (33cm) tiny lady who is quite different from the others in this section. This doll has a ball head with a dark blonde mohair wig and blue glass eyes with feathered brows and lashes. It is a shoulder head with a stiff neck on a kid body. The celluloid is more of a pink hue than ivory. She has been recostumed in bronze taffeta with green silk fringe.

All-Celluloid Dolls With Bent Legs

Popular play dolls were, of course, the all-celluloid babies that could be bathed by their little owners. They were made from around 1910 for a period of about 30 years. Earlier types are usually heavier and glossier while the later dolls have a matte finish and more natural coloring.

The Parsons-Jackson Company of Cleveland, Ohio, called their celluloid-like material "Biskoline," a name patented in 1913. According to the Colemans in *The Collector's Encyclopedia of Dolls* the company experimented for eight years before they marketed their dolls in 1910. They advertised in 1912 that their dolls would float in water.

These dolls were extremely well made of heavy celluloid and less likely to break than the thinner plastics (celluloid). In fact, they proudly advertised that their dolls were guaranteed for one year "not to crack, peel, break, chip or have the surface color wear off." Their slogan was "Kant Krack." But, they did.

THE PARSONS-JACKSON CO.
CLEVELAND, OHIO.

Illustration 17. The trademark of the Parsons-Jackson Company. The components of this mark are not always in this particular form and there is sometimes the addition of "USA" under "Cleveland, Ohio."

Parsons-Jackson dolls are jointed at neck, hip and shoulder and are put together with oil-tempered steel springs. To prevent damage, the holes where the limbs are joined to the body are lined with copper. Frederick W. Parsons applied for a patent to produce this type doll February 26, 1912, and was granted patent No. 1,120,331 on December 8, 1914. Parsons-Jackson dolls are usually marked on the back of the shoulders and head with the stork trademark. (See *Illustration 17*.) Sometimes there is "USA" added.

Jenny Polley in her article, "Ohio Dollmakers," in the Souvenir Journal for the 1972 Region 12 meeting of the United Federation of Doll Clubs pictures a doll marked: "PARSONS & PARSONS // CLEVELAND, OHIO USA." She says she has seen one with a stork but no printing on the shoulders.

In 1953 neither Mr. Parsons nor his son were living, but in response to a letter of inquiry, Miss Polley received the following letter from Mr. Dwight B. Easty, President of the Parsons & Parsons Company, Cleveland, makers of waterproofed fabric collars and cuffs:
"Dear Miss Polley:

"Thank you for your letter of February 17 regarding dolls made of *plastic* many years ago. (Italics by the author.)

"The Parsons Jackson doll has not been made since the year 1914 at which time the entire plant was destroyed by fire. The dolls under the label of Parsons & Parsons were made in later years by a group of fellows who thought the business could be re-established with equipment salvaged from the wreck and succeeded in making a few, one of which you might have, but their endeavor was not long lasting due to lack of enterprise and experience. The Parsons Jackson Company was

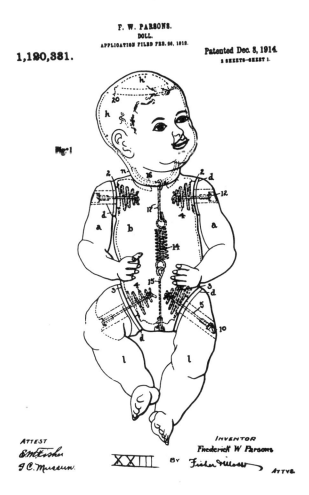

F. W. PARSONS.
DOLL.
APPLICATION FILED FEB. 26, 1912.

1,120,331.

Patented Dec. 8, 1914.
2 SHEETS—SHEET 1.

Illustration 16. Patent drawing for the Parsons-Jackson doll. Complete patent is in the section "Patents." *Photograph by Juanita Acklin.*

short lived, in fact only for a matter of two or three years, if we remember correctly, and possibly would have carried on for a much longer time had not a fire been disastrous for them.

"We wish we could give you more detailed information of an historic nature and regret it is not available.

Yours very truly,
The Parsons & Parsons Co.

(D.B. EASTY'S SIGNATURE)
by D.B. Easty"

(Used by permission of Miss Polley.)

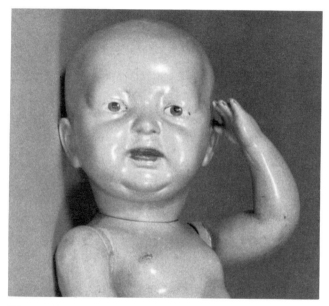

Illustration 18. 10½in (26.7cm) Parsons-Jackson baby. See caption page 2.

THE PARSONS-JACKSON CO.
CLEVELAND, OHIO.

Illustration 19. Components of the Parsons-Jackson trademark used on dolls in *Illustrations 18* and *20*.

The Parsons-Jackson Company at one time advertised 56 styles and sizes of dolls including fully-jointed straight-limbed dolls as well as babies.

There were, no doubt, many other firms in the United States making celluloid dolls, but only a few have been identified. The information would be interesting to

have, but lack of it should not lessen the appreciation for a fine doll or the affection one might have for a particular doll without pedigree.

The *1914 Marshall Field & Company Doll Catalog* reprinted by Hobby House Press, Inc. advertises hundreds of dolls, but there are only two bent-leg babies of "Celtid" which they advertise as being "equal in all respects to celluloid." Interestingly, a "Celtid" baby with moving eyes and mohair wig, 11½in (29.2cm) cost $17.00 a dozen. A "bisque head on a composition body" also with moving eyes and mohair wig is $8.00 per dozen.

The Parsons-Jackson patent may be seen in the "Patent" section.

From studying the catalogs of the day it would seem that there were fewer bent-leg celluloid babies produced than there were child dolls. We have examples from the four countries that were major manufacturers of these dolls. In addition to the United States, bent-leg babies came primarily from Germany, France and Japan. Probably there were others, but we have not seen them.

The Kämmer & Reinhardt catalog for 1928, reprinted by Patricia N. Schoonmaker, shows a full line of celluloid dolls. They advertised "the finest dull varnished celluloid heads with sleeping eyes with eyelashes will be made also with the 'Roli' head, our rosy darling, the most beautiful head ever seen." They also state, "The celluloid lines are made in our own celluloid work." We know that the Rheinische Gummi und Celluloid Fabrik Co. also made dolls for them.

The babies shown are all dressed in long dresses, but we can assume that some of them were bent-legged. They were available in bisque or celluloid. The same was true for babies with cloth bodies.

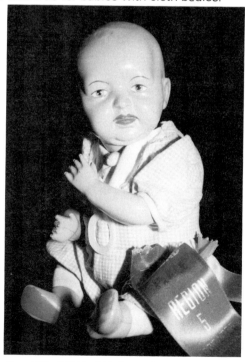

Illustration 20. 10½in (26.7cm) Parsons-Jackson baby with painted pink shoes with brown soles. The back of the head is marked: "(stork//TRADEMARK." The back is marked: "THE PARSONS-JACKSON CO.//CLEVELAND, OHIO//USA." *Pauline Bonnett Collection.*

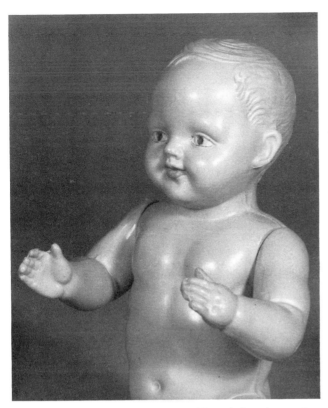

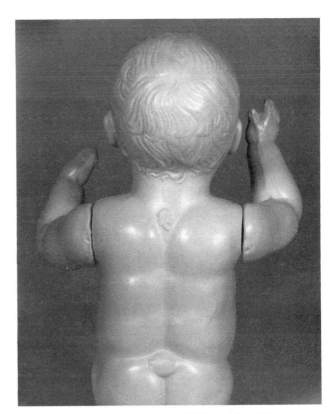

Illustration 21. This well-modeled little fellow is another example of an American-made baby. Indeed, that is his trademark. (See *Illustration 23*.) Unfortunately, this example of that trademark has lost his legs. He sits 6in (15.2cm) tall. His eyes are blue intaglio with black lid lines and his smiling mouth a rosy red. His deeply modeled hair is blonde.

Illustration 22. A back view of *Illustration 21* showing the fine modeling of the body and the location of the trademark. The Indian head symbol is at the center of the shoulders and the word "American" just below the waist.

Illustration 23. The Indian head trademark components. At present, the maker is unknown.

Illustration 24. 13in (33cm). This little boy has a great resemblance to the one in *Illustration 27*. He, too, was made in America, but has the trademark shown in *Illustration 25*. He is beautifully modeled and comparable to similar German Schildkröte dolls. Underneath the wispy brown human hair that has been glued to his head he has molded hair painted brown. His eyes are blue intaglio. The doll is jointed at hip and shoulder with elastic. He wears a contemporary handmade romper and an old straw hat. The large disc under his right arm is a pin holding the blue ribbon he won. *Mary Lu Thompson Collection. Photograph by John Clendenien.*

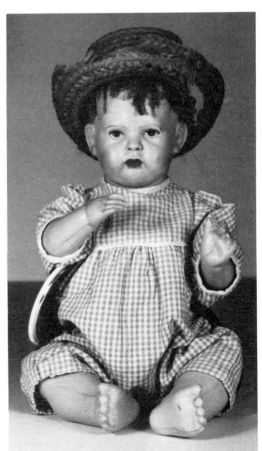

Illustration 25. The eagle mark found on the Thompson doll in *Illustration 24*.

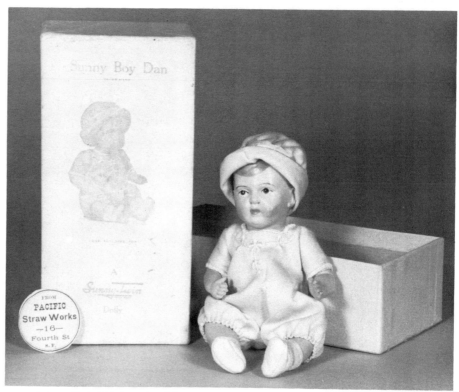

Illustration 26. 5¼in (13.4cm) *Sunny Boy Dan* is shown with his original box. The round paper label was found inside the box and may or may not be significant. He wears fine quality clothes. The romper and matching hat are of heavy pink cotton embroidered with white. The sox are white silk and the tiny ankle-strap shoes are white kid. The doll is medium weight celluloid jointed at hip and shoulder and is high quality in every respect. The seams are well finished and the features artistically painted, even to a slight pink shading over the blue eyes. He is marked on the back: "MADE//IN//USA." Printing on the box indicates that his name is a trademark as is "A Sunny-Twin Dolly." The words: "DES. PAT. APPL. FOR" appear below the picture. Patent No. 122,745 was registered to Lester Clark Brintnall of Los Angeles, California, September 16, 1919, for the words "Sunny Twin."

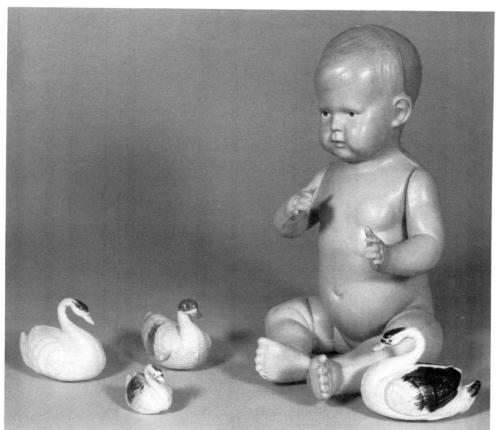

Illustration 27. 11in (27.9cm) tan-flesh colored baby boy of heavy celluloid. He is jointed at hip and shoulder. As with most of the celluloid dolls, the ball and socket joints are not visible. He has painted blue eyes with white highlights and black upper lid lines. His brownish painted hair is very lightly molded. The modeling of the body and features is exceptionally good. He bears a close resemblance to some of the German bisque dolls that collectors refer to as "characters." Marked on the back: "MADE// IN//USA." The toy swans and duck are typical of the tub toys advertised in the early decades of the 20th century. They are unmarked.

Illustration 28. This lovely 10in (25.4cm) little baby girl in her original dress of pale pink lawn has blue glass eyes and a brown mohair wig. Her mouth is the open/closed type. A most appealing little thing of high quality, matte finish celluloid that is tinted flesh-pink. She is marked on the back with the trademark of the Rheinische Gummi und Celluloid Fabrik Co.: "(turtle in diamond frame)// Germany//25//25." Notice the similarity to the little American dolls in *Illustrations 24* and *27*. *Jean Pritchard Collection*.

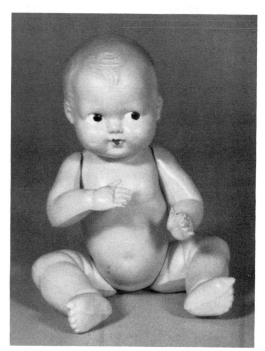

Illustration 31. Trademark found on dolls manufactured in the USA of what we term "heavy celluloid." It is a type of early plastic.

Illustration 29. 8in (20.3cm) early Irwin baby of fairly heavy celluloid, but not nearly as heavy as later Irwin dolls. We use the term generically in this case. The modeling is good with nails indicated on fingers and toes. The reddish-brown hair is lightly modeled in front and has a tuft at the nape. Side-glancing eyes are black dots. He is almost able to suck his thumb. Marked on left shoulder with the round mark (*Illustration 29*) and on the neck: *"NON-FLAM." John Axe Collection.*

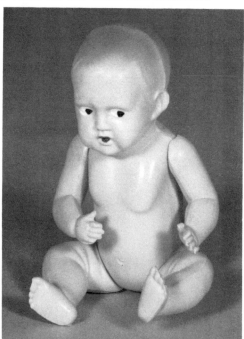

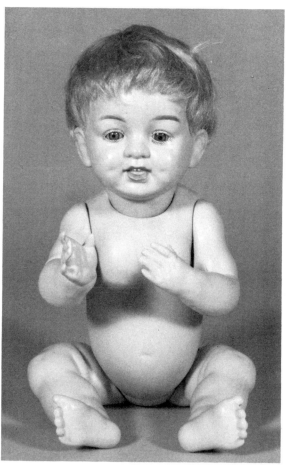

Illustration 30. Another Irwin baby, 5in (12.7cm), with the typical painted eyes that are simply black dots glancing to the side and reddish-brown hair. He is jointed at hip and shoulder. Although similar to the body of the doll in *Illustration 28*, the mold lines are different. Marked on back: *"(round Irwin symbol)//NON-FLAM." John Axe Collection.*

Illustration 32. An 11in (27.9cm) Kestner infant of the finest quality. The celluloid is a true flesh color and the modeling exceptional. Seams are beautifully finished and the doll is jointed at the neck, hip and shoulder. The head has the typical Kestner baby look with its open/closed mouth that shows two little modeled teeth and a tongue. His smile and dimples give this doll the gleeful expression that so many of Kestner's babies have. The stationary blue glass eyes have modeled upper lids, painted upper and lower lashes and feathered brows. His wig is made of blonde mohair strips sewn to a cap. The arms are positioned in the familiar Kestner manner: one folded to the body and the other outstretched. Mark on back: "J.D.K.//203/3//GERMANY."

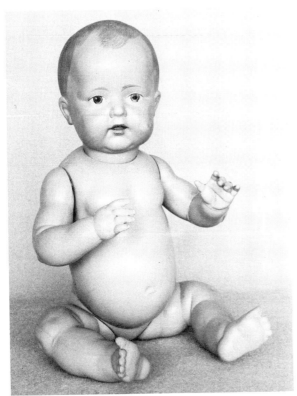

Illustration 33. 14½in (36.9cm) Kämmer & Reinhardt baby that is surely a boy. Of a pink-flesh color that was advertised as "My Rosy Darling 'Roli'," he is very high quality. Jointed at the neck, hip and shoulder, this doll is sculpted with great attention to detail, just as the Kestner baby was. His little fingers and toes are dimpled and have a faint pink tint on the nails. He is the ideal German baby with rolls of baby fat and dimples! The eyes are painted blue with white highlights and the brows are feathered. His mouth is slightly open disclosing two tiny celluloid teeth and the tip of his tongue. His hair is molded and painted brown. His markings are: Head: "K★R//727/36." Back: "K★R//36." A doll of this model with a bisque head and composition body would be marked "127." The celluloid dolls were the 700 series. *Photograph by Jane Buchholz.*

Illustration 34. Components of the Kämmer & Reinhardt trademark. The symbol may be found in conjunction with model numbers and may or may not have the word "Germany."

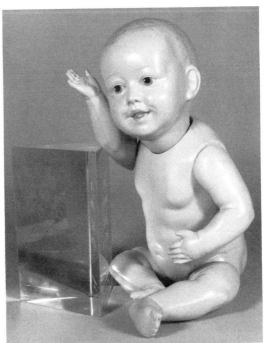

Illustration 35. This little 12½in (31.8cm) fellow is a heavier celluloid that is tinted dark flesh-pink. He is jointed at the neck, hip and shoulder and the seams are finished. His bottom is flattened more than most and this makes him sit firmly. The sculpting is excellent with well-defined musculature. He has brown painted hair that is only faintly modeled on top. His eyes are a deep blue with white highlights and black and red upper lid lines. This little boy has a wonderful smile that shows his dimples and an open/closed mouth with his tongue peeking out from under his gums. The head is marked: "GERMANY//(turtle in frame)//32." The body is marked: "(turtle in frame)//SCHUTZ - MARKE//32// GERMANY."

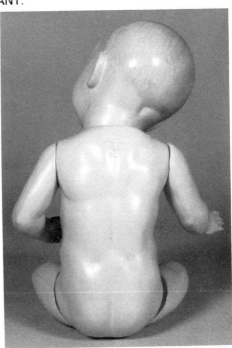

Illustration 36. Back view of *Illustration 35* showing the fine modeling and his turtle mark.

SCHUTZ-MARKE

Illustration 37. A form of the Rheinische Gummi und Celluloid Fabrik Co. trademark without the word "Germany."

Illustration 38. 9¾in (24.9cm) baby of deep chocolate brown transition celluloid. He is just a bit heavier than the earlier product, but not as heavy as those that came later. The seams are well finished and the molded ball tops of the arms and legs give the doll greater direction mobility. He has black painted hair, slightly modeled, and brown painted eyes and upper eyelashes. His open/closed mouth has a modeled tongue and is painted red as are the nostrils and corners of the eyes. He is definitely pointing with that right index finger! Marked on back: "(turtle in frame)//25." The paper wrist tag has a framed turtle on a blue field. Although the doll is black, it does not have ethnic features. It was purchased in Spain.

Illustration 39. 6in (15.2cm) all-celluloid *Bye-Lo*. This little treasure would be coveted by anyone! It would be a choice addition to a *Bye-Lo* collection, to a miniature collection or to a collection of celluloid dolls. It is a rare form of the *Bye-Lo*. John and Janet Clendenien Collection. Photograph by John Clendenien.

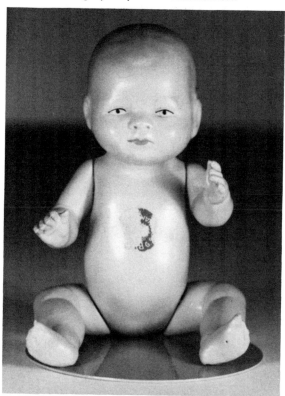

Illustration 40. Undressed view of *Illustration 39*. This tiny doll is high quality. It is well finished and the painting is good. The hair is only faintly modeled and painted light brown. The eyes are painted blue. In 1925 Karl Standfuss advertised he was the sole manufacturer of celluloid *Kewpies* and celluloid *Bye-Los*. The remnants of a paper sticker are visible on the front of the doll. The back of the torso is marked: "COPR BY//S. PUTNAM//GERMANY//14½." Possibly the "G" in the name did not "take" in the mold. *John and Janet Clendenien Collection. Photograph by John Clendenien.*

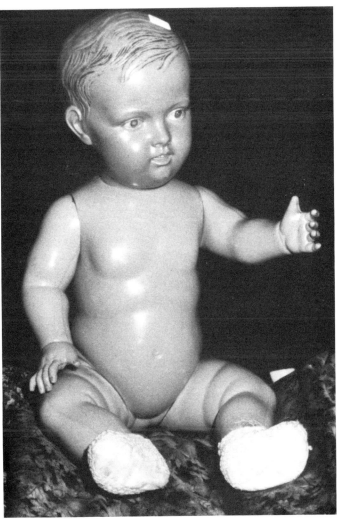

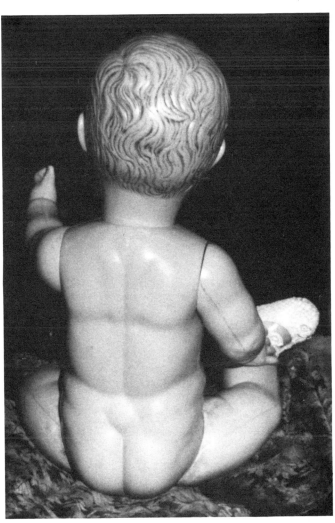

Illustration 41. This is the largest German baby, 25in (63.5cm), we have pictured. He is a beautiful example. The modeling of the entire doll, head, face and body are superb. He is jointed at the neck, hip and shoulders and, it would appear from the photograph, at the wrists. The author has not seen the doll and it is not available for examination. Information about this doll or a similar all-celluloid doll with more than five joints would be most welcome. Mark: "DRP//GERMANY//60//(symbol of crowned mermaid)." *Courtesy of Mary Skolfield. Photograph by Robert Beckett.*

Illustration 42. Back view of the doll in *Illustration 42*. The mark is faint, but appears to be the same as shown in *Illustration 43. Courtesy of Mary Skolfield. Photograph by Robert Beckett.*

Illustration 43.Trademark of the Cellba works found on doll in *Illustrations 41* and *42.*

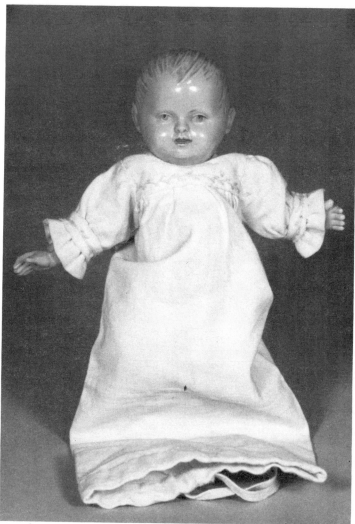

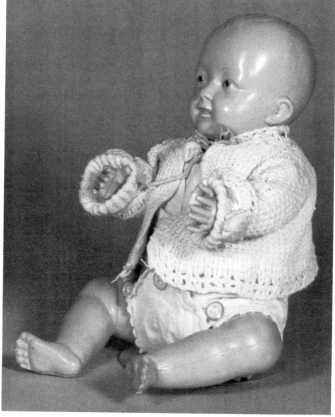

Illustration 44. 5in (12.7cm) flesh-colored baby of glossy, heavy celluloid that is extremely well modeled for its size, especially the hands and feet which have dimples and individually molded fingers and toes with nails indicated. Jointed at hip and shoulder, the doll has nicely modeled brown painted hair and blue intaglio eyes. The bottom is rather flat. It wears its old white wool dress with blue feather-stitch trim. It is marked with the trademark of the Cellba works of Babenhausen, Germany: "D.R.P.a.//GERMANY//(crowned mermaid in shield)//13."

Illustration 45. 9in (22.9cm) baby of heavy flesh-colored celluloid jointed at hip and shoulder. The hands on this doll are exceptional. Some of the fingers are completely individual (the two middle fingers are molded together). There are dimples on the little hands and the knuckles are indicated. The toes have joints modeled on the bottom as well as the top. The painted blue eyes have white highlights and black upper lid lines. Blonde hair is lightly molded. The clothes are old and are undoubtedly his original outfit, whether commercial or made by a very loving mother. He wears a shirt and a diaper of white linen trimmed with rickrack braid and fastened with five white buttons that are edged with deep pink. The sweater is machine-knitted white cotton tied with pink ribbons. The doll is unmarked but was probably made in Germany or the USA.

Illustration 46. LEFT: This little 11¾in (29.9cm) doll is French. It is lighter weight and has more yellow skin tones. The features are very like those of a real child. His blonde hair is slightly modeled but the modeling around his blue intaglio eyes is above average. One can almost hear his rich baby-chuckle. Jointed at head, hip and shoulder, he has the mark used by the *Société Industrielle de Celluloid.* Head marked: "30." Body marked: "(wyvern mark)//FRANCE//30." His lace trimmed net dress seems to be original. RIGHT: A 12in (30.5cm) German baby very similar to the doll in *Illustration 35.* The modeling of the face is a bit different. The eyes are dark brown and the mouth a much darker red. This little fellow has very slightly molded hair that is painted light brown. Although the bodies are almost identical, even to markings, this one is spring strung instead of the usual elastic. Mark on head: "GER-MANY//(framed turtle)//30." Mark on body: "(framed turtle)//SCHUTZ-MARKE//30//GERMANY." The celluloid swans are unmarked.

Illustration 47. The "wyvern" or "winged dragon" mark of the *Société Industrielle de Celluloid* of Paris, 1902-1925+.

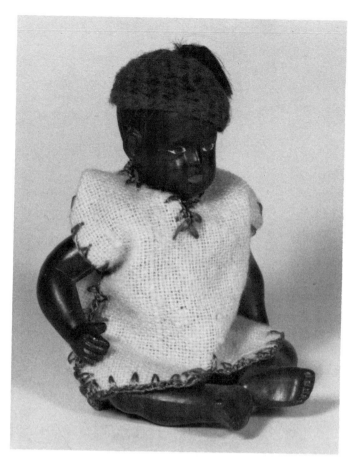

Illustration 48. A small 5in (12.7cm) black baby without ethnic features, he is made of heavy late celluloid. The doll is jointed at hip and shoulder and has black molded hair, brown painted eyes with black lid lines and brows. His mouth is red. He wears a red wool beret with a black tassel and a white wool dress with red buttonhole trim. Marked on back: "FRANCE//(S/C in diamond frame)." *Maurine Popp Collection.*

FRANCE

Illustration 49. Components of a trademark used by Société Industrielle de Celluloid. It is sometimes found in conjunction with the wyvern mark.

OPPOSITE PAGE: Illustration 50. A 14in (35.6cm) French baby that looks like they used a photograph of Charles de Gaulle as a baby for a model! He is made of heavy, glossy, flesh-colored celluloid and is jointed at head, hip and shoulder. The eyes are blue intaglio with white highlights and black upper lid lines. The open/closed mouth is very red with a white outline at the inner edge of the lips. His hair is painted brown and there are comb marks molded on only the front half of the head. This doll is beautifully sculpted, especially the ears and hands. The head is marked: "FRANCE//(S/C in diamond frame)//36//1." The body is marked: "FRANCE//(S/C in diamond frame)//36//3." Although the final numbers do not match, the head seems to be the correct size for the body.

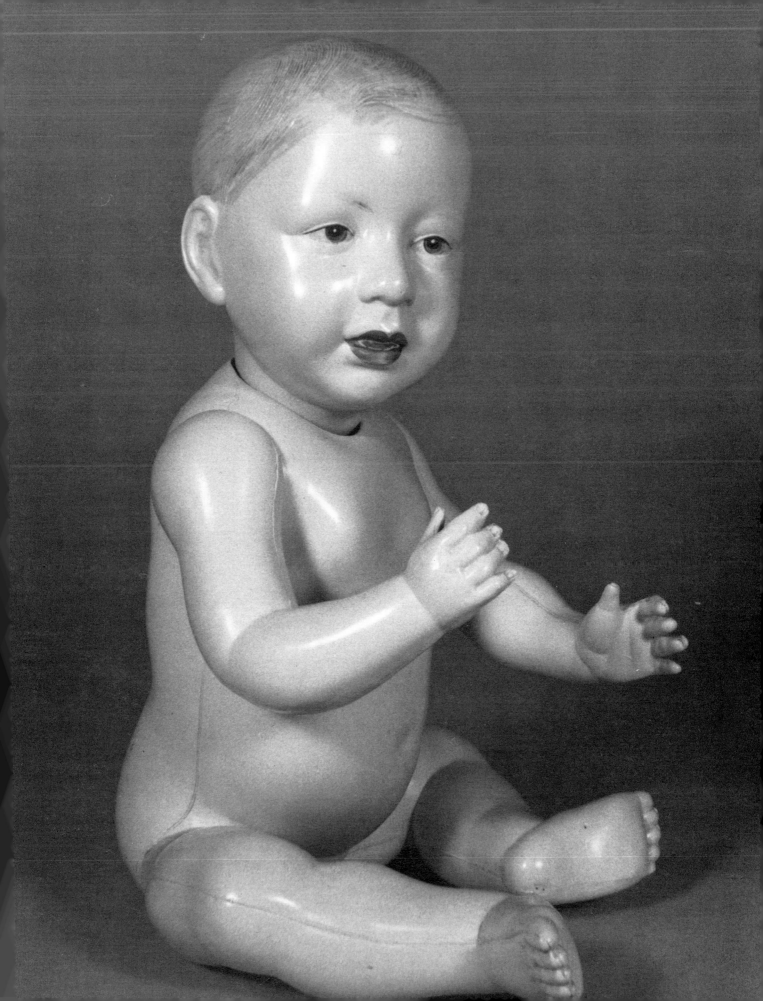

Illustration 51. 11in (27.6cm) bent-legged baby of lightweight, flesh-colored celluloid with a matte finish. It is jointed at neck, hip and shoulder and has molded light brown hair. The painted eyes are different from most because they have an extra ring of white between the black, highlighted pupil and the blue iris. The doll is richly dressed in a green wool dress with full red sleeves and bordered with gold silk that has a design of woven flowers. The apron is white lace-edged silk brocade that is trimmed with red velvet and gold lace. The shawl is made from the flowered silk of the skirt and is trimmed with gold lace. The little cap is also made of that silk material accented with green velvet and a ruffle of lace. Around the doll's neck is a "gold" metal tag that has a figure embossed in the center and the word "BREIZ" at the top and "BEPRED" at the bottom. (The final letter may be an "O.") The reverse side has engraved: "LE MINOR//CELT." The doll is marked on the neck: "(SNF in diamond frame)//27." This is the mark of Poupée Nobel. It was first registered in 1939 and later in 1960. This doll is one of the early types. It was costumed by Madam Le Minor of Pont L'Abbé, a famous French doll maker who used the dolls of Petitcolin and Poupée Nobel for costumes she designed.

FRANCE

Illustration 52. Components of the mark found on dolls made by Société Nobel Francaise.

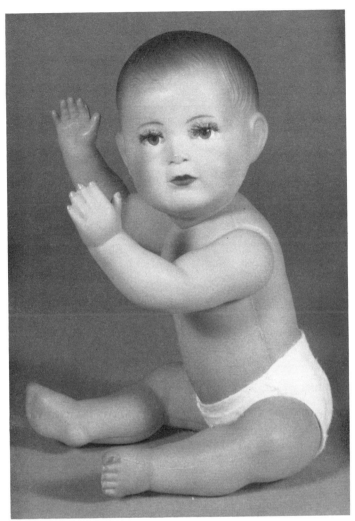

Illustration 53. Two small French babies of the late 1930s. The larger is 7in (17.8cm) and wears an original provincial costume similar to those found on the Le Minor dolls, brocade, velvet and lots of gold braid. She has molded hair painted light brown and blue eyes. Mark: "(SNF in diamond)//18//France." Her small companion, redressed, is only 4in (10.2cm) and also has the SNF mark of Poupée Nobel. *Edward Wyffels Collection. Photograph by Berdine Wyffels.*

Illustration 54. 10in (25.4cm) doll of a lightweight, well-finished celluloid with joints at neck, hip and shoulder. The hair is modeled brown and the stationary brown eyes are celluloid. Upper lashes are brown silk. The body is beautifully sculpted, even to having nipples. Not only are the features painted, the knees are tinted a delicate pink as are the nails of the hands and feet. Since the celluloid has a matte finish, this gives a most realistic appearance. Head is marked: "(SNF in diamond frame)//FRANCE//MOD 27 DEP." Body marked: "FRANCE//(SNF in diamond frame)//27//5."

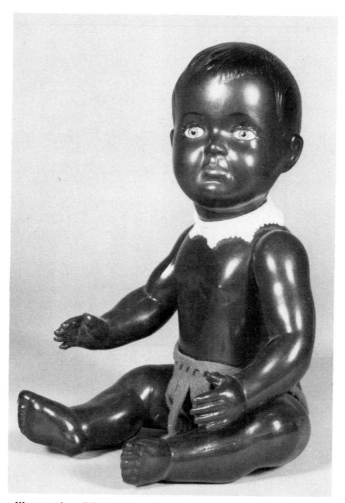

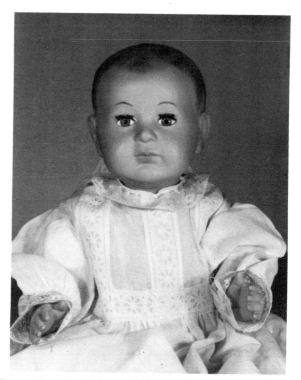

Illustration 56. A beautiful, big 23in (58.4cm) baby that has more of the look of a real child than the previous SNF examples. Head circumference is 17¾in (45.2cm). The celluloid is the later, heavier variety. He is completely jointed at neck, hip and shoulder and has blue sleep eyes with lashes. His molded hair is painted brown. The old "real baby" dress he wears shows how life-sized he is. A captivating doll, indeed. He is marked on back of neck with the Poupée Nobel mark: "(SNF in diamond frame)//1//MOD DEPOSE." *John and Janet Clendenien Collection. Photograph by John Clendenien.*

Illustration 55. 11¾in (29.9cm) dark chocolate-colored celluloid doll that must have been someone's idea of what an African "native" looks like! The original felt clothes are glued on. He wears a white collar and a blue waistband that has a red felt loin cloth stapled to it. He has black molded hair, celluloid eyes with silky upper lashes and is jointed at neck, hip and shoulder. This later doll is a shiny and fairly lightweight celluloid. The body of this doll and the one in *Illustration 54* seem identical in design. The heads are different, but the black one does not have ethnic features. Marked on back: "FRANCE// (SNF in diamond frame)//30//2."

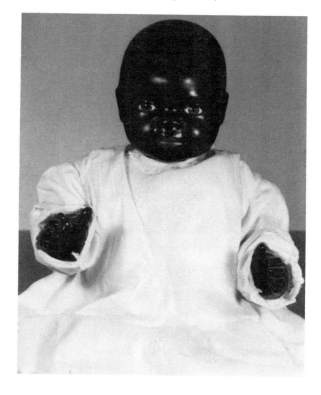

Illustration 57. A large 21in (53.3cm) black baby with ethnic features, this doll is a fine example of the wonderful modeling achieved with the use of plastics. (Remember, celluloid is a plastic.) The features are distinct and his hair is modeled in the tiny, tight curls associated with a black baby. He is a true representation of his race, not just a white doll painted black. He is completely jointed at neck, hip and shoulder and has stationary brown glass eyes. His arrival in the toy market of the mid 1930s was surely greeted with enthusiasm by black mothers seeking dolls for their little girls. Head marked: "FRANCE//(SNF in diamond frame)//50." *John and Janet Clendenien Collection. Photograph by John Clendenien.*

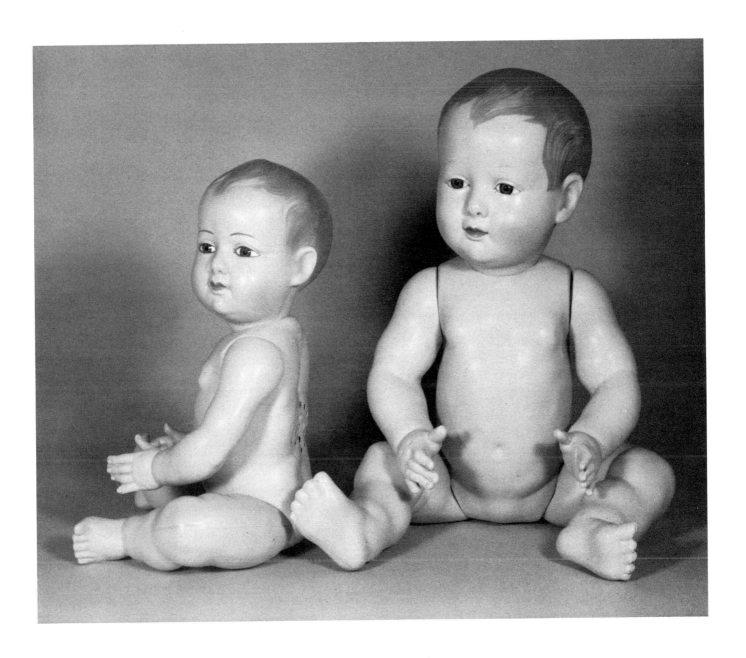

Illustration 58. These two French babies are of superior quality. The celluloid has a matte finish and the modeling is exceptional. Their brown hair has deep comb marks and their eyes are blue glass. The painting of the reddish-brown brows and lid lines is sharper on the smaller doll and its color is a bit pinker than the true flesh color of the larger example. Both are nicely tinted. The seams are well finished and great attention has been given to detail. The nails are molded and tinted and the breasts have nipples. The heads are attached to the leg elastic by metal springs. The hip and shoulder joints are the usual type. The smaller of the two dolls has a round perforated area in the back that has been cut out for the insertion of a crier and then has been replaced. The marks on the larger doll are indistinct, but presumably are the same as on the other with possibly different numbers. The small doll is marked on the head: "FRANCE//(head of eagle)//45//4." Body is marked: "45//(head of eagle)//FRANCE//2." These dolls were made by Petitcolin of Paris and probably date in the late 1930s. LEFT: 17½in (44.5cm). RIGHT: 21in (53.3cm).

FRANCE

Illustration 59. Tête L'Aigle (head of an eagle) is the trademark of Petitcolin. It will be found in conjunction with various numbers.

Illustration 61. The unfolded wrist tag that is shown on the doll in *Illustration 60*. Note that the company refers to the doll as "plastique." It is one of the type collectors refer to as "late celluloid."

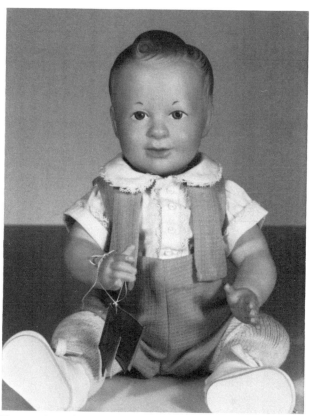

Illustration 60. Doesn't he look like a little French fellow? He is 16in (40.6cm) and is made of the later heavy celluloid of the 1930s. His features are beautifully molded. Notice the typical baby curl that mothers brushed around their fingers when baby's hair was still wet from the bath. How true to life! His hair is painted brown, as are the eyes. He is jointed at neck, hip and shoulder. He wears a real baby's clothing and has his original tag on his wrist. (See *Illustration 61*.) Marked on back of torso: "(head of eagle)//FRANCE//40" *John and Janet Clendenien Collection. Photograph by John Clendenien.*

Illustration 62. 7in (17.8cm) African mother and 4in (10.2cm) child. These little dolls are very good quality chocolate-colored celluloid. They are well made, with finished seams and attention to detail. They are jointed at hip and shoulder. The eyes are molded in an almond shape and painted. The mother's eyes have brown irises with white highlights and red corner marks. Baby's have only black pupils with highlights. Both dolls have molded black hair and red painted lips. Baby is undressed and slung on Mother's back in a colorful print shawl. She also wears red "panties," a pink and black plaid skirt and a brilliantly colored scarf. All clothes except the gold ribbon glued around her feet are sewn right into the celluloid. Mother marked on back: "18//(head of eagle)//FRANCE." Baby marked on back: "10//(head of eagle)//FRANCE."

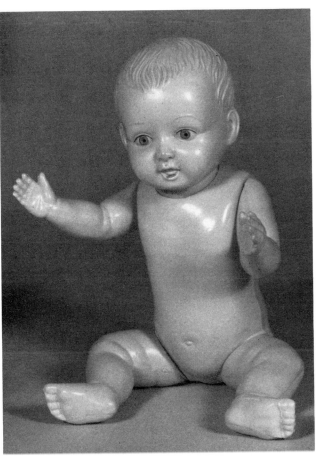

Illustration 63. 10in (25.4cm) baby that is jointed at neck, hip and shoulder. The modeling on this little Japanese doll is very good and the quality is also high, especially for its size. The hair, features and hands and feet are very well done. His eyes are blue intaglio with black lid lines and molded brows, not a usual feature. He probably dates from the 1920s. Marked on back: "(K in circle)//NIPPON." *John Axe Collection.*

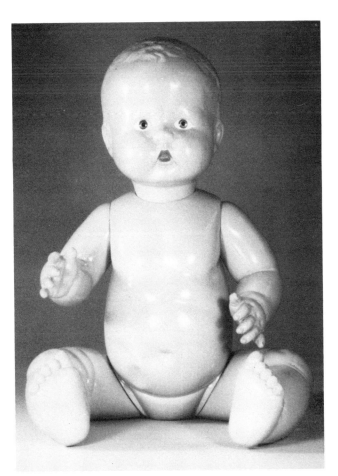

Illustration 65. A 20in (61cm) baby, one of the largest dolls we have seen. This baby is of heavy celluloid of the later type. It has been reported that dolls like this were used for display in the J. C. Penney Department Store in Oklahoma City, Oklahoma, in the 1930s and 1940s. It is beautifully made with light colored molded hair and eyes painted gray. As can be seen in the photograph, the fingers are individual and toes are even individually molded on the under side. It is jointed at neck, hip and shoulder. Mark: "(Fleur)//JAPAN//ROYAL." *Carolyn Baker Collection. Photograph by Ray Baker.*

Illustration 64. Marks found on the Japanese doll in *Illustration 63.*

Illustration 66. Mark found on dolls from Japan. (See *Illustration 65.*)

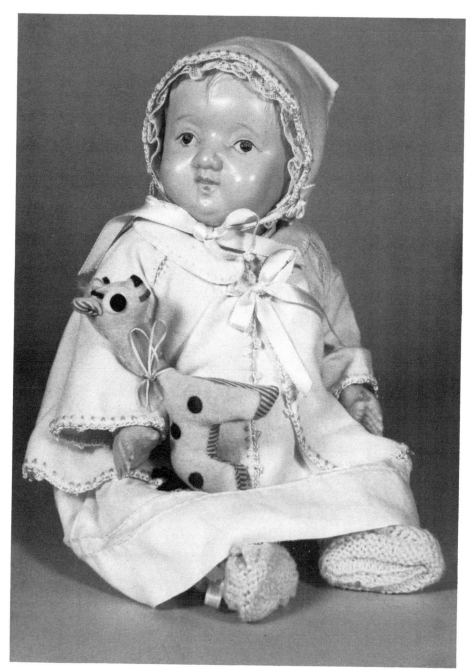

Illustration 68. Green and white paper label. (See *Illustration 67*.)

MADE IN JAPAN

Illustration 69. Trademark found on doll in *Illustration 67*.

MADE IN OCCUPIED JAPAN

Illustration 70. Trademark found on doll in *Illustration 71*.

Illustration 67. This 12in (30.5cm) Japanese baby is made of lighter weight celluloid than the comparable dolls of other countries. It is a flesh-pink tone. The body, jointed at neck, hip and shoulder, is quite well modeled with blonde hair and black intaglio eyes. Hands and feet are beautifully detailed with individual fingers and toes that have dimples and nails. The ears are overly large and the oriental appearance is obvious. Although made for Western markets, this baby just cannot deny his Japanese heritage. The clothes are old and were lovingly made for him of fine linen and wool with handmade buttonholes and pink trim. The doll is marked on the back with a stylized bird that resembles a bird of origami, the Japanese art of folding paper into forms. There is a green paper label on the bottom of the torso. It is shown in *Illustration 68*.

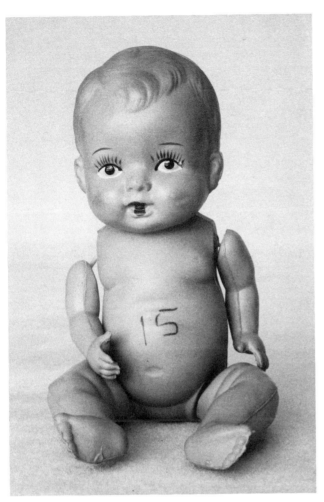

Illustration 71. This 7½in (19.1cm) little doll made of a lightweight pink celluloid is an example of the toys that were shipped from Japan during the Occupation after World War II. The modeling is good, but the workmanship is poor. Seams are rough and although the eyes with lashes are well painted, the mouth is simply a splash of very red paint where it is molded. Hair and eyes are reddish and the eyes are blue. Whether the "15" inked on his tummy was his original price or put on later is not known. Mark on back: "(Butterfly)//MADE IN//OCCU-PIED//JAPAN." *Photograph by Jane Buchholz.*

Illustration 72. This sweet little 16in (40.6cm) girl is one of the better dolls to come from pre-World War II Japan. Although the celluloid is not as heavy as that usually found in European dolls of this type, the modeling and finishing are superb. Her dark blonde hair is caught with a molded black ribbon, and there is a small cluster of molded posies on each side of her head. She is elastic jointed at the neck, hips and shoulders. Her clothes are not original. Mark: (See *Illustration 73*). The small doll in her lap is 6in (15.2cm). The head is very similar to the large one but this doll wears a molded bathing suit. Mark: (See *Illustration 74*). *Ursula Mertz Collection. Photograph courtesy of Ursula Mertz.*

Illustration 73. Mark found on the larger doll in *Illustration 72.*

Illustration 74. Mark found on the smaller doll in *Illustration 72.*

Illustration 75. This dear little 14in (35.6cm) boy with his molded fancy pink pants is another example of a better quality Japanese doll. He is from that period between the world wars. Fully-jointed, he has well-modeled features and blonde hair. He is marked: "Japanese symbol//MADE IN JAPAN//another Japanese symbol//129100//129101." *Ursula Mertz Collection. Photograph courtesy of Ursula Mertz.*

All-Celluloid Dolls
With Straight Legs

The dolls with straight legs came in various sizes from tiny to tall and were either jointed at the hip or had stiff legs that were apart. Many of these dolls were dressed in ethnic costume and these will be discussed, as the tinies will be, in other chapters.

The dolls with molded hair were advertised as marvelous companions for baby in his bath. The *1914 Marshall Field & Company Doll Catalog*, reprinted by Hobby House Press, Inc., shows two of these types. It is most likely that all the manufacturers produced these bath toys since they would have been quite marketable. In 1909 Karl Standfuss, who used the trademark "JUNO," obtained two German patents for jointed bathing dolls.

As the popularity of the new material grew, more manufacturers offered their typical play dolls in celluloid. Kämmer & Reinhardt and their "ROLI" line is a good example. Many of the bisque dolls were made in celluloid, too. Celluloid dolls appeared on the market from doll makers all over the world.

In Japan, Tokyo was the center of the celluloid, metal and rubber industries but their products were sometimes of inferior quality. The American companies Morimura, Yamoto, Tajimi and Haber distributed and sometimes designed dolls that were made in Japan.

CELTID BATH AND FLOAT BABIES

Stationary arms and legs; painted hair and eyes; painted shoes and stockings; balanced, so as to stand upright.

C67201 to C67210

	Inches	Boxed	Dozen
C67201.	4¾	1	.76
C67204.	5½	1	1.60
C67205.	6½	1	2.40
C67208.	8	1/2	3.80
C67210.	11	1/3	8.00

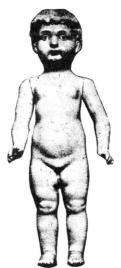

C67229 to C67239

CELTID BATH AND FLOAT BABIES

Best heavy quality, unbreakable, rubber cord jointed arms; painted hair and eyes; balanced so as to stand upright.

	Inches	Boxed	Dozen
C67231.	5½	1	1.60
C67233.	7¼	1	3.50
C67234.	8	1/2	4.00
C67239.	8¾	1/12	7.50
C67236.	10¾	1/12	7.80
C67237.	12¾	1/12	15.00

Illustration 76. *1914 Marshall Field & Company Doll Catalog.* Reprinted by Hobby House Press, Inc.

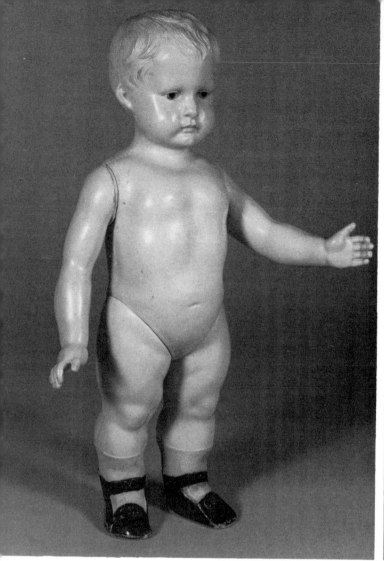

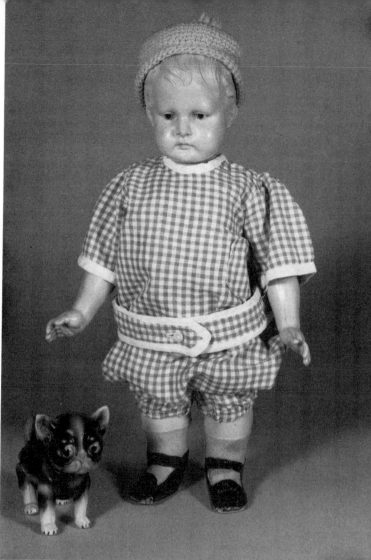

Illustration 77. This early 13in (33cm) doll made of heavy tan celluloid is a fine example of the realistic modeling made possible by the use of celluloid. The sculpture is exceptional with fingernails, knuckles and dimples on the well-formed hands. His hair shows curls and comb marks and the molded black shoes have bows, buttons and tan soles. All seams are finished. His eyes are painted blue with a black upper lid line. Where the limbs meet the body, it is flat, without the usual molded ball and socket. The doll stands very well alone. Mark on shoulders: "SCHUTZ-MARKE//(unframed turtle)."

Illustration 78. The little Rheinische Gummi und Celluloid Fabrik Co. boy is shown in his original blue and white gingham romper and knitted blue cap. His little Japanese dog is a later vintage. (See "Novelties.")

Illustration 79. The unframed turtle mark of the Rheinische Gummi und Celluloid Fabrik Co. as found on doll in *Illustration 77*.

SCHUTZ-MARKE

Illustration 80. This extremely rare little 9½in (24.2cm) doll is all celluloid. She is jointed at hip and shoulder and has a wooden dowel placed into her neck upon which any of five heads may be placed. She has molded tan ribbed sox and brown heeled boots with four buttons indicated on them. The upper legs where they fit over the torso are quite long and there is an indentation just below the waist to insure smooth fit. The head that is in place in the photograph has painted features, blue eyes and a light blonde mohair wig. The others are from left to right: a cat, by far the most unusual head. He has molded white fur with black ears and whiskers, green eyes and a little red mouth. His ribbon is red. Next is a girl's head with molded blonde hair and dimples. Her eyes are painted blue. The little boy's head has brown hair that is similar to flocking, but a bit rougher. He, too, has dimples and blue eyes. The last head is that of another little girl with molded hair, but in a different style and a bit darker in color. She lacks the dimples of her sister, but has the same blue eyes. None of the heads are marked. The doll wears replaced clothing. Mark on back: ''(unframed turtle)//SCHUTZMARKE//24//GERMANY//D.R.G.M. //447828.'' The 1911 *Youth's Companion* advertised this doll as ''The Five In One Doll.'' For 40¢ and a new subscription to the magazine a child could acquire one, or the purchase price was $1.25, postpaid. Their description of the dolls' hair was ''enameled'' and ''sandpapered'' in addition to ''real hair.'' They claimed that ''The children will never tire of this plaything, because of the number of different characters it represents. By changing the head, a different playmate is provided for almost every day in the week.'' *Courtesy of Ralph's Antique Doll Museum, Parkville, Missouri.*

OPPOSITE PAGE: Illustration 81. Collectors seeing this 11in (27.9cm) doll from a short distance usually say, "Lenci" and they are probably correct. The doll looks like felt since it is flocked in a flesh tone. She is made of medium weight celluloid and is jointed at hip and shoulder. The features are beautifully painted. Her cheeks have a pink blush and the mouth is red and well shaped. Her eyes are the most unusual feature. They are a long almond shape, glancing left and are blue with white highlights. Double black upper lid lines that are shadowed between the lines give her an exotic look. There are red dots in the corner of the eyes and at the nostrils. Her brown mohair curls are just that -- not a complete wig. They are glued to her head in front of her pink felt hat which is also glued to her head. Her pink printed organdy pinafore is trimmed with pink-edged white ruffles and she has a bouquet of two felt blossoms at her waist. Underneath she wears a petticoat of sheer pink and panties of pale pink rayon, both of which are sewn to the waist of the dress. Her sox are white silk and the shoes white felt with pink felt "buttons." She is marked on the back: "(turtle in frame //27½/28½." The arms and legs are marked: "20 28½ N." A doll similar to this was reported in its original Lenci box and with its tags. Lenci's granddaughter, Carla Caso, told the author that "they used a lot of celluloid."

Illustration 82. Here is a smaller pair of dolls, 8in (20.3cm), similar to the one in *Illustration 81*. They have the same eye painting and brown mohair wigs. They are also flocked to look like felt and are jointed at hip and shoulder. The celluloid is medium weight and molded beautifully. The hands are especially nice with separate fingers. Their provincial costumes are carefully made of good materials, but the boy's clothes are pinned to the body in the back. He wears brown felt lederhosen with a white shirt, coral vest and green suspenders. His hat is black caracul. The girl wears a maroon felt skirt, green bodice over a white blouse and a silky blue apron. Her large hat matches her skirt. She has nice lace trimmed undies. The only visible part of the mark is on the boy's back: "(turtle in diamond frame)." They were possibly made by Lenci.

OPPOSITE PAGE: Illustration 83. This 13in (33.0cm) doll is one of the rarest of the celluloids. She has been shown in competitive exhibits many times and is always a ribbon winner. The owner has never seen another, nor has any other collector been in touch with Mrs. Bonnett with information that another does exist. Undoubtedly more of these dolls were made. Where are they? The wigs are very fragile and possibly as they were broken the dolls were discarded. She has five wigs of different colors of blonde and brown that are styled in different manners. The doll is completely jointed at neck, hip and shoulder. Her eyes are painted blue and she wears a replacement dress of white dimity printed with pink rosebuds. The original dress was made of a pinstripe taffeta. The handmade underwear is good quality. The doll's head is the ball-type without hair so the wigs will slip on and off. The modeling of the hands is also worthy of notice. The fingers are well finished and some are separate. She was purchased in an antiques shop in New England in the 1940s. *Pauline Bonnett Collection.*

Illustration 85. These two charmers are nice examples of the little German dolls that were jointed only at the shoulders but have some sort of molded decoration to make them a bit special. LEFT: 7in (17.8cm) doll which reminds us of "September Morn" with her molded blonde hair caught up on top with a red bow. Her dark eyes and little watermelon mouth make her look like the bisque *Googlies.* Mark: "(turtle in diamond frame)//17." RIGHT: 7in (17.8cm) doll with modeled blonde hair which is held with a red ribbon in the manner of the bisque *Coquettes.* She has painted blue eyes and molded shoes and sox. Mark: "(helmet of Minerva)// 18//Germany." *Edward Wyffels Collection. Photograph by Berdine Wyffels.*

Illustration 84. A closer look at the doll in *Illustration 83* showing the fine modeling of the hands. *Pauline Bonnett Collection.*

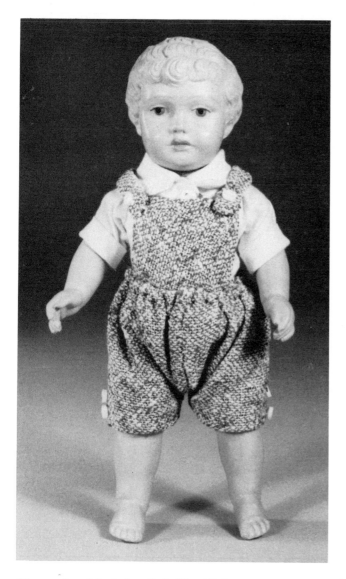

Illustration 86. A dear little 7in (17.8cm) early boy with molded curly hair and painted blue eyes with molded upper lids and black lid lines. He is jointed at hip and shoulder. His clothes are not original. He was made by Buschow & Beck whose trademark, "Minerva," has been in use since 1894. He is marked on back: "(helmet of Minerva//GERMANY//18." *Carolyn Baker Collection. Photograph by Ray Baker.*

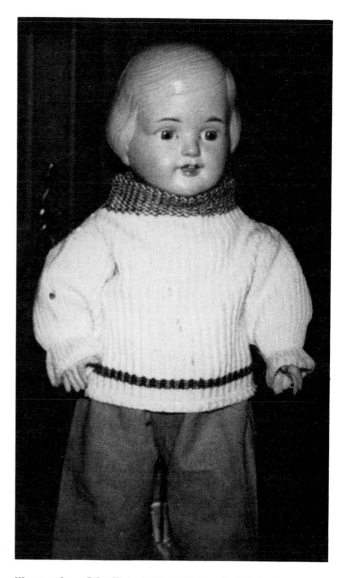

Illustration 88. This 14in (35.6cm) doll is from the Cellba works. He has molded blonde hair, blue glass eyes and an open/closed mouth with two molded teeth. He is marked on the back: "D.R.P.//(crowned mermaid symbol)." *Edward Wyffels Collection. Photograph by Berdine Wyffels.*

Illustration 87. Mark found on dolls made by Buschow & Beck. Their trademark was "Minerva" and they used the helmet of the goddess as a symbol.

Illustration 89. Crowned mermaid symbol used by Cellba of Babenhausen, 1952.

Illustration 90. In 1928 this 18in (45.7cm) toddler was advertised in the Kämmer & Reinhardt catalog as *Darling Learns to Walk.* The catalog, reprinted by Doll Research Projects, has illustrations of the dolls along with text in German, French, English and Spanish. Most of the dolls listed are either celluloid or bisque models that are available in celluloid as well. How could a toy buyer resist ordering her after reading the descriptions? "Our epoch-making novelty 'Darling Lerns [sic] to walk.' An epoch-making novelty of our firm. Our novelty 1928 'My Rosy Darling' the new unequalled standing and sitting Baby all of celluloid can be delivered in all sizes. It is of unsurpassable beauty and highest stability. The charming head of new modelling is a symphony of beauty. The celluloid lines are made in our own celluloid work." The last line is of particular interest, since we know that many of their dolls were made by the Rheinische Gummi und Celluloid Fabrik Co.

On another page additional information is given concerning this doll. This time, the spelling is correct. "'Darling learns to walk' with lifelike flirting eyes and selfacting mama voices. Will be delivered with 'Roli', our unsurpassable celluloid head 'My rosy darling', with flirting eyes. The [sic] prices see price-list. All babies in charming walk-clothes of the cheap and marketable to the preciously equipment [sic]. All Clothes, colours of Hair and the silk knots for the wigs are made in original as in illustrations only. Variations and extra wishes will be executed if possible."

The doll shown is of a pinkish celluloid jointed at neck, hip and shoulder. The blue glass flirting eyes have lashes and lids that move over the eyes. The wig is blonde mohair, but not in the same style shown in the catalog. They were the Buster Brown haircut -- straight short sides with bangs. The clothes, although old, are not original either. They were shown in short toddler dresses. Head marked: "K★R//728//GERMANY// 43/46." Body marked: "K★R//7." The bisque counterpart is model 128. The "Eskimo Boy" she carries is much older than she is. Dolls of this type were advertised in the 1912 Sears Roebuck catalog. The 13½in (34.3cm) doll sold for 39¢. This one is 6in (15.2cm) tall without his removable hat. The body is black plush on a white backing. The doll is jointed at hip and shoulder and has a celluloid mask face with blue painted eyes and brown molded hair. There is a squeaker in the tummy. The mask is marked on the lower flange: "(unframed turtle) 7-1/3//GERMANY." It is sewn to the cloth head.

GERMANY

Illustration 91. Symbol used by Kämmer & Reinhardt in conjunction with various numbers.

Illustration 93. Symbol found on dolls of early plastic. Post World War II.

OPPOSITE PAGE: Illustration 92. This 14¾in (37.6cm) doll would also seem to be one from the 1928 Kämmer & Reinhardt catalog, but not of the "Roli" line of rosy celluloid. Another advertisement in the catalog that was reprinted by Doll Research Projects, an enterprise of Patricia N. Schoonmaker, states that "Our exceedingly rich assortment of the highly popular dressed celluloid children with finest dull varnished celluloid-heads and sleeping eyes with eyelashes will be made also with the 'Roli' head, our rosy darling, the most beautiful head ever made." They said that their most popular size was 39 but that also the little sizes would be dressed. The "littlest sizes" were 24cm (about 9½in), 28cm (a little over 11in) and 33cm (13in). There was a remarkable variety of costumes for either boy or girl dolls and also several wig styles were available.

The doll shown is jointed at neck, hip and shoulder, has blue glass sleep eyes with lashes, an open mouth with teeth, blonde mohair braids and wears her original clothes: white combination slip and panties, rayon print dress with ribbon belt, white cotton sox with pink tops, white leather ankle-tie shoes that are marked on the sole: "Hermann Jurtz//Spielwarehaus//Stuttgart." Head marked: "K★R//717/39//GERMANY." Body marked: "K★R//39."

The 5½in (14cm) bent-leg baby in the woven straw cradle is what I call transition celluloid. It is the heavy early plastic that collectors still term celluloid. The doll is jointed at hip and shoulder, but there are molded hooks for stringing with rubber bands. New technology made the production of these little dolls of the postwar period a "whole new ball game," as the saying goes. The bodies were sturdy enough to simply leave holes where the arms and legs would be attached to the torso. No longer was a filled socket necessary to take the stress of stringing. The baby's hair is molded and he has black intaglio eyes and a little red mouth. The arms and legs seem to be of a different type of plastic. The body and head are a flesh color while the limbs are more orangish. Marked on back with Irwin symbol.

Illustration 94. This 16in (40.6cm) young lady comes from Poland. She is very well made of quality materials, completely jointed with brown glass sleep eyes and open mouth with teeth. Her wig has been replaced, but her clothes are all original and in the style of the late 1920s. The dress is made of a white silky material with red dots and red organdy collar and cuffs. She wears a combination slip and panties of white cotton edged with rayon binding. Her sox are white silk and the shoes are white leather with red stitching. She is marked on both head and body with the trademark of P. R. Zast: "(initials ASK in inverted triangle)//POLAND."

Illustration 95. The symbol found on dolls manufactured by P. R. Zast.

Illustration 97. Left: 10in (25.4cm) beautifully modeled French toddler. The dolls of Petitcolin usually are. He is jointed at hip and shoulder, has brown molded hair and painted eyes. He is marked: "(head of eagle)//France// 25."
Right: The small girl is only 5½in (14cm) tall. She has brown molded hair styled in the typical short bob that children wore in the early 1930s. Her eyes are painted blue and she has a molded silver bracelet on her right wrist and molded shoes and sox. She is jointed at neck, hip and shoulder, unusual for such a small doll. Mark: "15//(head of eagle//France." *Edward Wyffels Collection. Photograph by Berdine Wyffels.*

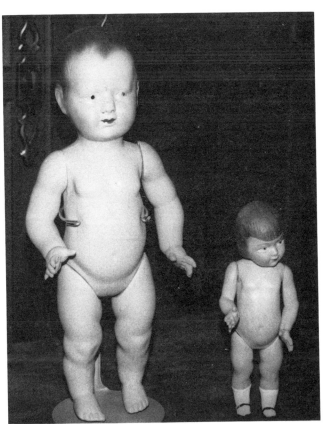

Illustration 96. 16in (40.6cm) "Ethiopia" was purchased in Italy during the Italian occupation of Ethiopia, about 1940. The owner thought it was a Lenci since she bought felt dolls at the same time. She says that there were window displays in the toy stores of Rome and other cities of these dolls seated in small chairs and being taught by white nuns. The doll is black celluloid with painted features and mohair wig. She is fully-jointed and has one ear pierced for a gold earring. She is unmarked and her clothes are not original. *Katherine Malcom Collection. Photograph courtesy of Albert Christian Revi.*

Illustration 98. The trademark of the French firm Petitcolin. It is often found in conjunction with size numbers.

Illustration 99. This 11in (27.9cm) little fellow looks like the older brother of the babies in *Illustrations 51* and *53*. He is completely jointed at neck, hip and shoulder and has painted features. His hair is brown and his eyes are blue. He wears handmade clothing. His shirt is yellow silk and his pants are tan wool. He has a dark brown wool vest. His knitted stockings are gold colored and the hand-sewn brown cloth shoes have brass flower buttons for decoration. Mark on back of head: "(SNF in diamond frame)//FRANCE//27 28". He carries a 3in (7.6cm) green celluloid teddy bear marked: "MADE IN JAPAN." The blue celluloid bear at his feet is unmarked, but is no doubt also Japanese. *Carolyn Baker Collection. Photograph by Ray Baker.*

Illustration 100. Poupée Nobel trademark of the Société Nobel Francaise.

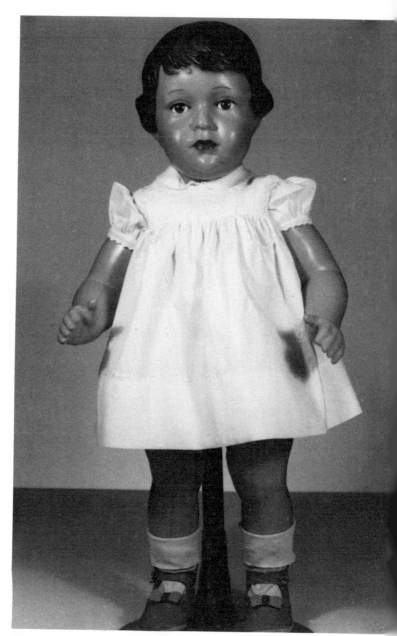

Illustration 101. One of two large 23in (58.4cm) Poupée Nobel dolls of identical model. This one is dressed as a girl. The unisex haircut was in vogue in the 1930s, too! This toddler and the one in *Illustration 102*, like so many of the French celluloid dolls, do not have the typical "dolly" look. It is of excellent quality, a character doll that looks like a real child. The modeling of the features and hair is extremely well done. The hair is brown and she has blue sleep eyes. She is completely jointed. Marked on back of neck: "FRANCE//(SNF in diamond frame)//59 59." *John and Janet Clendenien Collection. Photograph by John Clendenien.*

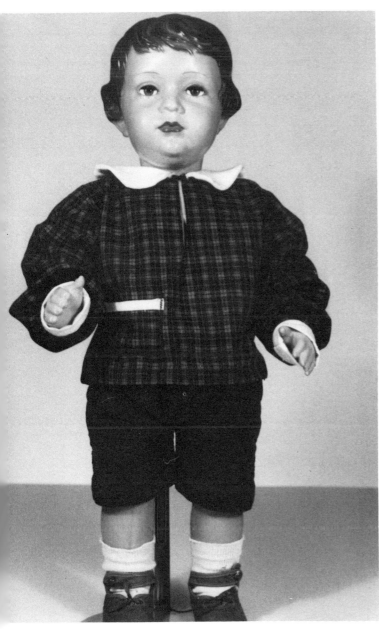

Illustration 103. These are most unusual dolls. They are all-celluloid that is jointed at neck, hip, shoulder and wrist. Another unusual thing about them is that their molded hair is painted black. They are beautiful toddlers of good quality.
Left: This 22in (55.9cm) one has stationary blue glass eyes and is marked on the body: "(windmill symbol)//France//55."
Right: The 17in (43.2cm) smaller doll has brown glass flirty eyes and is marked on back: "(windmill symbol)//France//45." *Edward Wyffels Collection. Photograph by Berdine Wyffels.*

Illustration 102. This is the second large 23in (58.4cm) Poupée Nobel doll. It is dressed as a boy and also has the unisex haircut like the toddler in *Illustration 101*. This character doll, also of excellent quality, does not have the typical "dolly" look either. He has brown hair and blue sleep eyes and is completely jointed. Marked on back of neck: "FRANCE//(SNF in diamond frame)//59 59." *Mary Lou Thompson Collection. Photograph by John Clendenien.*

Illustration 104. French trademark found on the dolls in *Illustration 103*.

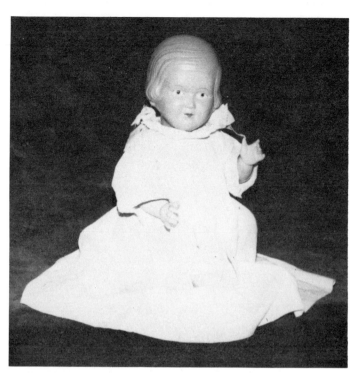

Illustration 106. Mark found on the doll in *Illustration 105*. It is unidentified.

Illustration 105. This 11in (27.9cm) child has molded blonde hair that is styled in the manner of the *Patsy* dolls and others of that era. She is jointed at neck, hip and shoulder. She has a nicely painted little red mouth and blue eyes. She has an unusual mark: "(letter 'S' within a double circle)//31." *Edward Wyffels Collection. Photograph by Berdine Wyffels.*

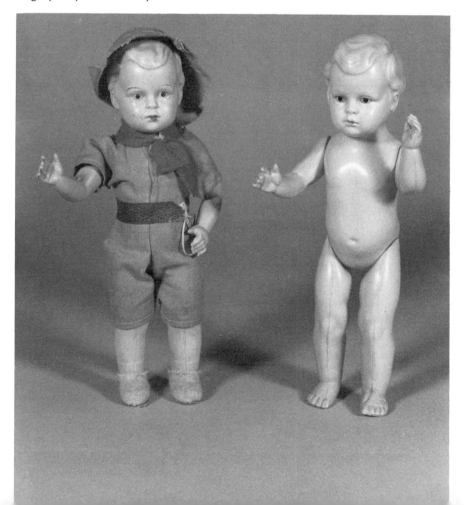

Illustration 107. Two almost identical 7½in (19.1cm) dolls. The one on the left wears what seems to be a Japanese version of a brown Boy Scout uniform with a red kerchief. Under the felt shoes he has molded shoes and sox. The doll on the right is the same, except that his feet are bare. They are made of heavy pink celluloid with molded hair, blue painted eyes with black lid lines and are jointed at the hip and shoulder. They are good quality dolls. The nude doll is marked with the Japan Royal trademark and presumably the other is, too. Boy Scout: *Rosemarye Bunting Collection.*

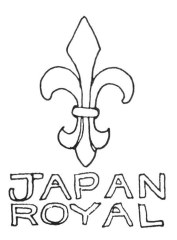

Illustration 108. Trademark found on Japanese dolls made of celluloid.

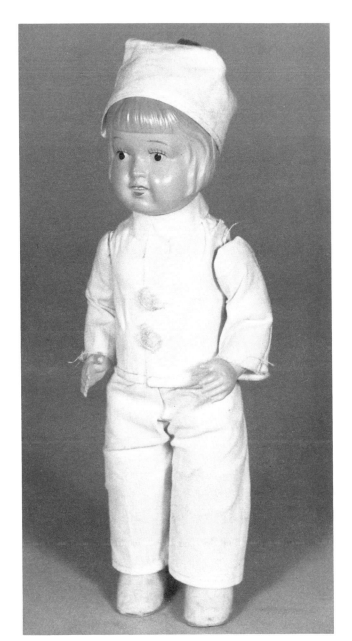

Illustration 110. This 7¾in (19.8cm) little fellow has his white suit glued right to him. He is of the same type thin celluloid as the doll in *Illustration 109* and the molded Buster Brown hair style is painted the same color of reddish brown. His eyes are blue and he has an open/closed mouth with molded teeth. The pompon on his hat is red, and no doubt the buttons, now faded, were too. No visible marks, but probably Japanese. *John Axe Collection.*

Illustration 109. This 6⅞in (17.4cm) boy has reddish hair and painted features. He is jointed at hip and shoulder and has molded black shoes and sox. He wears his original black felt suit, black and white shirt with a button made from a sequin and a red bead. He wears a silver link belt, a plaid tie and a red handkerchief in his pocket. The clothes are sewn on so if he is marked, it is not visible. He is probably Japanese of the pre-World War II era.

Celluloid Heads On Other Bodies

Heads made of celluloid appear just as often on other types of bodies as on those of celluloid. In most cases, the maker assembled the dolls with their bodies, but heads were always available for replacement and dolls were also able to be purchased in parts of one's choice and assembled. Custom designing! There is a good variety for study in this section.

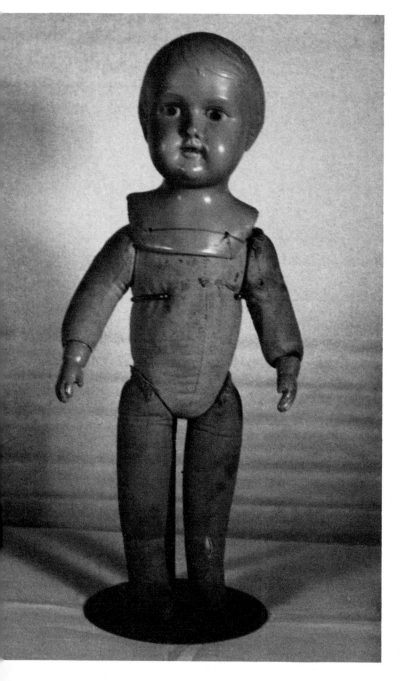

Illustration 111. The head of this 13½in (34.3cm) doll is no doubt a replacement on the cotton body with composition hands, since it fits so badly. However, the head is of interest since it bears the mark of an American manufacturer that is seldom seen, Marks Brothers Co. of Boston, Massachusetts. They made celluloid dolls from about 1918 into the 1920s. It has glass eyes, an open mouth and molded hair. Marked on back: "MADE IN//USA//MARKS//BROTHERS//CO//BOSTON." *Ursula Mertz Collection. Photograph courtesy of Ursula Mertz.*

Illustration 112. Trademark of Marks Brothers Co. of Boston, Massachusetts. (See *Illustration 111.*)

Illustration 113. This 12in (30.5cm) doll is a good example of how doll hospitals and mothers replaced heads that had been broken by accident or murderous little brothers. The label on the kid body with bisque arms tells us that originally the doll was a *Florodora,* a line of bisque-head, kid-bodied dolls that was made by Borgfeldt. Armand Marseille usually made the heads. The trademark on this particular body has a daisy, indicating that it was copyrighted in 1903 and probably before 1909. The head itself is one with an unframed turtle but also with the word "Germany." The doll dates around the turn of the century, a marriage.

The head has several interesting points. The hair, which is very deeply modeled with many comb marks, is basically the same color as all the rest of the head, a pink-tan-flesh color. It is difficult to tell if the darker spots were once paint or if it is merely some dirt in the crevasses. The fact that the blue painted eyes have not been washed off leads one to think the hair was probably not painted. Or did some of the paint adhere better than other? The open mouth has only faint pink lips and there are no whites in the eyes. The most unusual feature is the incised eyebrows. They are carefully done, hair by hair and their color is just a bit darker than the face of the doll. Did they use the method patented by Carpenter in 1880? The smiling open mouth shows six little celluloid teeth. The doll is marked on the back of the shoulder plate: embossed - "GERMANY// (unframed turtle)//SCHUTZ-MARKE." Directly under that is deeply incised in script "NO 11."

Illustration 114. Mark found on doll in *Illustration 113.*

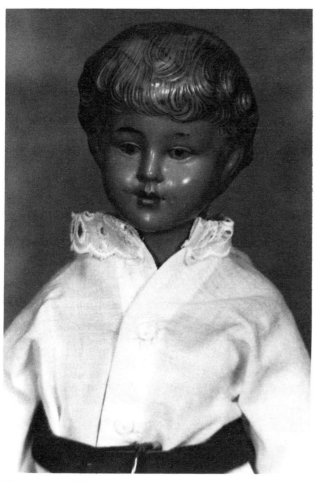

Illustration 115. Here is another early type boy, 14in (35.6cm), with beautifully modeled features and hair. He has blue painted eyes with molded lids and black lid lines. Near to the corners of his closed mouth lurk dimples caused by his hint of a smile. His hair was once painted. This head is on an old cloth body with the red and white striped stockings and brown leather boots made as part of the lower legs. The arms are celluloid that has been painted. He has been redressed, Mark: "(turtle)//24//GERMANY." *Irene Brown Collection. Photograph by Steve Brown.*

Illustration 116. This happy little 10½in (26.7cm) boy is ready to tell us all something funny. He is a real character! Just look at the dimples and the mouth with molded tongue and two teeth. Even his eyes are squinted because of that smile! He has brown molded hair and blue eyes and is on a cloth body with bisque forearms. His mark on the back of the plate is:

"(framed turtle) $\frac{X}{10}$ GERMANY."

The doll has been redressed. *Jean Pritchard Collection.*

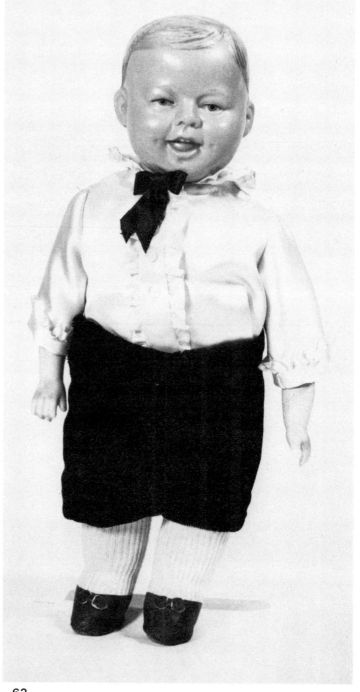

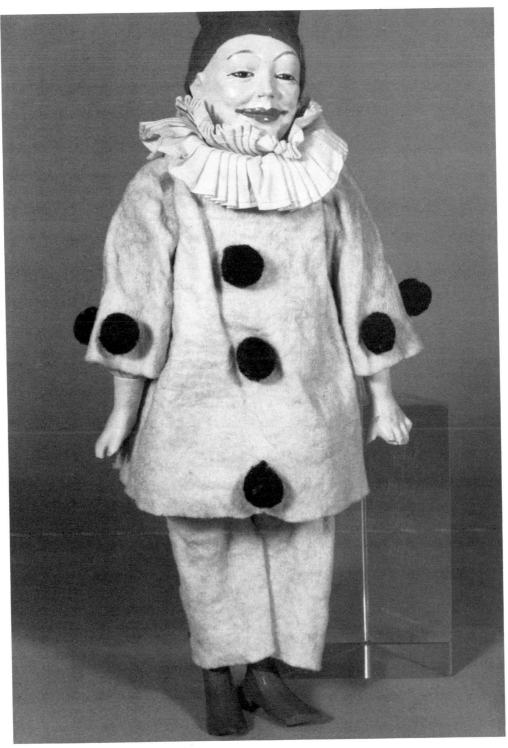

Illustration 117. Although this head bears the mark of the Rheinische Gummi und Celluloid Fabrik Co., the 12in (30.5cm) toy has much more of a French look --their "Pierrot." The head is made of white celluloid that has a vividly painted red mouth, eyes that have been outlined in black with highlighted black dots for pupils and red corner dots. The nostrils are also marked with red and the brows are painted a golden brown. The modeling of the face is extraordinary in that even the laugh lines around the eyes are present as well as dimples and laugh lines around the mouth. The head has a flange neck that is glued to the top of a round cloth-covered spring mechanism which houses a squeaker. When the head is pushed down as the doll stands, it makes a noise. The legs are wooden to the hip and they are shaped and have carved wooden shoes. They are painted red to the knee. The arms are stuffed pink cotton with composition hands that reach above the wrist. The original white felt clown suit has black pompons and a white ruffled cotton collar. The cap is red felt. He is marked around the flange on the neck: "(unframed turtle) 8½ GERMANY."

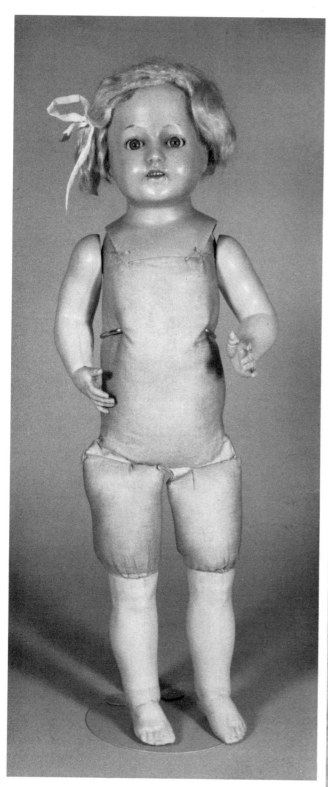

LEFT: **Illustration 118.** This lovely little 17½in (44.5cm) girl is a good example of a celluloid head and limbs in combination with a cloth body. She has blue sleep eyes with waxed lids and the remnants of hair lashes. Her mouth is open, disclosing four celluloid teeth. The brown brows are feathered with ever so tiny strokes and her mouth is a warm red. The blonde mohair wig is trimmed in the short style of the late 1920s. It is interesting to speculate whether or not this head may be one of the heads made according to Albert Beyler's patent of 1927. He filed for the patent in 1926 and those numbers appear on the back of the shoulder plate. Beyler's patent is probably the same one that Mary Hillier refers to as "MIBLU." The initials stand for Milch und Blut (milk and blood). It was a method of spraying the inside of the head with paint to give the celluloid the color of healthy skin. This head is painted inside with a fairly deep shade of pink. The difference in the painted celluloid and unpainted is quite obvious where the paint has peeled away. Those spots look grayish and dirty. *Illustration 120* shows the inside of the head. An unfortunate accident made it possible to share this with you!

The celluloid legs end in a flange just above the knee. The stuffed leg was hemmed and gathered onto the flange. The arms are in one piece. A tube of celluloid runs through the stuffing of the body at the top and the elastic is knotted and slipped into one arm, pulled through the tube and inserted into the other arm.

She is marked on the back of the plate: "(turtle in diamond frame)//GERMANY//12//1926."

OPPOSITE PAGE: **Illustration 119.** The gray areas where the paint has peeled from the inside are more visible in this close - up.

RIGHT: **Illustration 120.** When the head cracked, we pulled it forward far enough to photograph the interior to show the painting and eye insertion. The celluloid tube is visible at the point where it emerges from the shoulder. To clear up any mystery, the thumb and two fingers near the top of the doll's arm belong to her left hand. When it came off, we used it to steady the doll for this picture. She had suffered minor damage before the photography session. That really did her in, poor thing!

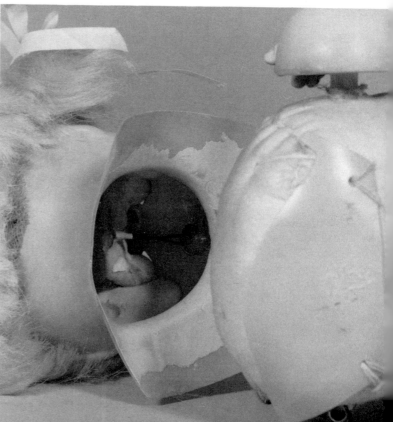

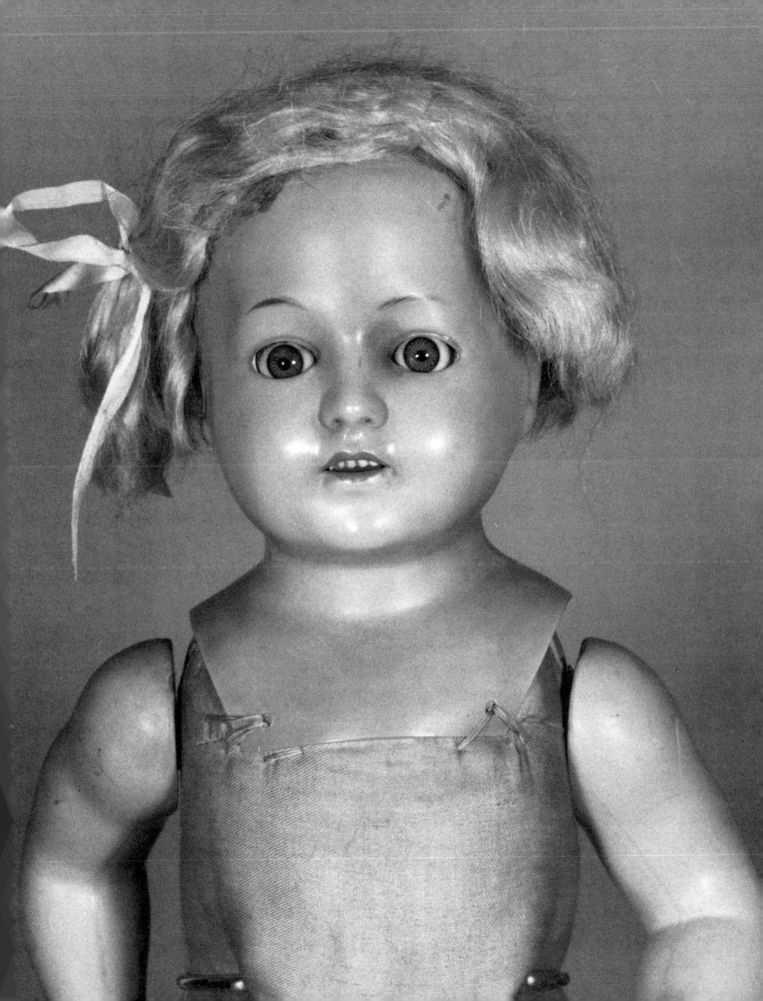

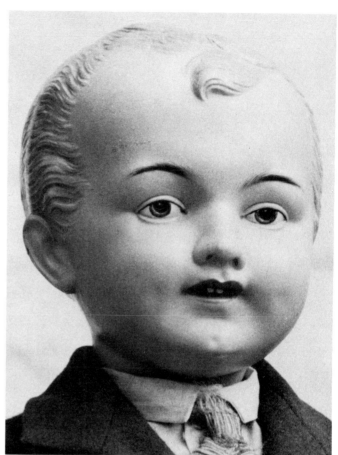

Illustration 122. A close-up of the little boy showing his fine sculpting. The little dimples in his cheeks and chin and the modeled eyelids are indications of a quality doll. *Photograph by Steve Brown.*

Illustration 121. This happy 19in (48.3cm) guy must be going to a party. He is certainly all dressed up in his best suit! Whoever dressed him did a fantastic tailoring job on the wool suit and cotton shirt. He has a very fine quality celluloid head on a regular composition ball-jointed body. The sculpting of the head is carefully and well done. He has blue intaglio eyes and an open/closed mouth with molded teeth. Mark: "(helmet of Minerva)// 6//Germany." *Photograph by Steve Brown.*

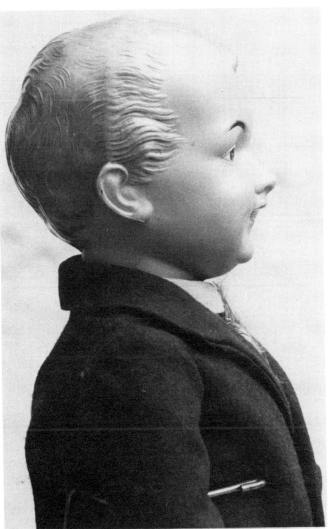

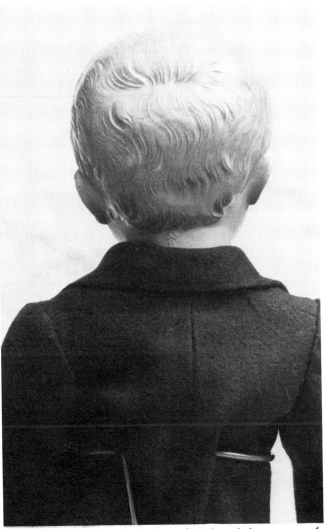

Illustration 123. A side view of the same doll. Notice the fine hair modeling. Isn't that profile the greatest? *Photograph by Steve Brown.*

Illustration 124. A back view of his head shows part of the mark in addition to the fine modeling of the painted hair. *Photograph by Steve Brown.*

Illustration 125. The trademark of Bushow & Beck of Germany.

Illustration 126. 12in (30.5cm) celluloid shoulder head tacked onto a crude papier-mâché body that is jointed at hip and shoulder. The legs are the straight stick type with very tiny feet. The clothes are original, of poor quality pink cotton. *Irene Brown Collection. Photograph by Steve Brown.*

Illustration 127. This close-up of *Illustration 126* is a good example of how a good head could be assembled with a terrible body. This head was no doubt meant for a boy doll. The deeply modeled hair with exposed ears and the heavy brows suggest it. It is a quality head with fine modeling and touches one would not expect on a cheap doll. The eyelids are sculptured and painted with both red and black lid lines. The mouth is open with three tiny teeth. He even has a dimple. The back of the shoulder plate is marked: "(turtle in diamond frame)//8½." *Irene Brown Collection. Photograph by Steve Brown.*

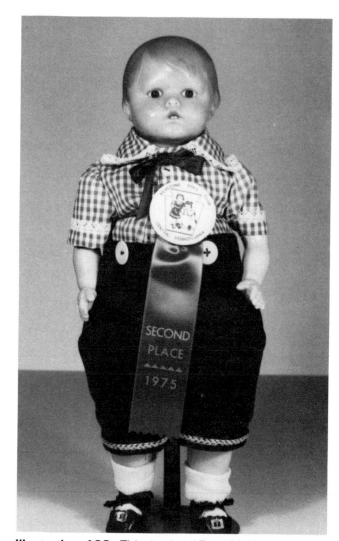

Illustration 128. This is the 17in (43.2cm) celluloid model of Joseph Kallus' *Baby Bo-Kaye*. The head was produced in Germany by Rheinische Gummi. Kestner manufactured the bisque head and Kallus' own company, The Cameo Doll Company, made the composition version. The dolls were assembled by the K & K Toy Co. who probably made the bodies and they were distributed by Borgfeldt. Mr. Kallus, a notable American doll designer, began his association with the Borgfeldt Company in 1912 when he was hired to work with Rose O'Neill on the production of the *Kewpies. Baby Bo-Kaye* was copyrighted in 1926, the year following its appearance in the toy world. The name was taken from the first two letters of "Borgfeldt" and the "K" in "Kallus"--BoK(aye). About 50,000 of the dolls were made. There must have been a huge mortality rate if their availability today is any indication!

This doll, dressed as a little boy, has the typical celluloid shoulder head on a cloth body with composition arms and legs. He has light brown molded hair, an open mouth with two lower teeth and stationary brown glass eyes. He is marked on the back of the plate: "BABY BO-KAYE//Reg. U.S. PAT. OFF.//COPYRIGHT BY// JOS. L. KALLUS//34//GERMANY (turtle in diamond frame)." *John and Janet Clendenien Collection. Photograph by John Clendenien.*

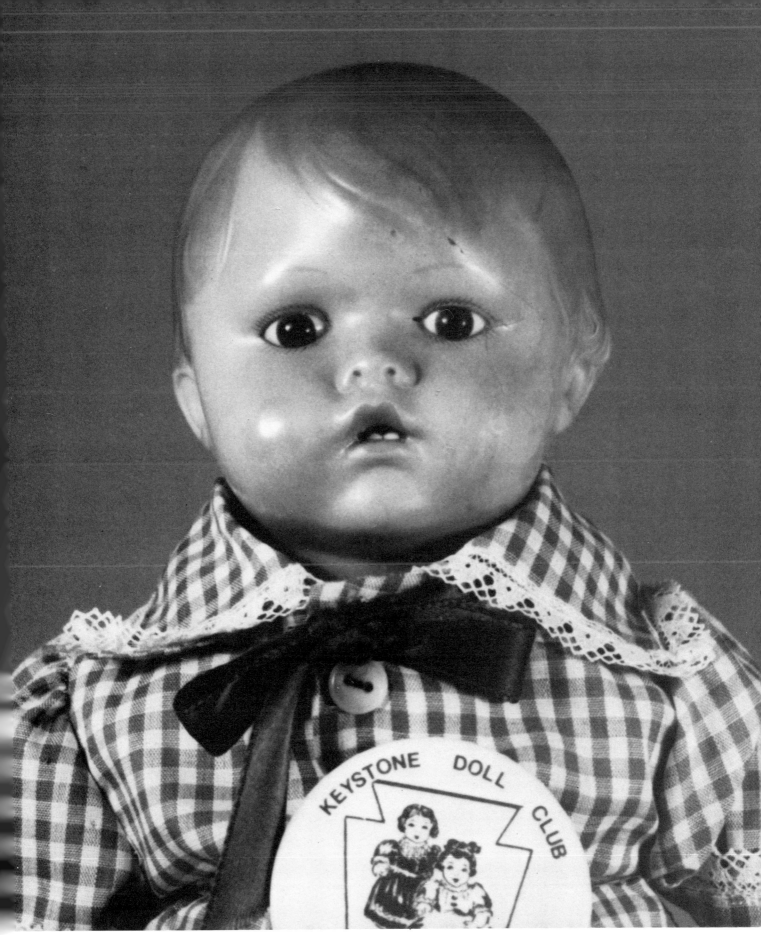

Illustration 129. A closer look at *Baby Bo-Kaye. John and Janet Clendenien. Photograph by John Clendenien.*

Illustration 130. This is 18½in (47.0cm) "DeHaven." He is named for his original owner. He came to me with a horrendous crack in his head that was beyond redemption, but I could not discard him. Fortune smiled one day at a flea market where I found a doll with a kid body wearing "DeHaven's" head! It was a perfect match. Moral: do not be too hasty to discard what seems to be hopeless. "DeHaven" was designed by one of America's foremost doll designers of the early years of the 20th century, Georgene Averill, who was doing business as "Madame Hendren." The toy at his feet is described in the chapter "Mechanicals."

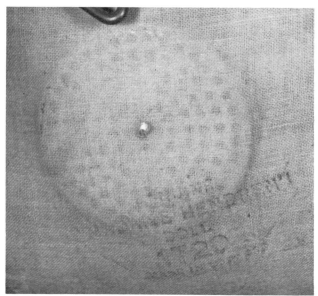

Illustration 133. Back view of the doll in *Illustration 132.* This shows the markings and the crier. The body is stamped with blue ink: "GENUINE//MADAME HENDREN//DOLL//1720// MADE IN USA."

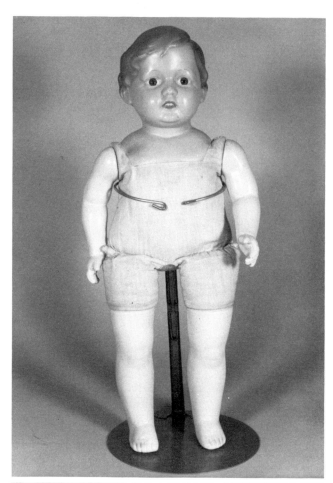

Illustration 132. "DeHaven" without his clothes shows the construction of his body with the "swinging" legs that toy makers advertised as "walking dolls." Georgene Averill patented the "mama doll" with crier in the latter part of the 1920s. This would agree with the information the original owner gave the author. She remembers it being purchased in "the late twenties." A 1929 retail catalog from a hardware store in St. Louis, Missouri, had 12 Madame Hendren dolls listed. Ten were girls and only two were boys. The only one that was given a name was the one like "DeHaven." All were titled either *Sunny Girl* or *Sunny Boy*. "DeHaven" additionally was called *Little Lord Fauntleroy*. There were two hairstyles shown. A girl with bangs also had sleeping glass eyes. Those with the hairstyle of the doll in this illustration were all listed with simply "glass eyes." The dolls ranged in height from 14in (35.6cm) to 21in (53.3cm). *Little Lord Fauntleroy* was shown in two sizes. The 19in (48.3cm) was described as wearing a black velvet suit with white lace-trimmed waist; black silk tie, black velvet tam; silk socks and patent leather slippers. His cost was $132.00 per dozen ($11.00 each). The 17in (43.2cm) size was described as having black sateen clothes and it cost $96.00 per dozen ($8.00 each). I have no explanation as to why a "retail" catalog would offer dolls by the dozen. It may be of interest to the reader to know that in the 1930 Montgomery Ward & Company catalog a "slender Little Girl doll," completely jointed with a bisque head, wig and sleep eyes was advertised at $2.29 for the 21in (53.3cm) size.

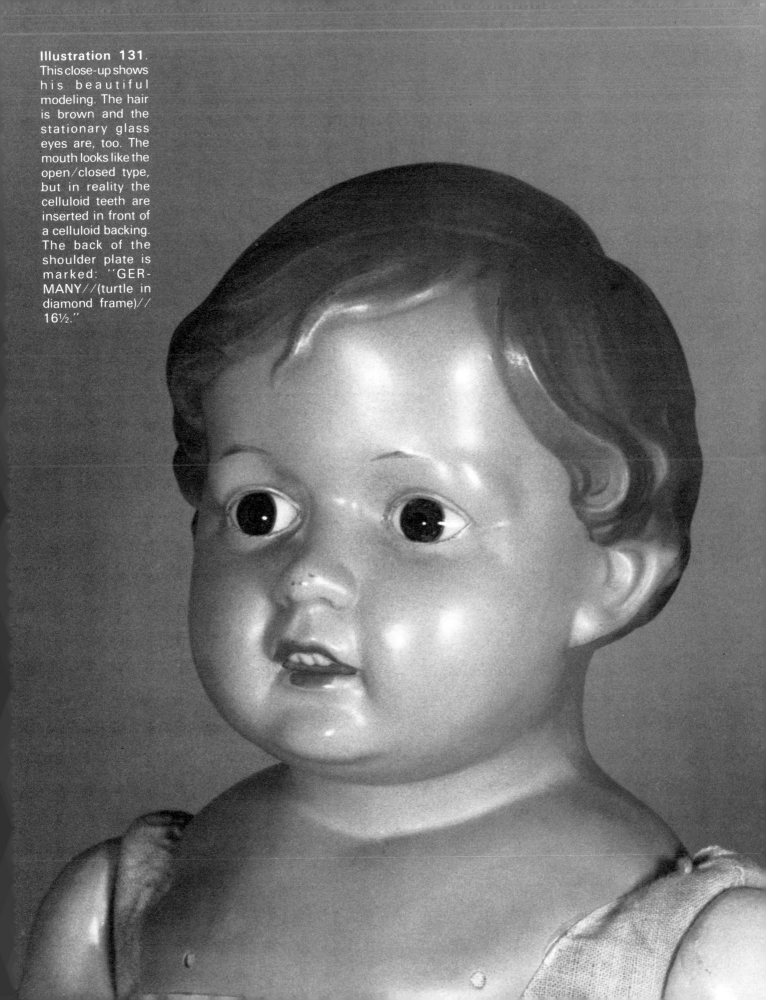

Illustration 131.
This close-up shows his beautiful modeling. The hair is brown and the stationary glass eyes are, too. The mouth looks like the open/closed type, but in reality the celluloid teeth are inserted in front of a celluloid backing. The back of the shoulder plate is marked: "GERMANY//(turtle in diamond frame)// 16½."

Illustration 134. Another 15in (38.1cm) doll designed by Georgene Averill. This is the celluloid version of the popular *Bonnie Babe.* It is a shoulder head on an all-cloth body. The eyes are brown glass and the little crooked open mouth shows two lower teeth and a tongue. The doll has been redressed. Marked on back: "BONNIE BABE, REG. U.S. PATENT OFFICE. Copyright by Georgene Averill. 34 Germany (turtle in diamond frame.)" *Information and photograph courtesy of the Margaret Woodbury Strong Museum.* Another example of a baby designed by Georgene Averill may be seen in *The Collector's Encyclopedia of Dolls* by Dorothy S., Elizabeth A. and Evelyn J. Coleman on page 401.

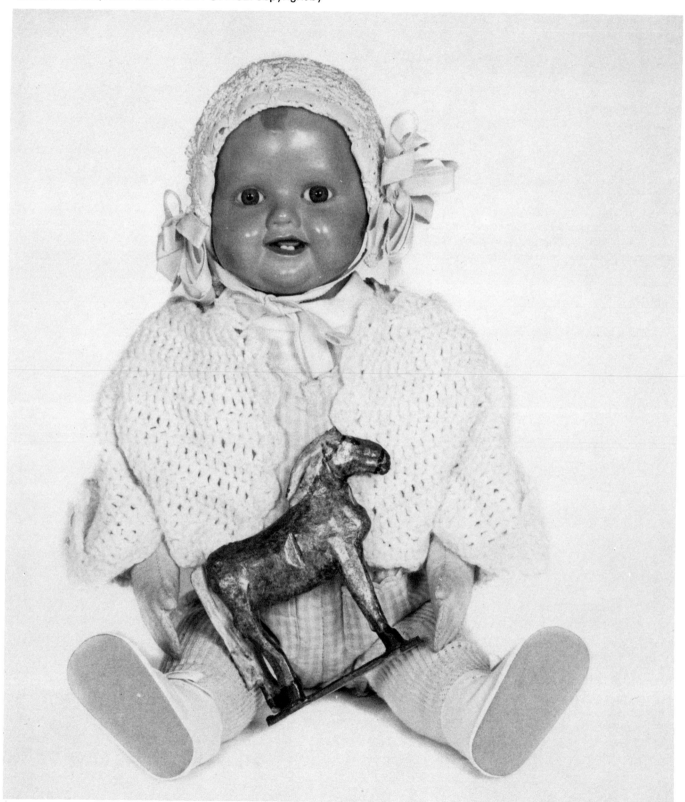

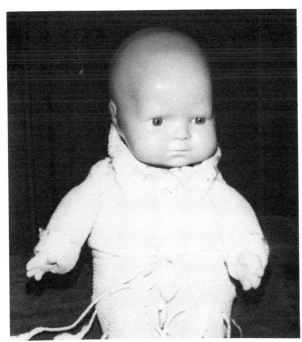

Illustration 135. This celluloid *Dream Baby*-type is on a cloth body with composition hands. It was probably made in the same era. The 1928 Kämmer & Reinhardt catalog shows a similar doll in the 100 series. This one is just like the one shown in the section "Heads Only." It has blue glass eyes and is marked: "(turtle in diamond frame)//103/14 Germany." Height of doll: 11in (27.9cm). *Edward Wyffels Collection. Photograph by Berdine Wyffels.*

Illustration 136. This is 18in (45.7cm) *My Rosy Darling* in her original box. She is the celluloid version of K★R 117. The dolls were advertised in the Kämmer & Reinhardt catalog of 1928 thus: "Dolls dressed according to artistic designs. 'My newest darling,' the charming slender doll, the modern line, the sweetest maiden's head. With living knavish eyes, of finest biscuit porcelain, the most enchanting model 117. All sizes are also delivered on request with the most beautiful head of celluloid 'My rosy darling,' model 117. Prices according to price list. Select clothes made to special original designs. Particularly painted on silk, also especial beautiful and yet praiseworthy clothes." She is called "117" in the ad. She is marked 717. The firm used the 700 series to denote the celluloid versions. She has the regular ball-jointed composition body that was used with the bisque heads.

The dolls shown in the catalog all wear dresses. This little charmer left the factory in a white cotton slip that is hemstitched at the top and also embroidered around the top and on the straps. She also wears her lacy white sox and white leather oxfords with two eyelets. Her huge hair bow is pale green silk. The doll had always been kept in her box, never played with. She still rested her neck on a pillow of pink tissue paper stuffed with excelsior. Because her stringing had gone completely, we used the similar pad which was at the top of the box to prop her shoulders. The other remains under her feet. She was tied into the box at the neck and

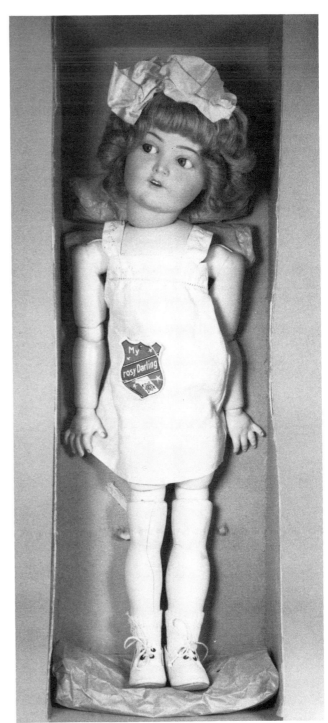

both legs. Temperature and humidity changes over the years have cracked the finish on her composition legs, but her blonde mohair wig is still unmussed and she flirts with one and all. She has metal eyelids that come down over her flirting blue glass eyes and her brown brows are feathered. She has an open mouth with four celluloid teeth. The back of the head is marked: "(K★R symbol)//46/717//GERMANY//(turtle in diamond frame)." The cardboard tag fastened to the slip with a brass spread pin is about 2in (5.1cm) high and printed with the company symbol and "My Rosy Darling" in a combination of blue, white and gold. *Evelyn Yalsch Collection.*

Illustration 137. The end of the box shows the Kämmer & Reinhardt trademark and the name of the line, "My Rosy Darling." Just above the label is another that proclaims, "The Flirt." The heavy cardboard box was made to simulate alligator skin. Its corners are reinforced with strong metal strips. The small label in the lower left indicates in German, English and French that she is a pale blonde. *Evelyn Yalsch Collection.*

GERMANY

Illustration 138. The Kämmer & Reinhardt trademark. It is found in conjunction with other words and numbers.

OPPOSITE PAGE: Illustration 140. One of the most sought-after infants in any medium is *Baby*. He is referred to in early doll books as *Baby Otto*. Later, collectors were to know him as *The Kaiser Baby* because of a fanciful story about the Kaiser's withered arm. Kämmer & Reinhardt called him simply *Baby*. He was the first of their very successful line of character dolls that was introduced in 1909. The bisque mold is No. 100. The character dolls came at a time when the doll market was in a terrible slump. When the Munich Art dolls of Marion Kaulitz caught the fancy of the public, Kämmer & Reinhardt were quick to see the possibilities and hastened to employ an artist to design a realistic infant for them. *Baby* was the fantastically successful result. In addition to the bisque model, he has been found in composition and celluloid. There is also a rare 200 series that is the shoulder head. Celluloid models were the 700 series. This doll has molded hair that is painted brown and blue painted eyes. He has a regular bent-leg composition body. Mark: "(K★R symbol)// 700/50." Height: 19in (48.3cm). *John and Janet Clendenien Collection. Photograph by John Clendenien.*

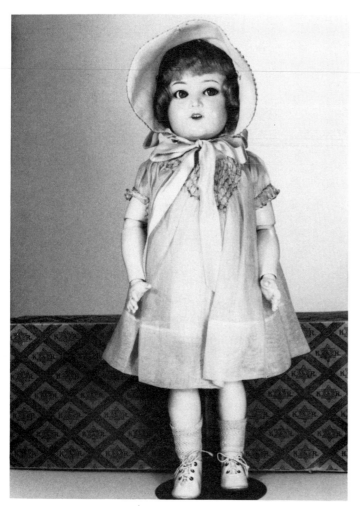

LEFT: Illustration 139. This 18in (45.7cm) doll is another K★R 717, but in a different type original box, and she wears her original outfit which consists of white lawn slip and pants that are lace trimmed and yellow organdy dress and bonnet that have lavender smocking and embroidery. Her bonnet ribbons are also lavender. She wears white leather shoes and white lace sox. Like the doll in the *Illustration 136*, she has a celluloid head on a composition ball-jointed body. Her flirty eyes are slate-blue and she has a wig of brown human hair. The Kämmer & Reinhardt trademark has been incorporated into the design of the box. Mark: "(K★R symbol) //46/717// GERMANY." *John and Janet Clendenien Collection. Photograph by John Clendenien.*

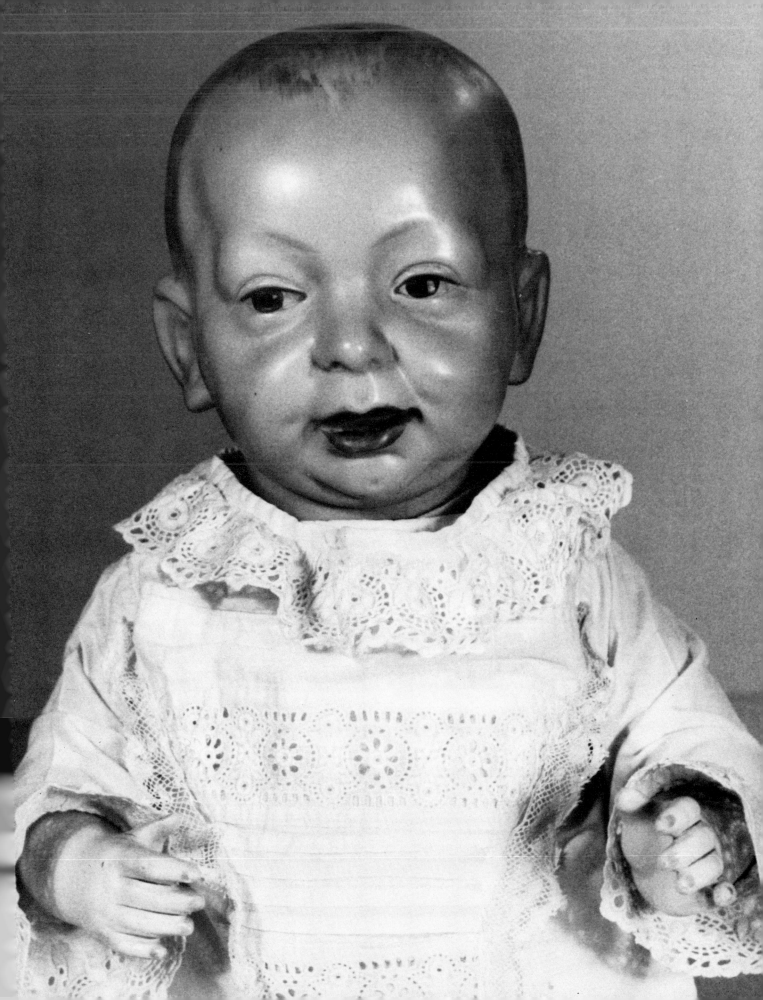

Illustration 141. This is the 16in (40.6cm) celluloid version of Kämmer & Reinhardt's popular model 101, *Peter.* He is on a completely jointed composition body and wears his original clothing, black felt lederhosen with red and white embroidered suspenders, a white cotton shirt and a black felt alpine hat. Because we are all so familiar with the doll, it is interesting to see how much better the modeling "comes through" in celluloid. His eyes are painted blue with molded lids and lid lines. The painting of the features is wonderfully lifelike. He has a brown mohair wig cut in little boy style. A truly beautiful doll. Marked on back of socket head: "(K★R symbol) 701//(turtle in diamond frame)//GERMANY." *Lois Fida Collection.*

Illustration 142. This is the 15in (38.1cm) celluloid shoulder head version of *Marie.* She is on a kid body that has cloth lower legs and celluloid forearms. She wears her original peasant costume of white blouse and skirt trimmed with black braid and red yarn embroidery. The bodice is black with gold buttons. Her shoes are carved of wood. *Marie's* head is made of the celluloid that has a slight gloss. *Peter's* is the matte finish. Her blue intaglio eyes have molded lids and painted lid lines. Her brown mohair wig is coiled in snail braids. She is marked on the back of the shoulder: "(unframed turtle)//(K★R SYMBOL)//301." Generally dolls made this many years after the turn of the century would have the framed turtle mark. Kämmer & Reinhardt introduced their character dolls in 1909/1910. *Irene Brown Collection. Photograph by Steve Brown.*

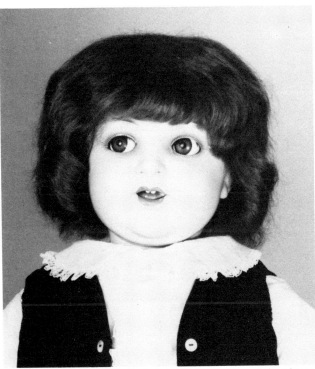

Illustration 143. This is the same model head that is on the all-celluloid toddler in *Illustration 90*, but this 27in (68.6cm) doll has a composition toddler body. He has a brown human hair wig, gray glass flirty eyes that sleep and an open mouth with a tongue that quivers. Mark: "K★R symbol)//728/11//GERMANY//62/65." *John and Janet Clendenien Collection. Photograph by John Clendenien.*

Illustration 144. The well-known symbol used by Kämmer & Reinhardt in conjunction with various numbers and marks.

Illustration 145. 20in (50.8cm). This is a splendid example of a celluloid shoulder head on a kid body. He wears a tan pongee middy blouse trimmed with red soutache braid and a red neckerchief. His pants are beige and tan checked wool and he wears tan silk stockings and brown leather boots with buttons and tassels. The clothing has been replaced but the footwear is probably original. The little dog is described in the chapter "Novelties." *Rosemarye Bunting Collection.*

Illustration 146. A close-up shows the excellent results that could be attained with the use of celluloid as a product for molding. The brown painted hair is modeled in a typical Buster Brown hair style with waves, curls and comb marks. His blue intaglio eyes with painted white sclera have remarkable depth. He has molded lids with red and black lines and red corner dots. His faint smile has produced tiny dimples at the corners of the open/closed mouth and the tip of his tongue is just visible. *Rosemarye Bunting Collection.*

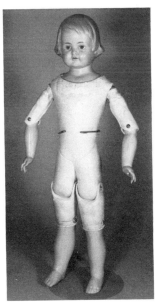

Illustration 147. Without clothing it is even more evident that this is a quality doll. The kid body is of excellent workmanship, similar to those used by Kestner on dolls of similar construction. This doll, however, is unmarked as to maker. The celluloid arms and legs are attached with wire and metal fasteners in the same manner as bisque limbs are. The back of the shoulder plate is marked: "GERMANY//7." *Rosemarye Bunting Collection.*

Illustration 148. *Hansi* is a 7in (17.8cm) little fellow with French and German connections. His head and arms are heavy celluloid. The modeling is quite good. The eyes are blue intaglio and the hair is molded and painted blonde. He has a real character face with the hint of a smile and two dimples. The flange neck is attached to a pink drill body and hidden by a collar of the same material. The neck is marked: "2/o//HANSI." The body is stamped: "GERMANY." The Colemans in *The Collector's Encyclopedia of Dolls* tell us that about 1917 L'Oncle Hansi made character dolls with heads and arms of celluloid and that among them were *Yerri* and *Gretel.* L'Oncle is French for Uncle. *Irene Brown Collection. Photograph by Steve Brown.*

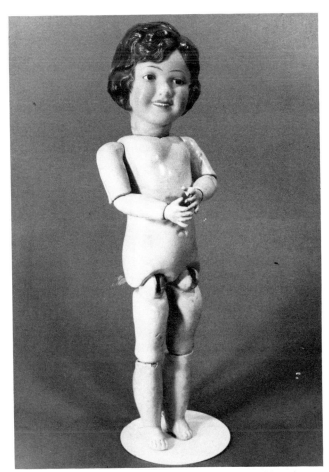

Illustration 149. This beautiful celluloid head has been put on a contemporary ball-jointed composition body. The modeling and painting are extremely fine. She has molded teeth and lovely inset brown glass eyes. Her curly hair is painted a deep auburn and the feathered brows are a bit lighter. She has rosy cheeks and red lips and eye corners and nostrils are indicated with red dots. Height of doll: 16in (40.6cm). Mark: "(head of eagle//FRANCE//43." *Courtesy of Ralph's Antique Doll Museum, Parkville, Missouri.*

Illustration 149a. Mark found on doll in *Illustration 149.*

Dolls in Ethnic Costume

The pair of dolls in Tyrolean outfits in *Illustration 150* are examples of the good quality that was available to the traveler looking for a souvenir of his journey or for something to take home for a child who asked the never-changing question, "What did you bring me?" These two, obviously a pair, were probably purchased from a jobber and dressed by another toy firm. Their costumes are matching, but their marks are different. Both are fine quality celluloid with very good modeling, the girl's slightly better than the boy's. The dolls are both all-celluloid, jointed at hip and shoulder. They have blue painted eyes with highlights, molded upper lids and black lid lines. The hair is well modeled on both dolls. They are the same color of rosy flesh with ruddy cheeks.

The boy is 9½in (24.2cm). His hair is a dark blonde. The hands are not nearly as nice as those of his companion. Although the fingers are separate, they were not molded as well and have celluloid left between them. His clothes are fantastic. He has white cotton underpants and a tan cotton shirt which is fastened with a snap. The shirt even has a little attached collar made just like one on a sport shirt, faced and turned and edge-stitched. He wears a tie of a bittersweet color that is repeated on his jacket collar, pockets, shoes and hatband. His lederhosen are gray suede trimmed with green kid and bound around the top with brown leather that matches the lacings. The suspenders are buttoned on with carved bone buttons. The little jacket is made of

gray felt trimmed with green collar and lapels and red and green decoration on the front. Hearts of gold colored metal are attached to the lapels. Above the red kid shoes that are stitched by hand are hand-knitted white and green wool cuffs for stockings. His little Alpine hat is made of green suede. He is marked on the back: "(crowned mermaid symbol)//25."

The girl is 9⅞in (25.1cm). Her hair is brown. The hands are much nicer, each finger separate almost to the base and in a more expressive position. Her clothing, while it is very well made, cannot compare with the boy's. She wears a little white cotton petticoat. One would assume that she originally had panties, but they are missing. Her dress has a skirt of gray taffeta trimmed with bright green braid with woven daisies and hearts. It is sewn to a red cotton top with white sleeves and she wears a white apron and a printed red shawl with white fringe. Her sox are white felt and she wears the identical shoes and hat that the boy does. Mark: "(turtle in diamond frame)//25½/26½." You will find this same mold used with variation in many of the dolls in this book. It is of interest that these costumes are sewn with a zigzag machine-stitch. Although the zigzag stitch sewing machine was not introduced in the United States until 1948, it had been introduced in Europe as early as 1882, so we cannot assume their date from the fact of the stitching.

Illustration 151. Trademark of the Cellba works in Babenhausen, Germany, found on the boy in *Illustration 150.*

OPPOSITE PAGE: Illustration 150. A 9½in (24.2cm) boy doll and 9⅞in (25.1cm) girl doll in Tyrolean costumes; both dolls were made in Germany.

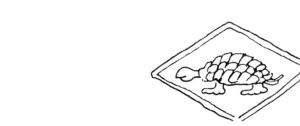

Illustration 152. Mark found on the girl in *Illustration 150.* It will be found on several dolls of the same model in this section. It is the mark of the Rheinische Gummi und Celluloid Fabrik Co.

Illustration 153. This 14in (35.6cm) young lady from Sweden has a celluloid shoulder head and forearms on a very good quality flesh-colored cotton body. The body is constructed to sit easily, and although it is seamed at the knees, there is not much mobility there. She has blue glass sleep eyes with hair lashes. The lower lashes are painted and the brows lightly feathered. Her lids are molded but do not have painted lid lines. She has an open mouth with six celluloid teeth. Her blonde mohair wig is styled in a straight bob. The costume is all original and quite eye-catching. Her dress is bright orange cotton flannel topped with a heavy woven apron of red and white and a white shawl printed with bright roses and yellow daisies. Her little cap is made of matching material and the ribbons are light brown. There is a tiny silver decoration on the front of the shawl and the same metal shaped into a heart is tied to her wrist. It is marked: "LISSKULLA//SVERIGE//(two crossed arrows.)" Her stockings are long white cotton and the shoes are brown leatherette with silver buckles. She wears white drawers and petticoat. The shoulder plate is marked: "(turtle in diamond frame)//GERMANY//9//1926." The same head is seen in *Illustration 119*. Her toy ducks are quite colorful and probably Japanese.

Illustration 154. Another little Swedish girl, this 6¼in (15.9cm) doll is all-celluloid, jointed at hips and shoulders. The face is the familiar one found on so many Rheinische Gummi dolls. We did not attempt to undress her to find a mark. She has painted features and a hank of yellow mohair glued to the head for a wig. Her feet are painted black to look like slippers and the legs are painted white to the knee. Her costume is very well made. There are even little lace-trimmed cuffs on the white cotton blouse. Her skirt is bright red wool topped with a gaily striped apron. She wears a little gray sateen bodice and cap, both bound with green. Silver metal eyelets hold the ties for her bodice. A gold paper label on her skirt bears the words "Swedish//hand-work//HERRESTAD//Goda Ideer." There is a Kimport label under her apron. *Photograph by Jane Buchholz.*

Illustration 155. Three little all-celluloid dolls dressed in provincial costumes. The girls, shown front and back are 6in (15.2cm). They are jointed at hip and shoulder. Under the synthetic wigs the hair is molded in the familiar style found on this model doll made by the Rheinische Gummi und Celluloid Fabrik Co. Their features are painted and so are their bare feet -- to represent shoes. They wear the straw hats with huge pompons that were typical of the Black Forest. Marked on back: "(turtle in diamond frame)//13½/14." Typical souvenir dolls, they have loops on their hats so they may be hung on something. The 5½in (14cm) boy is made of thinner and lighter colored celluloid. He, too, is jointed at hip and shoulder and has painted features. He is a bit different in that he looks to one side, smiles and the left arm is bent more than the right. He wears yellow cotton flannel pants with black felt jerkin and hat trimmed with red. He, too, has feet painted to look like shoes. His wig is blonde mohair. He is marked: "D.E.P.//GERMANY//(crowned mermaid symbol)//13//13½."

Illustration 156. This pair of little German children are also of the later variety. LEFT: The 15in (38.1cm) boy has a swivel head, blue sleep eyes and has no markings on his body. He has a wrist tag that reads: "From Bavaria, original Schmeder, Trachten, Loisi Oberbayerr Mit echter Lederhose." RIGHT: The 16½in (41.9cm) girl has a swivel head and blue flirty eyes. She is marked on the back: "(Emaso within a circle)//40." It was the trademark of E. Maar & Sohn of Monchroden, near Coburg, Thur. *Edward Wyffels Collection. Photograph by Berdine Wyffels.*

Illustration 157. Trademark found on doll in *Illustration 156.*

Illustration 158. These two girls in their provincial costumes would seem to be the same doll that is in *Illustration 340*. Both are 14in (35.6cm) and are marked: "(turtle in diamond frame)//T-36." The later Schildkröte dolls of the transition type were made of Tortulon and marked with a "T". The Käthe Kruse dolls were advertised as being made of this material and were so marked. *Edward Wyffels Collection. Photograph by Berdine Wyffels.*

Illustration 159. Another pair of all-celluloid dolls in Tyrolean costume. These are also in original clothes and probably pre-date the pair in *Illustration 150*. They are 7¾in (19.8cm) with brown glass sleep eyes, open mouths with two upper teeth and mohair wigs. Hers is brown and his is blonde. They are marked: "(K★R symbol//728/5/0//GERMANY//19." The 1928 Kämmer & Reinhardt catalog mentioned this type doll but stated the smallest sizes were 24, 28 and 33cm (about 9½in to 13in). They were probably added later to the line. *Jimmy and Faye Rodolfos Collection.*

OPPOSITE PAGE: **Illustration 161.** These two in Dutch costume are completely different types. The little boy is 9in (22.9cm) and has a celluloid head with a flange neck on a cloth body. He has painted molded brown hair and blue intaglio eyes. He wears brown felt pants, a blue felt jacket with pearl buttons and a print tie. His shoes are carved wood. The head is marked: "(helmet of Minerva)// No. I//23//GERMANY." *Lillian Mosley Collection.* The girl is 11in (27.9cm). She is all-celluloid, jointed at hip and shoulder. Her hair is deeply molded and she has brown intaglio eyes with brown lid lines. Her brows and hair are very light brown. She wears a typical Volendam costume. The skirt is brightly striped cotton flannel. The top and apron are black felt trimmed with a floral print cotton. She has pink silky underwear and black stockings and wears wooden shoes. Her cap is lacy starched white cotton. Her mark is only partly legible. Only "land" in the country of origin is clear. Marked on back: "LUCKY//LIFE//MADE IN//---LAND" in a heart. (See *Illustration 163*.) *Penny Caswell Collection.* The little dog is Japanese.

Illustration 160. Kämmer & Reinhardt mark used in conjunction with other numbers and marks. Found on dolls in *Illustration 159*.

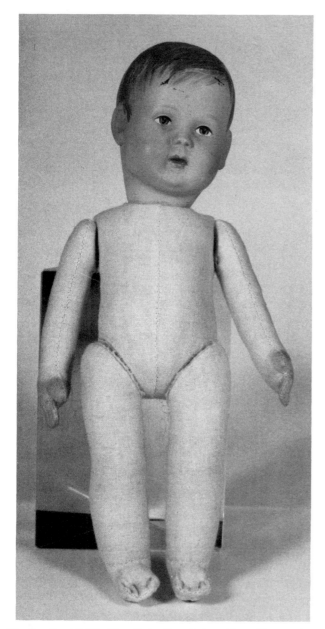

Illustration 162. The little Dutch boy (See *Illustration 161*) shown undressed. His body is very well constructed of flesh colored cotton with disc joints. The fingers and toes are indicated by stitching. *Lillian Mosley Collection.*

Illustration 164. The boy doll's trademark (See *Illustration 161*.) The helmet is the Minerva trademark of Buschow & Beck.

Illustration 165. These two little girls in their colorful outfits are similar to the little Dutch boy. These, however, have celluloid heads and also hands on cloth bodies. They both have painted brown eyes and brown mohair wigs and are in all-original condition. Both are about 14in (35.6cm) tall and are identically marked: "(helmet of Minerva)//No. 4//30." *Edward Wyffels Collection. Photograph by Berdine Wyffels.*

Illustration 163. Unidentified trademark found on the girl doll in *Illustration 161*.

Illustration 166. Underneath this girl's costume from Czechoslovakia is a little 6in (15.2cm) all-celluloid boy. He has a boy's short haircut (unpainted) and exposed ears. His eyes and brows are painted gray. One-strap black shoes and knee stockings are painted black. Jointed at hip and shoulder, he has nicely modeled hands and the left arm is bent more than the right. A white cotton petticoat is stamped: "CZECHOSLOVAKIA." This stamp is also on the doll's left thigh. The costume is bright with a blue skirt trimmed with yellow and print blouse and bonnet. Mark on back: "15."

Illustration 167. Another large 21in (53.3cm) all-celluloid doll with beautifully modeled brown hair, painted light blue eyes and wearing an original costume of Poland. She is unmarked. *Edward Wyffels Collection. Photograph by Berdine Wyffels.*

Illustration 168. LEFT: This 16in (40.6cm) all-"celluloid" girl wears a colorful costume of Poland. She has a brown wig, blue sleeping glass eyes with lashes and an open mouth with upper teeth. She is jointed at neck, hip and shoulder. No mark is visible, but a tag on her wrist reads in Polish: "Kaliskie Zaklady Tworzyw Sztwcznch." RIGHT: The 16in (40.6cm) companion doll is from Czechoslovakia and wears a costume of that country. She is a transition doll with painted molded brown hair and unusual painted green eyes. The head is marked: "40" and the body is marked: "40//(techplast symbol//MADE IN CZECHOSLOVAKIA." Both dolls from the *Edward Wyffels Collection. Photograph by Berdine Wyffels.*

Illustration 170. This little 7in (17.8cm) black boy seems to be dressed in fishermen's clothes. He wears his original red pants and shirt with patches, a straw hat and has a yellow net draped over his shoulder. He has molded hair and painted features. The all-celluloid body is jointed at hip and shoulder. He is marked: "(head of eagle)// FRANCE//1 75//3." *Carolyn Baker Collection. Photograph by Ray Baker.*

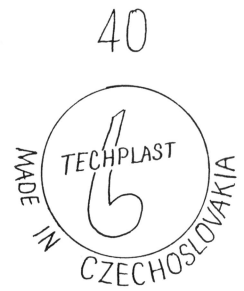

Illustration 169. The trademark found on the doll from Czechoslovakia. (See *Illustration 168.*) It is unidentified.

Illustration 171. The Téte L'Aigle (head of eagle) mark used by Petitcolin of Paris. This mark, in conjunction with other numbers and words, is found on several dolls in this section.

Illustration 172. Three little 5in (12.7cm) dolls whose provincial costumes give them added height. They are all-celluloid, jointed at hip and shoulder. They all have molded white ribbed sox and black one-strap slippers. The doll on the right seems to be a bit earlier than the others. She is lighter in color and has a mohair wig. The other two have synthetic wigs. She also has a costume of just a bit better quality. It is blue velveteen with a red wool hood/cape. The one on the left wears a dress of green rayon with a white organdy headdress. Both have woven labels: "MADE IN FRANCE." The doll in the rear (middle) wears a bright red cotton print dress and black rayon apron with "VENCE" printed in gold paint. She wears a lace-trimmed cap under her straw hat. A little paper gold cross is tied with a black thread around her neck. Although the clothes have not been removed to check, these dolls identical to the larger dolls in this section that have the Petitcolin mark.

Illustration 173. Another pair of the same model doll in a different size, 6¾in (17.2cm), and costume. They are made of the same lightweight celluloid and have the same characteristics. They have brown mohair wigs and the costumes are of much better quality. The girl wears a cream wool skirt with a deep red band. Her blouse is white cotton with cuffs of embroidered braid. The red wool apron and white shawl collar have hand embroidery. Her cap is lace-trimmed white satin. The boy wears yellow twill trousers with red ties, a white shirt with a little turned collar, a blue felt vest trimmed with red and a matching felt hat. They are marked on the back: "(head of eagle)//FRANCE//(numbers hidden by clothing.)"

LEFT: Illustration 174. Two or more dolls in provincial costumes, 10½in (26.7cm). Again they are Petitcolin dolls. Quality seems to vary a great deal in these dolls' costumes. A little 7¾in (19.8cm) doll which is not shown has clothing made of heavy black bengaline, felt and slipper satin, all well finished and trimmed. A paper wrist tag reads: "Poupée//Noelline." These show quite a difference, too. The flower-seller has semi-finished cotton clothing that is pinned directly into the doll. The other doll wears a dress of maroon rayon trimmed with heavy gold braids of various designs. The best thing about her is her rolled velvet headdress that is also ornately trimmed with gold. Both wear metal crosses. They are marked on the back: "(head of eagle)//FRANCE //270."

OPPOSITE PAGE: Illustration 175. This 15in (38.1cm) doll is spectacular. She is all-celluloid and jointed at neck, hip and shoulder. She has painted features with modeled eyelids with lid lines and a brown mohair wig. Surprisingly, she has molded shoes and sox like the others, but her hands and arms are more slender and adult-looking. The costume can be seen elsewhere in color. It is beautifully made with lavish use of fine materials. Her gold wrist tag reads: "Je m'appelle//THUMETTE//mon pays est// Pont-L'Abbé//en Bretagne." (My name is THUMETTE. My country is Abbey Bridge in Brittany.) On the back of the dress is a gold heart with the words: "M.A. LE MINOR//PONT L'ABBE" A woven label in the skirt says: "MADE IN FRANCE." She is marked: "(head of eagle)//FRANCE//35." *Margaret Wirgau Collection.*

FRANCE

Illustration 177. Components of the mark used by Société Nobel Francaise.

Illustration 176. This 5¾in (14.7cm) saucy miss is that well-known Parisian entertainer, the Can-Can Dancer. She is all-celluloid, jointed at hip and shoulder. Her features are exotically painted with even a beauty mark. The costume on this tiny lady is very well made of good quality materials. Her outer dress is scarlet taffeta trimmed with black lace. Underneath she wears the typical petticoat with many rows of full lace ruffles, lace panties and black mesh stockings. She has a blue silk garter on her right leg. She has molded high laced black boots and wears black mesh mitts. The wig is blonde mohair and she wears a high headdress of red and white feathers. The little checkerboard she stands on is a piece of cardboard covered with red faille and black celluloid squares. A nail through the bottom into her foot holds her in position. She is marked: "(head of eagle)//130."

Illustration 178. This 8in (20.3cm) doll is shorter than her clothing. She is 9in (22.9cm) in her costume. She is all-celluloid, jointed at hip and shoulder. Her eyes are heavily painted black to look oriental. The black brows sweep up and add to the look. Her black synthetic wig is dressed in a Japanese style. Her blue silk print kimono is lined with stiff buckram and trimmed with bright red silk. A willow pole with a multi-colored paper lantern is thrust through a hole in her wrist. She has very firm bust pads to give her an adult shape and underneath she wears the typical white sox these dolls all seem to have. Her shoes are the usual molded wedge-heeled slippers painted burgundy. She has a small length of white ribbon with the words: "MADE IN FRANCE" inked on it and stapled to the lining of the skirt. The mark is not visible but she is probably marked with the Nobel mark since her legs are the kind they used.

Illustration 179. These two 8½in (21.6cm) dolls are lightweight, pale celluloid. They are jointed at hip and shoulder and have molded shoes with wedge heels. The shoes are painted the burgundy color that seems to be usual with this type doll made by Poupée Nobel. They have painted white sox. The features are painted with varying degrees of skill. (Not really the greatest.) They have brown mohair wigs. These provincial costumes are very well made from fine materials. The dresses are silk velvet trimmed with gold with pink braid. One dress is light blue with a white satin apron and the other is black with a pink faille apron. Only the collars and headdresses are different. They have lace-trimmed blue panties and starched cheesecloth petticoats, also lace-edged with woven "MADE IN FRANCE" labels. Gold paper labels are tacked to the hems of the dresses. They read: "POUPÉE MARTEL." The dolls are marked: "FRANCE// 7//(SNF in diamond)//21." Paper wrist tags are printed: "MADE IN FRANCE" and have the model numbers inked in. Black dress: "1658/1//Briton." Blue dress: "1658/2."

Illustration 180. Mark found on dolls made by Société Industrielle de Celluloid.

Illustration 181. These two 11¾in (29.9cm) dolls are interesting because they are evidently from the same mold. One doll looks taller because her skirt holds her up. The bodies are identical with painted white sox and molded, flat one-strap shoes that are painted the familiar burgundy color. They are fairly lightweight celluloid that is tinted an orangish-flesh color. The dressed doll is just a bit lighter color and has a gloss finish. The other, which seems to be of later vintage, has a matte finish. Both dolls have inset celluloid eyes with silk lashes. The dressed doll's eyes look like pale blue glass with stria. The other's are more like the plastic eyes we see in today's dolls. The bodies are presumably the same. The modeling is fairly good. The nude is marked: "FRANCE//(SNF is diamond)//30//2." The only visible mark on the dressed doll's back is: "FRANCE//(SNF in diamond)." This is the mark of Société Nobel. The dressed doll's head is marked: "4//FRANCE." The nude's head is marked with the trademark of a different firm altogether: "5//FRANCE //3//(S/C) in diamond)." It is the trademark of Société Industrielle de Celluloid. Both have brown synthetic wigs. The costume on the one doll is extremely fine. Her dress is made of scarlet felt trimmed with heavy gold braids and silk ribbon woven with a design of pink and blue, edged with gold lace. The stomacher is white satin edged with lace and gold braid. The collar is pleated linen with lace edging. A starched lace headdress completes the outfit. A woven label is sewn into the skirt: "AU NAIN BLEU//406a412 RUE ST. HONORE. PARIS" is the label of a famous toy shop in Paris. The doll is very probably one costumed by Madam Le Minor.

BELOW: Illustration 183. This little 7in (17.8cm) black toddler is all-celluloid, jointed at hip and shoulder. His hair is molded into tiny, kinky curls that are painted black. He is a rich chocolate brown. He has true ethnic features, painted eyes and lips. He wears his original outfit. The white cotton top is part of his underwear. There is also a lace-edged stiff petticoat under that long vividly striped skirt of red, white, green and black cotton. His necklace is a string with two silver glass beads similar to those used on the old Christmas garlands. Glue marks on his head indicate that he probably wore a turban of some sort. No marks.

Illustration 182. This is another doll costumed by Madam Le Minor. Her overall height is 17in (43.2cm). The skirts of these fine dolls are usually quite full and so stiff that the doll's legs do not reach the floor. The doll actually measures 15½in (39.4cm). She is all-celluloid, jointed at neck, hip and shoulder. Her molded flat slippers are painted burgundy and she has white painted sox. The celluloid is a tan-flesh color. She has inset brown celluloid eyes with silk lashes and painted brows. Her lips are very deep pink and the cheeks lightly blushed. Her wig is brown synthetic. The head is marked: "FRANCE//(SNF in diamond)//38." She is clad in the costume of Savoy. Her dress of heavy blue/green changeable silk is fully-lined with buckram and trimmed at the hem with bands of intricate silk braid in a design of orange, gold and green. These, in turn, are banded with narrow gold braid. Her heavy black velvet apron is edged with gold lace and the matching shawl has black silk fringe. The dress front is starched white lace and her cap is black velvet with gold braid. A tiny gold metal cross hangs at her throat. A heart-shaped paper tag on her right wrist is gold on the obverse and reads: "Me m'appelle//MARION//mon pays est//LA//SAVOIE." (My name is Marion. My country is Savoy.) The reverse is white with: "LE MINOR." Her original price in the 1940s was $25.00. *Photograph by Jane Buchholz.*

All-Celluloid Tinies and Kewpie-Types

The tiny dolls in this section are 4½in (11.5cm) tall at the most. The *Kewpie*-types are larger, but do not go up to the size of a 22in (55.9cm) example that was reported by a doll club in Arizona. Wouldn't that one be fun!

Tiny dolls like this have always been favorites of children. There is something about having a doll small enough to cuddle in one's palm or slip into a pocket that is almost irresistible. The survival rate was not as good for them as for the larger dolls, but some managed to avoid destruction by being stashed away in funny places like button boxes. (For the benefit of the younger readers, a button box, usually an empty, round tin candy box, was where one kept buttons that had been cut off discarded clothes. Possibly only one of a hundred of those buttons might find use, but NOTHING was wasted. A lot of little things were dropped into button boxes because no one could think of a better place to put them! Today's collectors love it.)

Many of these dolls were sold in dime stores. The *Kewpie*-types were especially plentiful. The girls with waved hair were very popular with little girls of the Depression era.

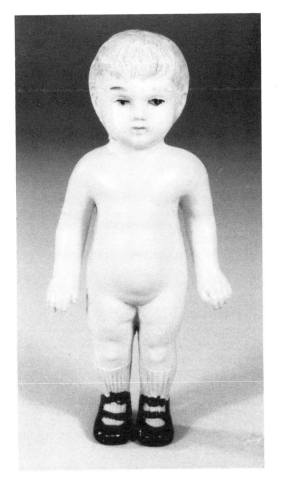

Illustration 184. This little 4½in (11.5cm) bathing doll is one of the early dolls produced by the Rheinische Gummi und Celluloid Fabrik Co. His mark was registered in 1889. The tortoise with a diamond frame (the more familiar "turtle mark") was registered in 1899. He has well-modeled hair and shoes and sox. He is made of the heavy early celluloid. Mark: "(turtle)//SCHUTZ MARKE//11." *Carolyn Baker Collection. Photograph by Ray Baker.*

GERMANY

Illustration 185. One of the marks that may be found in conjunction with numbers on dolls manufactured in Germany by the Rheinische Gummi und Celluloid Fabrik Co.

SCHUTZ-MARKE

Illustration 186. Another mark of the German firm, the Rheinische Gummi und Celluloid Fabrik Co.

Illustration 187. The taller doll is 4½in (11.5cm) and is identical to the one shown undressed in *Illustration 184*. This one is dressed as a girl in a flannel combination (undies) and a cotton dress with a silk sash in just the manner that a little girl might have sewn for her dolly. The baby sitting at her feet is 2¾in (7.1cm), jointed at hip and shoulder. She has very good modeling for such a tiny thing. The blue intaglio eyes have black lid lines and her little mouth is dark red. She wears an original outfit of a pink and white checked dress and a white bonnet with a pink ribbon. She is the heavier early celluloid, but not as early as the other. The short baby dress would indicate the 1920s, at least. We did not attempt to remove the original clothes to find a mark. She is probably German. *Maurine Popp Collection.*

Illustration 188. This is a 3in (7.6cm) little sweetheart. She has so much presence for her size. Her modeling is extremely good with deep comb marks in her blonde hair and nicely painted features. She has blue intaglio eyes with black lid lines and red corner dots. Her little mouth is a rosy pink and she has pink nostrils. We really should have removed her green velvet coat for her photograph. Underneath she wears her original knit underwear. (Her dressmaker many years ago added a diaper!!) She also wears a lace-trimmed lawn petticoat and a little white dress with a woven white stripe made in the low-waisted style so popular for little girls just before the turn of the century. Her bonnet is lace with pink ribbons. It was possible to dress her this way because she is jointed at hip and shoulder. She has little tan molded sox that are meant to look like they are knitted and black Mary Janes. Her tiny hands are molded front and back; even the knuckles and pads on the palms are there! A good guess would be Rheinische Gummi; the boy in *Illustration 77* has the identical shoes and sox. *Photograph by Jane Buchholz.*

Illustration 189. Another tiny German lass, 3in (7.6cm). This little girl is jointed only at the shoulders. Her molded brown hair has an orange band around the head and she has brown painted eyes. She wears panties made from a bit of lace and a green cotton dress. She is marked: "(helmet of Minerva)//8//GERMANY."

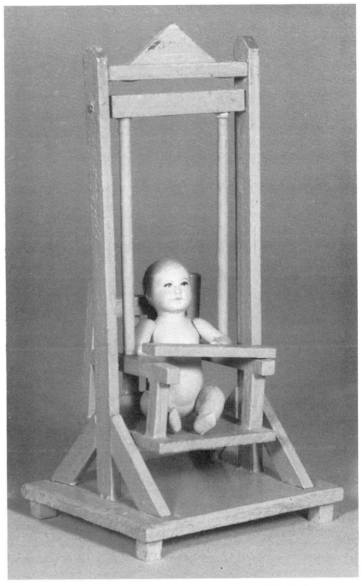

Illustration 191. 3in (7.6cm) baby made of fairly heavy celluloid with matte finish. He is jointed at hip and shoulder and has brown painted hair that is only slightly modeled in the front and facial painting that is unusually detailed for this size doll. Many times the eyes on these little fellows are just black dots. He has blue eyes with pupils, molded lids and black lid lines. The modeling of the body is above average, too. He is marked just above the waist: "MADE//IN//USA." printed in an oval. His swing is pink wood from the 1930s.

Illustration 190. Trademark of Buschow & Beck. Germany.

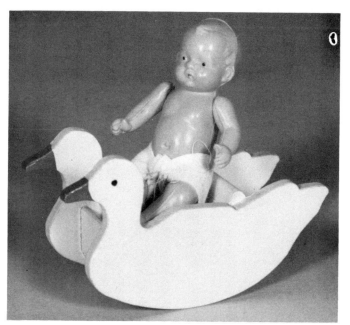

Illustration 193. A little 3⅛in (7.9cm) Japanese baby of light pink-flesh celluloid. His hair is molded blonde. His painted eyes are just black dots. Jointed at hip and shoulder, he wears his original flannel diaper. Mark: See *Illustration 194*.

Illustration 194. Mark found on *Illustration 193*. Not identified.

Illustration 192. A pair of 3¼in (8.3cm) bathing dolls, but in factory clothes. They are identical except that the girl has the remnants of a blonde mohair wig, not merely a hank of the material glued to her head, it was sewn to a mesh cap and tied with a red ribbon! They have molded hair, painted eyes and modeled shoes and sox. The clothing is sewn on the dolls. She wears a white cotton dress with a pink sash and his pink suit is embroidered with white. It would not have been an easy job to dress these tiny dolls without breaking their arms. One snapped off as I examined it to see how close they were to the bodies. This kind of work was usually done by women in their homes. The pay was a few cents for a certain number. Girls in factories dressing dolls made only a few cents an hour. One wonders if the workers were ''docked'' if they broke any dolls. Just visible on the boy's back is the framed turtle.

RIGHT: Illustration 195. This little 2½in (6.4cm) boy with his molded Dutch costume (he even has wooden shoes) was probably painted originally. Only his intaglio eyes are distinct now. He is made of a heavy ivory-colored celluloid. He is marked on the back of the left sleeve: ''GERMANY'' and with the symbol shown in *Illustration 196* on the back. *Photograph by Jane Buchholz.*

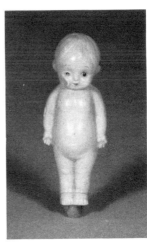

Illustration 196. The mark found on doll in *Illustration 195*. It is the mark of Dr. Paul Hunaeus of Linden (near Hanover) in Germany. According to *The Collector's Encyclopedia of Dolls* by the Colemans, he made celluloid dolls from 1900 past 1925. In 1900 he was granted two German patents. One was for sleeping eyes in celluloid heads and another concerned the torso and arms and leg joints of celluloid dolls. In 1901 he was granted another patent concerning sleeping eyes. He made celluloid dolls' heads and complete dolls. Some of these heads were also marked: "IGODI" which was the trademark of Johannes Dietrich.

Illustration 197. The unusual thing about this little 2⅜in (6.0cm) rigid Japanese doll are his molded eyeballs! There are other surprises, too. He has modeled pads on his little palms. The hair is sculpted in a short wavy style and painted blonde. He has a definite tooth mark on his cheek. (That baby was no doubt cutting his first teeth --none on the other side!) The doll rattles, whether by accident or intent is not known. Mark: "MADE IN JAPAN" in a half circle on the back.

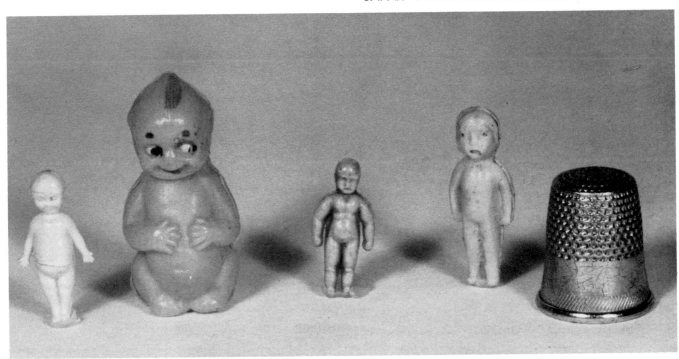

Illustration 198. These four dolls are examples of the small dolls that have somehow survived being lost. They are all unmarked, and probably vary in age by 20 or more years. They are, left to right: ⅞in (2.2cm) made of heavy white celluloid with *Kewpie*-type molded hair and features. 1⅜in (3.4cm) *Kewpie*-type squatting on his haunches. There are molded tufts of hair on his head. ¾in (2.0cm) a very small version of the bathing doll. He is deeply modeled. His arms are away from the body. 1⅛in (2.8cm) not nearly so nice. It has just a bit of molded hair in back and blue eyes and red mouth. *Maurine Popp Collection*.

Illustration 199. Four minis of varying degrees of quality, none very good. Left to right: 2in (5.1cm) made of heavy flesh-colored celluloid with well modeled, typical *Kewpie* tufts of hair and pale blue wings. The arms are rigid. The mark is indistinct, but it is not Japanese. 1⅜in (3.4cm) small and awful, but jointed at the shoulders. It has a single molded forelock. Mark: "JAPAN." 1⅜in (3.4cm) another S&A (small and awful). This has the *Kewpie* tufts and wings. Also jointed at shoulders. Mark indistinct. 2in (5.1cm) *Kewpie* with green wings perched on his shoulders right under his ears. Jointed at shoulders. All three are made of lightweight celluloid. This one has the mark in *Illustration 200*.

Illustration 200. Japanese trademark found on celluloid dolls. Unidentified.

RIGHT: Illustration 201. An unjointed 2⅜in (6.0cm) *Kewpie* of heavy flesh-colored celluloid. He has the *Kewpie* tufts, but not as well modeled as the one in *Illustration 199*. They are painted brown, as are the faint wings on his shoulders. The red shield has been painted on with a stencil. There is a white circular label printed in black: "COPYRIGHT ROSE O'NEILL" glued to his back, which is embossed: "10/0."

Illustration 202. This is the 3in (7.6cm) black version of the *Kewpie* known as the *Hottentot*. These little dolls came into being about a year after the first *Kewpies* were introduced. They were made from 1914 to about 1925 and usually came as a pair in a blue and white checked blanket. Their eyes glanced in opposite directions. They had white wings and the hair was painted black. They were jointed only at the shoulder. This one has vestiges of his original paper sticker, a black-edged red shield. He is marked on the back: "8/0" and has a circular paper label as seen in *Illustration 203a*. We should have removed his fancy straw hat for the photograph.

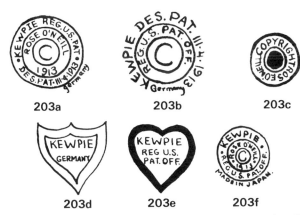

203a 203b 203c

203d 203e 203f

Illustration 203. Paper labels found on *Kewpies*. The *Hottentots* were found with a and b. The labels c, d, e and f are *Kewpie* marks and, according to *The Collector's Encyclopedia of Dolls* by the Colemans, the unauthorized versions carried the marks e and f. *Used by permission of the Colemans.*

Illustration 205. Another bride and groom, 4in (10.2cm), dressed in their crepe paper clothes. This couple does not have as much of the *Kewpie* look, but they come from about the same era. She has a light brown mohair wig with a wreath of posies around her head. They were also probably used as decorations for a wedding cake or favors. Mark: See *Illustration 206. Carolyn Baker Collection. Photograph by Ray Baker.*

Illustration 204. 3½in (8.9cm) wedding couple from the early 1920s. They are dressed in their original crepe paper clothes. The happy bridegroom wears tails and a top hat. The sleeves are glued to his arms. Black satin ribbon binds the edges of his coat and he has a little fuzzy cloth flower on his lapel. No doubt the same florist provided her bouquet. Her veil of tulle is held to her head with bands of pale green chenille. They probably graced a wedding cake. There is still paper stuck to their feet. Although they look like the *Kewpies*, they do not have wings. Mark on back: See *Illustration 207.*

Illustration 206. Mark found on Japanese celluloid dolls in *Illustration 205.* Unidentified.

Illustration 207. Trademark found on dolls in *Illustration 204.* Unidentified.

Illustration 209. This little 3½in (8.9cm) two-faced doll is an example of the Japanese tendency to copy anything they thought would sell. One side has a *Kewpie* face and the other side is a *Billiken* (see *Illustration 210)* and has the word embossed on the right leg. Additionally, it is marked: "(CK in a diamond// PAT.11217 (or 14217)." These would not be United States patent numbers; they are not high enough. The wings of the *Kewpie* side are painted green. *Kewpies* were distributed by George Borgfeldt. *Billiken* was a copyrighted doll of the Horsman Company. Both were popular dolls in the same era, *Billiken* from 1909 to 1912 and *Kewpie* in 1913. The doll would probably date from the early *Kewpie* period, before *Billiken* was passé. *Judith Whorton Collection. Photograph by Judith Whorton.*

Illustration 208. 6in (15.2cm) made of very pink-flesh celluloid with molded tufts of hair in the *Kewpie* manner, over the ears and on the forehead. No peak on the head or tuft in the back. He is jointed at the shoulders. The seams are very poorly finished and the painting only fair. He should have individual fingers, but they still have chunks of celluloid between them. Marked on back: See *Illustration 205.*

RIGHT: Illustration 210. *Billiken* side of the two-faced doll shown in *Illustration 209. Judith Whorton Collection. Photograph by Judith Whorton.*

Illustration 211. This 3¾in (9.6cm) *Kewpie* is made of the same heavy celluloid as the little one on the left in *Illustration 199*. The shape of the mark, although not entirely legible, is the same. He has the well-modeled blonde tufts and dark blue wings on the back of his neck. His painting is what is most unusual about this little fellow. He has very heavy, black, curly lashes and heavy brown dots for brows. He is jointed at the shoulder. Mark: "(looks like "DESON")//43680//PATENT." Because it does not have enough numbers for an American patent of this era, and because it does not look Japanese, a good guess would be German.

C67310—Celtid Baby, painted hair and eyes, jointed arms, knit mercerized rompers, cap and bootees, 6 inches; ½ dozen in box ......
...........Dozen 4.00

C67310

C67312—Boy and Girl, Bisque heads: sideways glancing glass eyes; mohair wig; jointed limbs, pressed paper body, striped cotton cloth dresses; 6½ inches; 1/6 dozen assorted in box ....Dozen 4.00

Illustration 212. A comparison of prices in the *1914 Marshall Field & Company Doll Catalog*, reprinted by Hobby House Press, Inc., shows that a 6in (15.2cm) Celtid doll with moving arms cost a fraction more than 33¢ each, wholesale. This is the same price for 6½in (16.5cm) bisque head *Googlies* that resemble those made by Armand Marseille. 8in (20.3cm) celluloid dolls with molded clothes and moving arms were 62½¢ each and the familiar bisque girl with bangs made by Heubach was only 4¢ more in the same size. It becomes obvious that these small celluloid dolls were considered quite comparable to their bisque counterparts.

Illustration 216. A large 11in (27.9cm) all-celluloid *Kewpie*. It is dark pink with blue painted eyes and brown hair. The molded wings are green. He is a very well-modeled doll with individual fingers, rolls of fat and a sweet little mouth. It is probably one of the dolls from the era between what we called celluloid and what later came to be known as plastic. He is jointed at the shoulders and still wears his original tag that reads: "'KEWPIE'//DESIGNED//and//COPYRIGHTED//by ROSE O'NEILL.//ARNART IMPORTS INC.'" Marked on back: "(oriental design)//No 92189// PAT. NO.// 380851//No. 24. 12." *Carolyn Baker Collection. Photograph by Ray Baker.*

Illustration 213. This is another *Kewpie*-type, 9in (22.9cm), without the peak and wings. His brows are double strokes and he has painted lashes. The hands are in the typical starfish position, but have the fingers modeled straight together instead of spread apart. The celluloid is fairly heavy and quite pink. He is jointed at the shoulders. Mark: See *Illustration 214*. Green and white paper label on feet is shown in *Illustration 215*.

Illustration 214. The embossed "A" is a mark found on celluloid dolls. It is probably Japanese.

Illustration 215. Green and white paper label found on Japanese dolls.

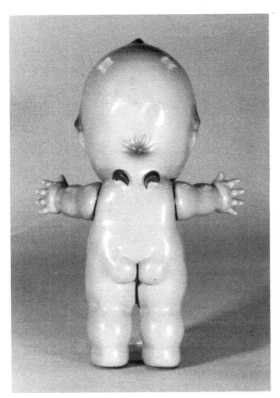

Illustration 217. Back view of *Illustration 216. Carolyn Baker Collection. Photograph by Ray Baker.*

Illustration 218. Trademark found on doll in *Illustration 216.* Unidentified.

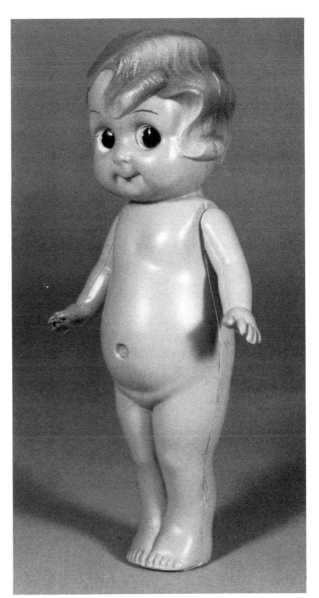

Illustration 219. 8in (20.3cm) and every inch a 1920s flapper! She has red marcelled hair, the huge painted googly eyes with lashes that were considered "it," and a smiling, heart-shaped mouth. The celluloid is fairly heavy and a ruddy color. She is jointed at the shoulders. Her navel is a deeply incised curlicue and she has tiny, fat buttocks. Quite a gal. This type doll was a favorite of little girls of the late 1920s and early 1930s. Young seamstresses then were not so industrious as their mothers. Many of these dolls acquired huge wardrobes made from scraps from adult sewing projects. They were mostly of two designs: a straight piece of material with a hole in the center and a slit to make it large enough to slip over the head. This poncho-like dress was then tied with a sash. The fancier outfit was a circle of material with a hole in the middle for a skirt. A matching smaller circle made a dandy wide-brimmed hat and a straight piece with two holes for arms made a bolero. There were a lot of variations of this basic design, large circle -- long evening skirt, small circles of tulle -- a ballerina's tutu. She is marked on the back and has a paper label on the feet. (See *Illustrations 220* and *221*.)

Illustration 220. Unidentified mark found on celluloid dolls.

Illustration 221. Paper inspection label.

Illustration 223. Mark found on Japanese celluloid dolls. Unidentified.

Illustration 222. Another doll of the same type, 6½in (16.5cm). Her hair style underneath that cap is rows of marcelled waves. It, too, is painted red. The celluloid is the same ruddy color and she is jointed at the shoulder. This doll wears a dress and hat crocheted from gold wool yarn trimmed with pink. Her hat is joined to the top of the dress and it has a yarn covered loop on a length of yarn attached to the top. She was made to hang from something. Mark: See *Illustration 223*.

Illustration 224. This is a typical example of the cheap souvenir doll, 3½in (8.9cm). She is made from very lightweight celluloid, jointed at the shoulders. She has marcelled hair that is painted gold. Her eyes have black pupils and blue sclera, red lashes and brows. She wears molded red shoes and white sox. Seams are rough. The stiff cotton lace dress is gathered and stapled. She wears a thread with glass "Christmas beads" on it around her neck. She is attached to a badge by a rubber band that is held by a loop of ribbon. Her flowers are thin plastic. Mark: "MADE IN JAPAN."

Illustration 225. A couple more S & As (small and awful) 3⅝in (9.2cm) souvenir Indians -- right off the "Japanese Reservation!" They are tan celluloid with molded straight bobs under their black yarn wigs. They are jointed at hip and shoulder and wear their original cotton flannel Indian suits.

BELOW: Illustration 226. These four MUST be the nadir of the world of celluloid. We would have to rate them S & TA (small and terribly awful!). They range in size from 3⅝in (9.2cm) to 2⅜in (6.0cm). The larger dolls are jointed at hip and shoulder, the smaller at the shoulder. They are all made of very light celluloid that is poorly finished and badly painted. The garish clothes are glued on. Paper labels with "JAPAN" are glued to the backs of the large ones. These would have been available for children to play with. They are not a souvenir-type doll. I cannot imagine that a child would want them for more than a few moments. But, they are part of the celluloid story.

All-Celluloid Dolls With Molded Clothes and Accessories

Celluloid lent itself well to making dolls with molded clothes and accessories such as balls, bottles and toys held in the doll's hand. This was another way to sell more dolls. If a child had a doll with no clothes, why not make dolls available that had clothes molded on? This would create a demand for more dolls as children always want what is new or different and parents are usually able to be manipulated, especially if the cost is not too great.

One wonders if the reason there are so many more of these little dolls from Japan was because the German doll makers were directing their efforts in the era of celluloid's great popularity to making better quality dolls, larger and more expensive models.

Illustration 227. A group of small all-celluloid dolls with molded clothes ranging in size from 3in to 9in (7.6cm to 22.9cm). This group shows the wide variety in style and type. Rear, left to right: The first three have only moveable arms. The next two are jointed at hip and shoulder. The four in the front row are unjointed. *Edward Wyffels Collection. Photograph by Berdine Wyffels.*

Illustration 228. This poor little 4½in (11.5cm) fellow with his flattened head is one of the few examples of a doll with molded clothes that has an American trademark. His sailor suit is blue and he wears tan shoes and white sox. The flowers are unpainted flesh-colored celluloid. Mark: See *Illustration 229*. Maker unknown. *Maurine Popp Collection.*

Illustration 229. American trademark found on the celluloid doll in *Illustration 228*.

Illustration 231. Indian head trademark found on celluloid dolls. Unidentified.

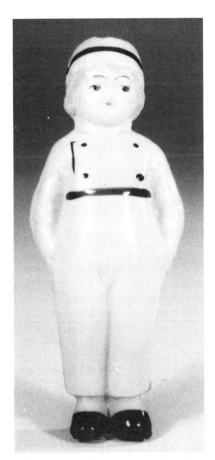

Illustration 230. This little 4¼in (10.9cm) boy has another American mark. He has a yellow hat and suit accented with the same color as his blue shoes. Mark: See *Illustration 231*. *Carolyn Baker Collection. Photograph by Ray Baker.*

Illustration 232. This 9in (22.9cm) *Kewpie*-type is holding a molded violin. He and his jointed dog are from Japan. He has no wings. Both he and the dog have the mark shown in *Illustration 233*. The dog is jointed at head and legs. He is pink with white markings. 5in (12.7cm) long and tall. The doll was advertised in *Playthings* in March 1920, by Foulds & Freure, Inc. *Carolyn Baker Collection. Photograph by Ray Baker.*

Illustration 233. Mark found on Japanese celluloid dolls. They are usually of a higher quality. Unidentified.

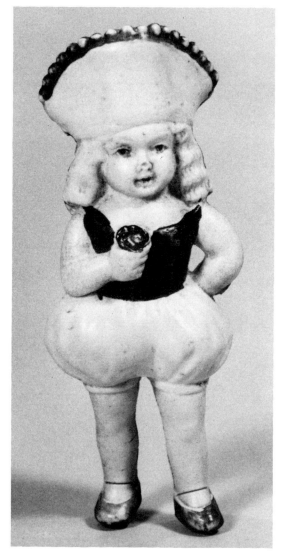

Illustration 234. This 4¼in (10.9cm) little girl is unusual in the non-articulated dolls with molded clothes in that she has separated legs and an arm partially away from her body. She is cream-colored heavy celluloid with good modeling. Her hat is pink with gold trim; her bodice is blue and the bloomers are cream. Her shoes and the rose in her right hand are red. The left hand is clenched behind her back. Mark: See *Illustration 233. Marjorie Smith Collection.*

Illustration 235. This 4in (10.2cm) little girl reminds one of the Campbell Kids. The modeling is extremely detailed. Her flirty eyes are intaglio black dots and much of the trim is outlined in black. The basic color of the doll is white. Her bonnet, dress and shoes are blue-green. She has two rows of tiny rosebuds on her bonnet which also has pink ribbons. She carries pink roses. Her cheeks are painted with bright pink circles, but she is still smiling. Mark: See *Illustration 236.*

Illustration 236. Trademark found on Japanese doll in *Illustration 235.* Unidentified.

Illustration 237. Another little unjointed *Kewpie*-type, 2¾in (9.6cm). He has a molded hat, belt and spear, but no wings. The mark is undecipherable but no doubt Japanese. *Carolyn Baker Collection. Photograph by Ray Baker.*

Illustration 239. The 4½in (11.5cm) post World War II football player still wears the same uniform, purple shirt and stockings, white pants and sox and helmet, shoes and football of an orange-brown shade. He is the same player but now his shoes are better molded and he has jointed arms to carry his football. The number "8" on his back is painted gold in addition to being molded. Mark: See *Illustration 240.* Made in Occupied Japan.

Illustration 238. These three 4½in (11.5cm) football players are also non-articulated but with separated legs. The modeling is very good on the costumes and fair on the features. The dolls probably date from the 1930s and these helmets were what the Japanese thought our players were still wearing. They all have different numbers molded on their backs and loops for hanging them on something are molded on their heads. Compare these with the doll in *Illustration 239.* Mark: See *Illustration 240. John Axe Collection.*

Illustration 240. This mark is found on the dolls in *Illustrations 238* and *239.* The former is marked with the word "JAPAN" and the latter with the words "MADE IN OCCUPIED JAPAN."

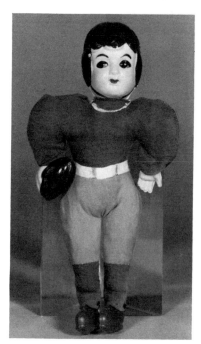

Illustration 241. Another athlete, 8in (20.3cm) with his antiquated helmet. Only the head, hands and feet are celluloid. The body is a very crude cotton uniform stuffed with lumpy straw. He is colorful, though. His pants are orange and the top is purple. The celluloid is lightweight and not too well finished. His shoes, ball and helmet are brown. He has black eyes and rosy cheeks. Mark below helmet: "JAPAN."

Illustration 242. A perky little 7in (17.8cm) girl from the 1930s. She is jointed at the shoulders. Instead of having color, the celluloid, which is thin, is white. She has blue painted eyes and brown hair. The romper is green with a molded pink flower that is the same shade as her large hair bow. Mark: See *Illustration 233. Carolyn Baker Collection. Photograph by Ray Baker.*

Illustration 243. Here is the very recognizable *Skippy*. The 5½in (14cm) doll has molded clothes and painted features which capture the comic strip character's spirit. He is jointed at the shoulder and wears a raspberry coat, blue pants and tie, white shirt and tan hat and shoes. He is marked on his collar. "JAPAN" and on the back: "SKIPPY//(symbol in *Illustration 233*)." There is part of a paper label on the feet that reads: "TRADE..SKIPP..// COPY..//PERCY...//MADE I..." *Jean Pritchard Collection.*

Illustration 244. This 7in (17.8cm) colonial couple, jointed at the shoulders, are good examples of quality dolls from Japan. This firm, using the symbol in *Illustration 233* seems to be a cut above most of the other companies that were producing celluloid dolls in Japan. There is a great amount of modeling on both dolls and they are carefully finished and painted. Both dolls have intricate hair styles that are painted white, simulating powdered wigs. The girl has either a tiny hat or a huge jewel on her head. It is blue, banded with gold and held in place by a molded blue ribbon. Her underskirt is white with a molded pink design on the folds. The outer dress is blue with pink trim and stomacher and deeply molded folds and a pink bow in the back. Her little black shoes have gold buckles on the straps. The boy is every bit as colorful. His breeches are hot pink with gold at the knee. The vest is pink and coat and hat are black. The coat has a molded design around the edge that is painted the same blue as the ribbon on his peruke. His linen is white. The back of the coat is modeled to show the curved seams, pleated tails, buttons and pockets. The only thing they neglected to paint is the pompon on his tricorn. He, too, has gold buckles on black shoes. Mark: See *Illustration 233*.

Illustration 245. This scout is 9½in (24.2cm) without his hat, 10in (25.4cm) with it. He is jointed at the shoulders. He is another fine Japanese doll. His features are sculpted and carefully painted. He has blue eyes and blonde hair. There is considerable modeling of folds and creases in his uniform and every detail they could think of is there. The uniform is brown and his sox and kerchief are blue. He has a molded pack on his back, leggings, a whistle or knife at his belt, and the wonderful celluloid hat is removable. The clenched right hand has a hole for holding something. The flag is not original, but probably accurate. He can be seen in the color section. *Jean Pritchard Collection.* Mark: See *Illustration 246.*

JAPAN

Illustration 246. Mark found on Japanese doll in previous illustration. Note that the central portion is the same as the mark found on the little girl in *Illustration 251.*

Illustration 247. A mahogany-colored 3¾in (9.6cm) boy jointed at the shoulders. He wears only a rough red shirt and a smile. He has molded eyeballs with black "googly" dots for eyes and a little red mouth and dimples. His molded hair is painted black and his little behind is peeking out below the shirt. Mark: See *Illustration 248.* This doll, like many of the others, is found in various sizes.

Illustration 248. Mark found on Japanese celluloid dolls. Unidentified.

Illustration 249. The 6in (15.2cm) aviator in his molded pink flight suit is jointed at the shoulder and is a rattle. The dark pink of the suit is accented with black shoes, collar and helmet strap. He has blue painted eyes. There is a paper inspection sticker on his feet and he is marked on the back: "Made in Japan//PATENT." *Carolyn Baker Collection. Photograph by Ray Baker.*

Illustration 250. 4in (10.2cm) This is the little girl who had a little curl right in the middle of her forehead. Right now she is very, very good playing with her dolly. The lightweight celluloid is a brownish-pink and her hair and brows and lashes are painted red. The eyes are bright blue circles with black dots. She wears her original yellow rayon dress which is glued on. She is jointed at the shoulders and carries a colorful baby rattle in one hand and the baby in its pink bunting in the other. Her hair style is that of the late 1920s or early 1930s. She is marked on the neck: "JAPAN//PAT."

RIGHT: Illustration 251. A group of dolls with jointed arms. They all have different unidentified marks. LEFT: This 6in (15.2cm) girl is all dressed up in her 1920s style yellow hat and blue coat. Mark: See *Illustration 252*. CENTER: This 5in (12.7cm) little tyke could have been a golfer from the look of his outfit and the little white ball in his left hand. He has a brown shirt and yellow hat and pants, also brown shoes. Notice that the pants are plaid and the sox are argyle!! Mark: See *Illustration 253*. RIGHT: Her 6in (15.2cm) mother is going to have a fit. She is all dressed up in her red dress and pink hat and is holding a football in her right hand. Mark: See *Illustration 254*. All from the *Carolyn Baker Collection. Photograph by Ray Baker.*

Illustration 252. Mark found on Japanese celluloid doll on the left in *Illustration 251*. Unidentified.

Illustration 254. Mark found on Japanese celluloid doll on the right in *Illustration 251*. Unidentified.

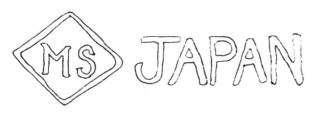

Illustration 253. Mark found on Japanese celluloid doll in the center in *Illustration 251*. Unidentified.

Illustration 256. Although this 5½in (14.0cm) *Kewpie*-type is jointed at both hip and shoulder, he cannot stand up; he must sit. The bottom of the doll is flat and the legs are attached at an angle coming out from the sides. It was probably easier to joint the doll than to try to mold the legs in an outstretched position. He is very well finished with good modeling and careful painting. The romper is pink and the hat is gray. Mark: "MADE IN// JAPAN." *Carolyn Baker Collection. Photograph by Ray Baker.*

Illustration 255. The happy little 4½in (11.5cm) German clown is a very nice doll. He is made of a peachy-flesh color celluloid and has intaglio eyes that are painted brown with black pupils and lid lines. It is unusual to find two colors in the eyes of so small a doll. His hair and brows are light brown and the hat with black accent is a dull red. There are vestiges of the same red paint on his clown suit with its painted silver ruff and buttons. He is jointed at the shoulder and is stamped on the seat "GERMANY."

Illustration 257. Another mark found on celluloid dolls made during the period directly after World War II. Mark found on the doll in *Illustration 258.*

Illustration 258. 5¾in (14.7cm) baby toy with a molded cream-colored snowsuit with scarlet trim. He has pale flesh-colored face and hands. His eyes are green with a paler green ring around the pupil. The hair, lashes and brows are the typical reddish color. Jointed at hip and shoulder, his outstanding characteristic is the separately molded fingers on his hands. Mark: "(500 in a diamond)//MADE IN//OCCUPIED//JAPAN." He must have been on sale with the doll in *Illustration 70.* They both cost the same and were disfigured in the same manner.

Illustration 259. These two dolls were probably made for baby's play. They look like the type that would be sold in an infants' department. They both wear their original outfits. The larger doll wears a blue organdy dress and bonnet that are trimmed with white lace. Underneath a square of white flannelette with the edge blanket-stitched in pink by machine is folded to make a petticoat. The smaller doll wears a white cotton dress with green and brown print and a matching bonnet trimmed with coral braid. The undies are part of the dress. The dress is obviously made for this doll, or this type doll. It has been shortened, but seems to have been done when she was dressed.

Illustration 260. The dolls from the previous illustration are shown without clothing. LEFT: This small 7in (17.8cm) doll is very good quality. She is well modeled and jointed at the neck, hip and shoulder. She is made of a fairly heavy pink-flesh celluloid and has a lot of detail in the painting. The blue eyes have highlights in the pupils and white sclera. Many times the eyeballs of these dolls is simply left the color of the celluloid. The black, neatly painted upper and lower lashes and the pink corner dots and nostrils are not often found on Japanese dolls. Mark on back: "(Fleur)//JAPAN//ROYAL." Stamp on left foot: "JAPAN." Red inspection label on right foot. RIGHT: This 8in (20.3cm) one could have been an Easter toy. The face is a pale flesh color with the huge googly eyes. The irises of the eyes are lavender and there are highlights on the pupils. She, too, has the white sclera, but only long, curly upper lashes. The whole body is molded to look like a pink teddy bear, for the hands are shaped like paws. It is jointed at hip and shoulder and contains a rattle. Mark on back: "(Fleur)//JAPAN//ROYAL." Stamp on left foot: "MADE IN//JAPAN."

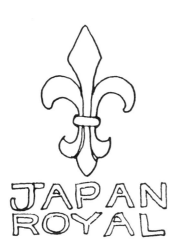

Illustration 261. Trademark often found on celluloid dolls from Japan.

Illustration 262. Red inspection sticker often found on celluloid dolls from Japan.

Illustration 263. Two more of the jointed babies with molded snowsuits. The large one is 8in (20.3cm). He is made of heavy celluloid. The snowsuit is pink with red trim. His boots are brown. The little bit of hair that shows is heavily modeled. The painting of the molded eyes is interesting. Black, highlighted pupils have a ring of pale blue and then the slightly darker blue iris. The rest of the eyes are white with black lid lines and the typical long, curly reddish lashes. Marked on back: "(N in oval)//MADE IN//OCCUPIED//JAPAN." The smaller baby, 5½in (14.0cm), wears a yellow molded snowsuit. The face is very pale flesh color and the eyes are simply black dots. He is jointed at hip and shoulder and marked on the back: "(trefoil)//MADE IN//OCCUPIED JAPAN."

Illustration 264. Mark found on celluloid dolls made during the period when Japan was occupied by the American forces directly after World War II. This mark was found on the doll on the left in *Illustration 263*.

Illustration 265. Mark found on celluloid dolls made in the period directly after World War II when Japan was occupied by the American forces. Mark found on the doll on the right in *Illustration 263*.

Novelties

Novelty dolls are not new. The term in this section refers to dolls that were used for another purpose than "playing dolls." Adults in the French courts amused themselves with dolls; the Swiss clock makers tinkered with them and produced the wondrous automatons of the 19th century; Victorian ladies made dolls into sewing aids; bakers decorated cakes with them; the list is endless.

In addition to the dolls there are some little toys that would have appealed to children of all ages. They are not shown in a particular order for they are too diverse to categorize.

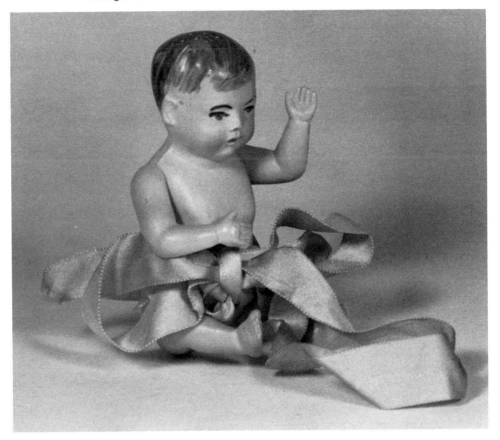

Illustration 266. This little 4¾in (12.2cm) boy baby has been transformed into a powder shaker. He is jointed at hip and shoulder and has painted features. There is an opening in the center back where the powder was put in. It has a paper glued over it, hidden by the gold satin ribbon that is tied around him. Pin holes in his head allow the powder to escape. He seems to be a commercial item. Mark on back: "MADE//IN//USA." *Maurine Popp Collection.*

RIGHT: Illustration 267. Mark found on celluloid doll in *Illustration 266*.

Illustration 268. A toy designer with a wonderful sense of humor designed this 5½in (14.0cm) celluloid duck, probably for Easter. Our no-nonsense officer of the law is a chartreuse duck who has a purple bill and sports a bright pink coat and hat. His eyes are molded and painted in such a manner that they resemble glass. He is jointed at the legs. Mark on his tail: (symbol shown in *Illustration 270*.)

Illustration 269. The other side of Officer Duck. He is ready for business with his night stick. Notice the molded buttons and star on the coat and even a stripe on his green pants.

Illustration 270. Mark found on celluloid dolls and toys made in the USA. Unidentified.

Illustration 271. Toy animals have always fascinated children. One of the most enduring toys has been the Noah's Ark with its line of animals marching in twos. Celluloid was a popular medium for them. The rhinoceros in the illustration is 3in (7.6cm) tall. Strangely, although few dolls are found with United States' trademarks, most of these animals have them. They are made from heavy celluloid and are realistically modeled and painted. They were purchased a few at a time, so we cannot assume they came from a single set or any specific sets. The two trademarks are: "(MADE//IN//USA in an oval form)" and the one found in *Illustration 270.*

Illustration 272. Farm animals are also loved by boys and girls. They came in play sets for farms and singly, the way they are still available today. They, too, have mainly the same United States' trademarks and the Japanese mark that is so often found "(cross in a circle.)" The large horse is Japanese. The quality is not nearly as nice as those of American manufacture. Animal figures were also made with rattles inside. None of the animals in the collection are from Germany although they were surely produced there. Both the domestic and wild animals were advertised in the *1914 Marshall Field & Company Doll Catalog.* An assortment of the domestic animals came nine to a box. Wild animals were 12 in an assortment. Both wholesaled for $4.00 per dozen boxes. The ram in the picture is 3¾in (9.6cm) high.

Illustration 273. 10in (25.4cm) high woven cabinet with molded twin babies inside in the bed. It is all-original except for the paper inside the door. It must not have been the best seller on the shelf for it is marked down successively from the original price or $4.98 to $3.32, to $2.50 and finally to $1.00.

Illustration 274. This is the cabinet shown opened with one of the dolls standing and the other still tucked in the bed. The doll is 3¼in (8.3cm) made of pink, heavy celluloid. Mark on back: "BEST//USA." Best and Company were New York, New York, distributors of dolls from 1902 to past 1925. According to the Colemans in *The Collector's Encyclopedia of Dolls* they registered the trademark, "Snuggles" to be used on dolls of many materials, including celluloid. There is a white flannelette bunting fastened to the bed. The two little dolls were tied in with a pink cord.

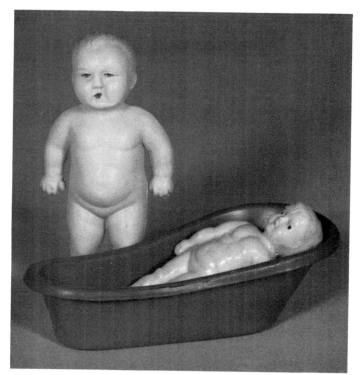

LEFT: Illustration 275. Among the many small "homey" items that were offered for children to play with in that less complicated era before World War I were the little dolls' bathing or toilet sets. (See *Illustration 277*.) These were probably from that kind of toy. The tub is 3in (7.6cm) and made of brown celluloid. The 2in (5.1cm) bather is the heavy, glossy celluloid with considerable modeling for such a small fellow. His arms and legs are separate from the body much like the one standing behind the tub. Neither the doll nor the tub is marked. The second doll is 2½in (6.4cm) and made of a matte finish flesh color celluloid. He has molded blonde hair and blue eyes. Mark on back: "(helmet of Minerva)// 6¾." From the number of teeth marks on these little dolls, they must have presented an irresistible urge to babies to put them in their mouths. Another one in the collection (also bitten) is only 1⅛in (2.8cm) and lives in a white 1⅝in (4.1cm) tub. (Not shown.)

C60705—Dolls' Bathing Set; Celtid doll; 1⅝ inches; bath tub 2½ inches; mirror; towel; each set in compartment box, 4x5 inches; 1 dozen in package.....**Dozen 1.60**

C60709—Dolls' Bath Set; Celtid baby, 1 in; tub, 1½ inches; soap dish, soap, towel, sponge; on card; 1 dozen cards in box........................**Dozen 70c**

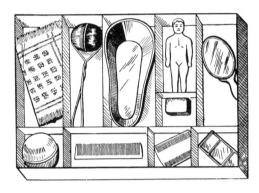

C60707—Dolls' Bathing Set; Celtid doll, 1⅞ inches; bath tub, 3 inches; comb, fine comb, mirror, soap tray, powder box, towel and soap, rattle; in compartment box, 5½x8¼ inches; ½ dozen in package.................**Dozen 3.80**

Illustration 276. In the *1914 Marshall Field and Company Doll Catalog* reprinted by Hobby House Press, Inc., these little bathing sets are shown with all the little trinkets that were included. With the smallest sets, the child could simply wash and dry baby. As the sets increase in size and cost, the baby can be bathed, powdered, combed, fed and entertained with a rattle. It is interesting to see that included in one set is a fine comb. We rarely hear of them today. Not only were they used for the fine baby hair, but also for a scalp condition known as "cradle cap" which babies tended to get and that mothers combed out with a fine comb.

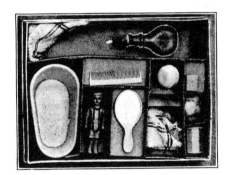

C60708—Dolls' Toilet Set; jointed Celtid doll, 3 inches; bath tub, 5 inches; mirror, comb, powder box, fine comb, soap tray, towels, soap, nursing bottle; in compartment box, 7¼x9¾ inches; ½ dozen in package......**Dozen 8.00**

Illustration 277. The helmet of Minerva. Symbol found on dolls made by Buschow & Beck of Germany.

LEFT: Illustration 278. These toys were called "Rollies." A "Roly" had a weighted bowl on the bottom so that when it was pushed it would roll over and come back to an upright position. These with the molded celluloid dolls were quite popular in the period before World War I. They came in a variety of sizes and types. Many were comic looking characters; some were animals and birds, and there was a type on two wheels that could be pulled. The axle ran through the figure just above the weight so it would swing back and forth as the child pulled it. The 2in (5.1cm) man on the left wears a green hat and black pants and smokes a long pipe. He is marked: "(PH symbol of Paul Hunaeus.)" The Scot with the protruding ears and kilts is 3½in (8.9cm) and is marked on the back: "PALITOY//MADE//IN//ENGLAND." *Carolyn Baker Collection. Photograph by Ray Baker.*

RIGHT: Illustration 279. The mark found on dolls made by Paul Hunaeus in Germany.

Illustration 280. Older children with a bit more dexterity were able to amuse themselves with hand puppets such as these Palmer Cox characters. The molded celluloid heads are about 2½in (6.4cm) with a flange that holds the heads in the cotton mitts. The heads are all well molded with brightly painted faces. They are marked differently. The fellow on the extreme right has a very small flange and nothing is visible. He has an unframed turtle on the back of his bald head. The other three are marked on the flange thus: Woman: "GERMANY K.H. (turtle)." Man with cap: "(turtle) K.E. GERMANY." Man with hat: "GERMANY K.F. (turtle)." A toy with the identical head of the man with the hat was advertised in 1914.

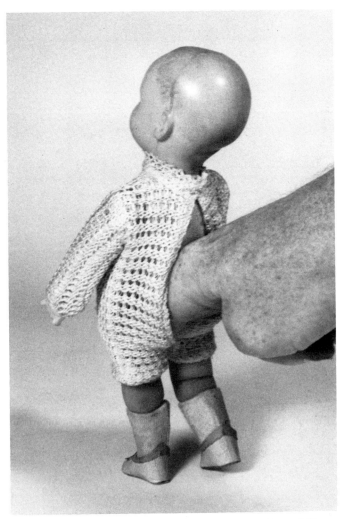

Illustration 281. Another fun toy in the same era was *Our Tiny Toddler*, shown here with the original box. By inserting the first two fingers into the legs of the crocheted romper and then into the cardboard-stiffened sox and shoes, the doll could be made to walk very realistically. The celluloid head is attached to a cardboard half-body which is covered with the romper. The sleeves of the romper are stuffed to make arms, and the celluloid hands are fastened at the ends. He has blue painted eyes and blonde hair and an open/closed mouth. Marked at neck: "GERMANY (turtle mark)/8½." The box has no marks. He measures 6½in (16.5cm) from the top of the head to the bottom of the pants. *Jean Pritchard Collection.*

Illustration 282. And here is the *Tiny Toddler* toddling. This doll in every respect resembles one shown in the May 1912 *Playthings* with a warning to the trade that Geo. Borgfeldt & Co.".. are the sole owners of the United States Patents of 'FINGY-LEGS' The Tiny Tot." They stated that the patent covers the "feature in a plaything whereby the fingers of the person holding it form the legs of the doll, figure or animal." They threatened action against anyone handling infringing articles. Under the photograph, similar to the one above, is printed: "U.S.Patent No. 752607." *Jean Pritchard Collection.*

Illustration 283. These three puppies were made in the 1920s. They are all jointed at the legs and neck. The little one on the left seems to be a bulldog. He is brown and white and has a bright pink nose and very bulgy eyes. Mark on under side: "(cross in circle) // JAPAN." 3¾in (9.6cm). The other two dogs are the comic character "Bonzo." They are a good quality cream celluloid with brown ears and features. The modeling is superb. His squinty eyes and laugh wrinkles tell us he is a happy mutt. One dog is modeled to sit and the other to stand on his rear legs. Both have their original blue ribbons and labels that are printed in two circles: "BONZO JUNO Schutzmarke GERMANY COPYRIGHT." Mark on head: "(JUNO in oval)." Mark on body: "GESCH-SCH // GERMANY." 4in (10.2cm).

JUNO

GESCH-SCH

Illustration 284. Mark found on dolls and celluloid toys made by Karl Standfuss.

Illustration 285. A different type candy container is this egg of white papier-mâché sprinkled with mica to give it a bit of glitter. The celluloid head is held to the egg by means of the pink flannelette hood with stiff bunny ears. There is a cardboard plug in the bottom that can be removed to fill the egg with candy. The container is unmarked, but is probably German. Length of egg: 5in (12.7cm).

Illustration 286. 5½in (14.0cm) plush babies such as these were advertised in many sizes in the years just preceding World War I. The heads are heavy pink-flesh colored celluloid. The hair is deeply modeled and the eyes are painted blue. The flange on the neck is fitted into a white plush pillow-shaped body that is tightly stuffed. The stiff arms are separate, but sewn into place. They have tiny felt feet and hands. The plush bonnets and felt collars are removable. One has bells attached to blue cords with pompons and the other to pink. If they are marked, it is on the flange under the plush. Undoubtedly German.

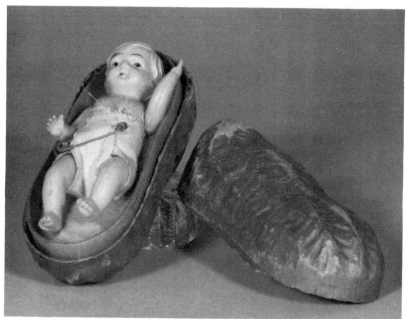

Illustration 287. Popular play and souvenir items were the little celluloid babies hidden in unexpected places like peanuts. The modeling on this 4in (10.2cm) one is good; the little fingers are individual and the hair is well defined. Jointed at hip and shoulder, he wears his original diaper with a gigantic (for him) brass safety pin. The 4¾in (12.2cm) pressed paper peanut has its original cotton pad. The doll is marked on the back: See *Illustration 288.*

Illustration 288. Mark found on the baby in the peanut.

Illustration 290. Shamrock-like mark (trefoil) found on dolls made in Japan. Un-identified.

Illustration 289. What else? A 3¾in (9.6cm) black baby in a watermelon of green pressed paper with a pink interior. The baby is coal black celluloid with molded hair and eyeballs. He has a tiny red mouth and red brows! Although he is black, he does not have ethnic features. He is jointed at hip and shoulder and wears his original diaper with its huge pin. He has managed to keep his little glass nursing bottle with him. Mark on back: "(trefoil.)"

Illustration 291. In the 1920s party favors made of crepe paper were quite the rage. They could be purchased for almost any occasion and some were, no doubt, craft items. This group includes the little bridal couple that is described in the "Kewpies and Tinies" section. LEFT: 6in (15.2cm) is the total height of the doll. Underneath the elaborately ruffled white skirt is a half doll, jointed at the shoulder. The undressed doll may be seen in *Illustration 292*. The doll in the middle is the same head, but on a long tubular body with wire legs that make her 15½in (39.4cm) tall! The legs can be seen on either side of the bride and groom. The arms are also attached to long wires. It is dressed in blue and pink crepe paper. RIGHT: This is an 8in (20.3cm) whole doll with jointed arms dressed in a fancy blue paper dress and bonnet. All of the three are marked: "MADE IN JAPAN." *Carolyn Baker Collection. Photograph by Ray Baker.*

Illustration 292. This is the same type doll seen dressed in *Illustration 291*. She is 3in (7.6cm) and has molded hair and painted features. The celluloid is lightweight and rough. She is jointed at the shoulders. The marks are from the paper that was glued to her, not a molded or painted hair band. Mark: "(diamond with unreadable symbol)//MADE IN JAPAN."

Illustration 293. Another favorite toy of the crib crowd, this 5¾in (14.7cm) molded celluloid rattle is really quite artistic. The handle is a molded pale pink stem and opening blossom of a flower. The bud that has just burst forth is a little schoolboy with rosy cheeks, blue eyes, molded blonde hair and a bright red cap with a black visor. Mark on hat: "MADE IN//JAPAN."

TRADE MARK

MADE IN JAPAN

Illustration 295. Trademark found on the box in *Illustration 294*. Unidentified.

Illustration 294. This 6½in (16.5cm) celluloid bear is bright red with a molded green bow at his neck. He is made in two sections so that when a child pushed him down, the legs were depressed into the torso and he squeaked. The arms are jointed at the shoulders. The original box in the photograph shows a group of other toys. It is possible that they were available also. Mark on back: "MADE IN JAPAN." The box has a trademark that looks like a bunny. *Carolyn Baker Collection. Photograph by Ray Baker.*

MADE IN JAPAN
O PAT NO 54317

Illustration 297. Trademark found on celluloid dolls and toys made in Japan. Unidentified. The particular mark with the patent number is found on the buggy in *Illustration 296*.

Illustration 296. The little 4½in (11.5cm) blue celluloid buggy is a miniature of the type used in the 1920s and 1930s. It is lightweight celluloid that is molded to look like the wicker buggies that were in vogue then. The hood is movable and has isinglass portholes. It is marked on the bottom: See *Illustration 297*. *Photograph by Jane Buchholz.*

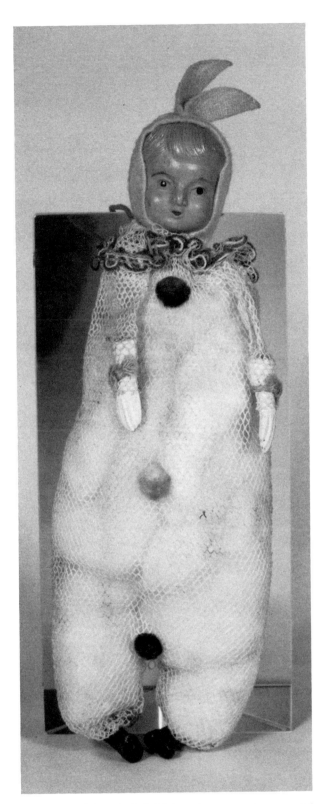

Illustration 299. This tiny 1⅝in (4.1cm) half doll is made of strong celluloid that is a pale flesh color. Her modeling is much more defined than shows in the photograph. She has yellow hair, rosy cheeks and a bodice of two shades of pink with blue molded flowers. She was probably used as a party favor with a fluffy skirt of crepe paper or ribbon or some other novelty item. Unmarked.

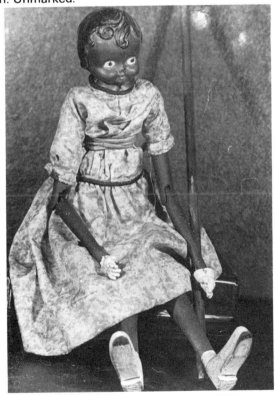

Illustration 298. Celluloid heads were also used for candy containers. This particular 8¾in (22.3cm) doll is only a mask with the rest of the head covered by a cotton flannel bonnet with bunny ears. The hands and feet are molded composition. The mesh bag, now filled with cotton, once held hard candy. A drawstring at the back of the neck opens the bag. A paper label on the back collar reads: ''MADE//IN//JAPAN.'' *Maurine Popp Collection.*

Illustration 300. This unmarked 18in (45.7cm) toy is similar to the Tennessee Mountain dolls known as *Limber Jacks*. They are loosely jointed and dance when jiggled by a stick attached to their bodies. This doll has a black celluloid head with painted features. Her molded black hair is almost the style of *Betty Boop*. The wooden body has pegged joints at the shoulders, elbows, thighs and knees. The body is painted black and the carved shoes are white. She wears white celluloid ''gloves.'' A 19in (48.3cm) stick fits into a hole in her back to hold and make her dance. She wears a pink taffeta petticoat and a red print taffeta dress. The clothes are nailed to the body. *Yolanda Simonelli Collection. Photograph by Yolanda Simonelli.*

Illustration 301. The bridal couple and minister are 13in (33cm) to 14in (35.6cm) tall. The dolls have flexible wire bodies and celluloid heads. The bridegroom's hat and the minister's pince nez are also celluloid. They have painted features. The minister is bald; the bridegroom has painted black hair and the bride's wig is made of russet color crepe paper. These dolls were once in the collection of Mary E. Lewis, founder of The United Federation of Doll Clubs and author of the book *Marriage of Diamonds and Dolls* (H. L. Lindquist Pub., 1947.) They were described thus: "Happy-Go-Lucky-in Love. The little figures which represent the young Speakeasys were very modern for their day. They were a shade grotesque and foreshadowed that whole generation of exaggerated long-necked characters which appeared in store windows, advertisements and fashion illustrations following the exposition of 'art moderne' in Paris in 1925. The bridegroom is in tails made of black felt, his linen of stiff white paper. The bride is too thin, too dead-white, her bobbed hair too brassy-red. She symbolizes a strange, hard type of femininity that we called the flapper. Her dress is made of one of the early forms of Argentina cloth. The same transparent film was used to make protective covers for the elaborate silk lamp shades which gathered dust in the drawing rooms. The gown is veiled in fine cotton net and the bride wears a short tulle veil bound tight around her bushy bob." *Yolanda Simonelli Collection. Photograph by Yolanda Simonelli.*

Mechanicals

Toys that do things have always been favorites of young and old alike. (Why does the new daddy run out and buy the new baby boy a train?) They have the capability of entertaining not only the child who is playing with them, but the playmates who may be watching. For the few moments it takes for the springs to unwind, not only the toy is in the spotlight, so is the person who turned the key or pressed the button. In that brief moment he has power over an inanimate object; he can make it move!

These little celluloid toys were certainly not the most expensive mechanicals that could be had. Quite the contrary; they were among the least costly in most cases. They did provide a lot of fun for their owners.

Illustration 304. The symbol found on heavy celluloid type dolls made in the United States just after World War II.

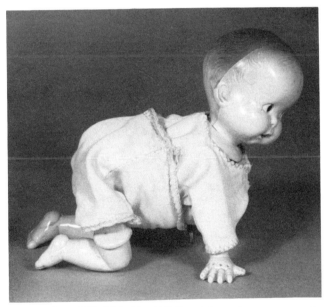

Illustration 302. This 6in (15.2cm) American creeper is a bit larger, heavier, and probably later than the Japanese version in *Illustration 318*. He is made of a heavy flesh-colored celluloid with painted features. He still wears his original pink rayon knit shirt and pants. Marked on back: "(Irwin symbol)."

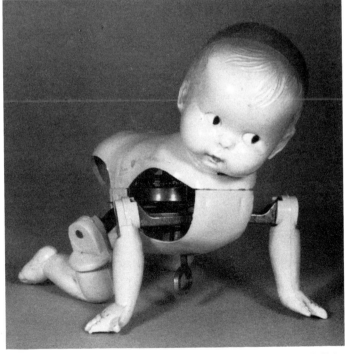

Illustration 303. Undressed view of the Irwin doll in *Illustration 302* showing his construction and part of the mechanism.

Illustration 305. The little 5in (12.7cm) Dutch boy is all metal, including his head. Only the arms move. His felt clothing is glued and sewn into place. He has a plush wig. The wooden shoes are glued to his feet. When the spring inside his torso is wound with a key, he tosses the little celluloid girl into the air. He is unmarked. *Jean Pritchard Collection.*

Illustration 306. A back view of the metal boy shows the
little 3¾in (9.6cm) girl. She has molded hair and shoes
and sox and is jointed at the shoulder. Her felt clothes
are sewn on and attached to the boy's hands. She is
marked on the back: "(Minerva helmet)//10." The left
leg is marked: "GERMANY." The doll was made by
Buschow & Beck who made both celluloid and metal
dolls, so it would be reasonable to assume that the
entire toy was made by that firm. *Jean Pritchard
Collection.*

Illustration 307. Symbol
found on dolls made by
Buschow & Beck.

-137-

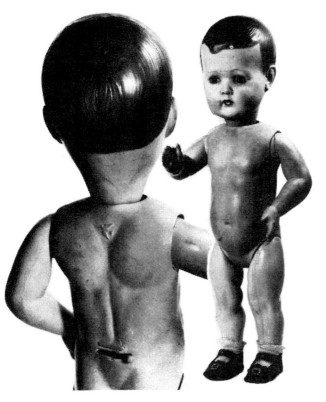

Illustration 308. 19in (48.3cm) This little fellow with his painted dark hair and stationary glass eyes is interesting in that only his legs are elastic strung. His head and arms are attached in such a manner that when the lever in the center of his back is manipulated, his head and arms move. The trademark of a bird in flight on his back is the only mark. It is unknown. *Ruth Whittier Collection. Photograph by Richard Merrill. Courtesy of "The Handbook of Collectible Dolls" by Madeline O. Merrill and Nellie W. Perkins.*

Illustration 309. Flying bird trademark on the mechanical boy in *Illustration 308*.

Illustration 310. This little 7in (17.8cm) miss from the Black Forest in Germany is what could be termed a "transition" doll. She still has the look of the celluloid dolls, but her plastic is strong enough to have hooks on the arms for stringing. It would be practically impossible to put a dent in her without a lot of pressure, and then, it is probable that she would crack. She is very well made and nicely dressed in a provincial costume. Her black cotton skirt is lined with stiffening and she wears a white blouse, black felt bodice and green silk apron. Her straw hat has the huge red pompons worn by women in the Black Forest area. In contrast to the celluloid heads that had to have metal bodies to house the spring mechanism, the plastic torso on this doll is capable of containing it. When wound with a key, she twirls in circles. She is really a charming little girl with her blue eyes and brown mohair braids. Unmarked.

Illustration 311. An early 9in (22.9cm) celluloid version of Donald Duck and Pluto. The little green metal cart is a wind-up toy from Japan. Later versions of Donald portrayed him with a much shorter neck. Although the dog, Pluto, is rigid, Donald is jointed at hip and shoulder. He is made of white celluloid with pink legs and bill and a blue sailor jacket and hat. Pluto is yellow celluloid with black ears. A gold cord is knotted through Donald's gloves so he does not drop the reins. The duck is marked on the bottom: "(circle with symbol seen in *Illustration 312*)//MADE IN JAPAN//© WD." Pluto is marked: "MADE IN JAPAN."

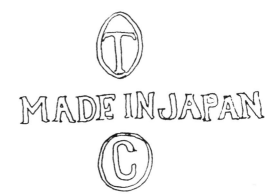

Illustration 312. Mark found on the Donald Duck in *Illustration 311*. The upper portion is found on the football players in *Illustrations 238* and *239*.

Illustration 313. Clock work toys have intrigued young and old alike for years. The new technology that developed after World War II soon replaced the hand-wound springs with battery and then computer operated toys. The little cyclist is 4½in (11.5cm) high. He is jointed at the shoulder. The head and torso are a single piece that extends just below the hips with little stumps to hold him on the seat. His molded sailor top is red and the cap is blue. Brown shoes are attached to the ends of his red polka dot pants and to the pedals. When wound, he pedals the green bike with its red wheels and the thin silk American flag flutters as he goes. The side of the bike is stamped: "MADE IN JAPAN."

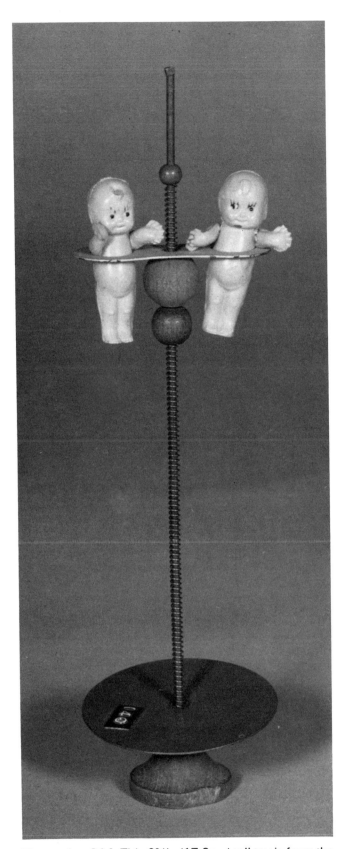

Illustration 314. This 6¾in (17.2cm) tall toy is from the early 1930s. The two little 1½in (3.8cm) *Kewpie*-type dolls slip into the holes in the disc. As it is pushed up the spring-covered pole by the wooden beads, the dolls spin around. Dolls are marked: "JAPAN."

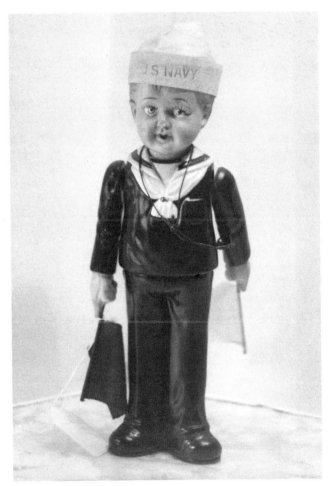

Illustration 315. This is a 12in (30.5cm) Japanese version of a sailor in the United States Navy. The string around his neck holds the key which winds him up and sets him in action, waving his signal flags. He is another excellent example of the Japanese dolls with molded clothes. His suit is blue and white, the shoes black and his hat, which boldly says "U S NAVY" is cream. He waves red and yellow flags. *Mary Piper Collection. Photographer unknown.*

Illustration 316. The little 6in (15.2cm) sailor boy is a real character. From the quality of the modeling and the clothes, one would immediately assume he was made in either Germany or the United States. Not so. No marks are visible on him, but the dog tells the story. The two little boys share the nasty bulldog who has a penchant for pants. He is marked underneath: "MADE IN//OCCUPIED//JAPAN." The sailor has a blonde mohair wig over molded hair. His eyes are molded slits painted blue. There are two little white tears molded on his cheeks and you can almost hear his shrieks of indignation. Celluloid head, arms and legs are attached to a metal torso that contains the spring mechanism. When wound and the dog is attached to the rear by inserting a protruding metal rod into the dog's mouth, the boy's legs move and he runs around with the dog fairly firmly attached to the seat of his blue wool pants. The toy is of much higher quality than is usually found in the Japanese imports.

Illustration 317. The little 6in (15.2cm) chocolate-colored boy is the same high quality as his sailor friend. His hair is molded in the tight little curls that were seen on the black French doll. He, too, is screaming with anger because the dog is at the seat of his pants and he just wants to eat his watermelon! He has the same type modeled slits for eyes and ethnic features. His little romper is red with cream dots that match his shirt. The celluloid watermelon has a pink center, white edge and green rind. They did not forget the seeds, either. The dog came with this doll. It was a fortunate find, since the sailor was the first acquisition and the dog must have a certain metal clip in his mouth to hold him to the doll. Both dolls have movable arms and legs.

OPPOSITE PAGE: Illustration 319. This is a very interesting 13½in (34.3cm) doll from Japan. She dates about the late 1920s or early 1930s. There is a great similarity to the baby in *Illustration 45*. Her head, arms and legs are made of glossy flesh-colored celluloid and the torso and feet are metal. The body is not just a metal case, though. It is shaped like a body and painted the same flesh color. Metal bars run from the body to the feet and are covered with tubes of celluloid fashioned-like legs. The red metal shoes have four wheels on each. When the spring is wound with a key, the doll walks, swings her arms and turns her head. She wears her original white rayon panties and a fine quality cotton print dress and matching cloche hat. She is marked on the bottom of the feet: "MADE IN JAPAN."

Illustration 318. This little 4½in (11.5cm) long creeper has head, arms and legs made of thin pinkish celluloid. They are attached to a metal body that contains a spring which is wound by a key on the under side. This sets the baby creeping along the floor. He still wears his original white romper with red dots, a bib and one sock. He is marked on back of his head: "JAPAN."

RIGHT: Illustration 320. The original box says she is a "Walking Mama Doll." She measures 11in (27.9cm). The head, arms and upper torso are celluloid. The lower torso is shaped like a metal can with two wheels on the bottom. It contains the mechanism that when wound moves the baby along the floor with a slow, rolling gait. The toy is jointed only at the shoulders and she carries a nursing bottle that is molded into her right hand. She wears her original long light blue flannel gown with rayon ribbon edging. The bonnet is of the same material, but edged with white rabbit fur. She wears a white flannel bib, also trimmed with ribbon. All clothes are original. The doll is unmarked, but the box is marked: "JAPAN." *Carolyn Baker Collection. Photograph by Ray Baker.*

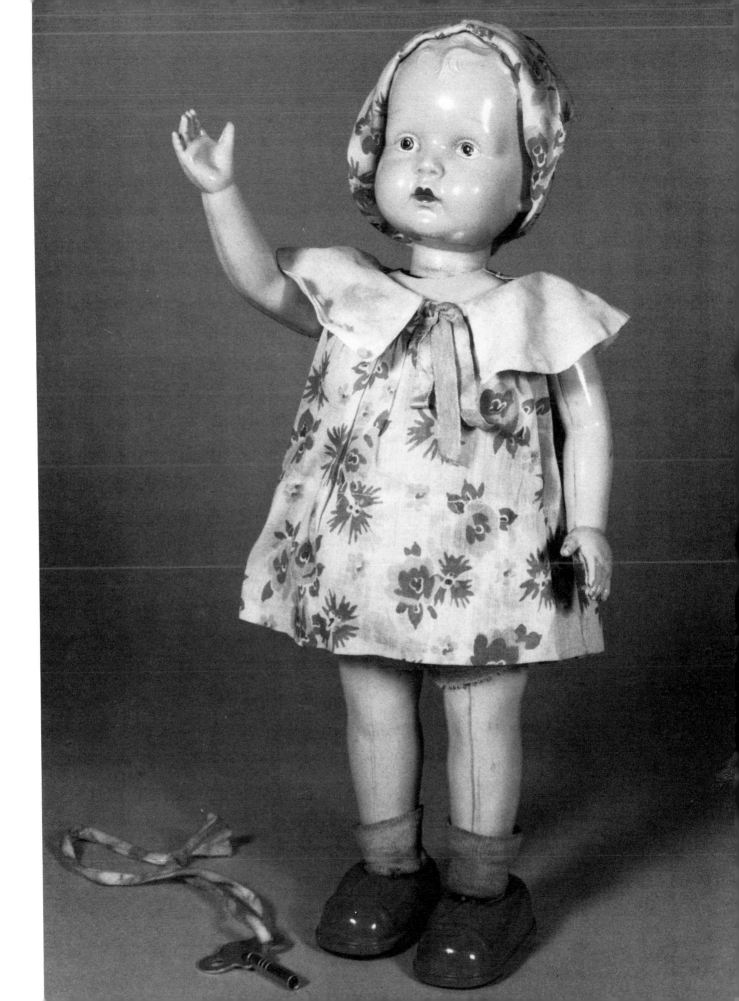

Copy Cats

Toy manufacturers were in business to make money. A successful model of a doll would be used as long as it was popular and, most important, profitable. As new materials became available and there was a demand for them by the public, or if their products could be made more cheaply in another medium, the doll makers would authorize new versions.

As we have seen, some firms made their own celluloid copies of their popular bisque models and some contracted with other manufacturers of celluloid such as the Rheinische Gummi und Celluloid Fabrik Co. to have them made. It was all quite legitimate when toy companies marketed celluloid versions of their dolls, but theft of design has never been uncommon. Any successful product will usually have imitators. The toy industry has always been notoriously secretive for this very reason.

Before World War I when Germany was the acknowledged leader in the doll making field, importers would buy exclusive sales rights to a design and patent a trademark for it to protect themselves against other importers, but there were always those who would change a model slightly and go ahead with production.

During World War I when the German supply of dolls was cut off, the Japanese stepped in and tried to fill the demand. They copied the models they used so precisely that they sometimes even used "MADE IN GERMANY" on the dolls they pirated.

Prior to this period, the Japanese dolls had not been terribly popular because of occasional inferior quality and oriental features.

The piracy was not limited to the Japanese, of course. Others, the Americans among them, gave it a try.

The dolls shown in this section are a few examples of how original models were copied in celluloid. There are other obvious examples in the book, some of the babies and *Kewpie*-types, especially. The practice was not limited to only celluloid. Wherever it was practical, they tried it. It was not all illegitimate, but there was a good deal of questionable copying.

Illustration 322. Trademark found on the celluloid doll in *Illustration 321*. Unidentified.

Illustration 321. The little 6½in (16.5cm) celluloid doll is a steal from her 7in (17.8cm) bisque look-alike. The modeling of the heads is almost identical; only the little curl of hair at the outside bottom on each side of the face has been tapered to give it the look of shorter hair. All the other curls, waves, bows and ridges match. The whites of the celluloid doll's eyes have been painted over the molded bottom lid line and this makes them seem larger. The lower portion of the torso has been adjusted to take the bent legs of a baby; it has been widened and flattened. The legs seem to be much too short for the length of the torso. She has also been given new bent arms in her transformation to celluloid. The bisque girl has the typical slant one finds on bisque dolls with wired-on legs. Another amusing point of comparison is that the navel of the bisque is indented and that of the copy protrudes. A doll advertised in the *1914 Marshall Field Doll Catalog* reprinted by Hobby House Press, Inc. seems to be the same as the bisque. She sold for about 15¢ wholesale. Her hair bow is blue and she is marked inside the leg socket: "653/4." The celluloid has a red bow and is marked on the back: "(symbol seen in *Illustration 322*)//MADE IN//USA."

Illustration 323. This is the first example of one model doll being offered in several forms by different manufacturers. There are numerous other examples of this particular head throughout the book. She is the typical little German girl. This one, 6in (15.2cm), is in a provincial costume of extraordinary detail. There are six layered flounces sewn to her petticoat representing the six petticoats that would be worn under this costume. Four are of white cotton, each with a different lace trim. The other two are pink flannelette with crocheted edges of green and blue yarn. The black cotton skirt is printed with white and has two rows of thin braid around the hem. Her blouse is trimmed with the same red silk that fashions her apron. The black flannel cape attached to her hat covers a kerchief. Under it all is the familiar hair style that will be seen in the next illustrations. She is made of regular weight, pink-flesh celluloid that was used prior to 1940 for dolls of this type. She is marked "(framed turtle)//16/16½."

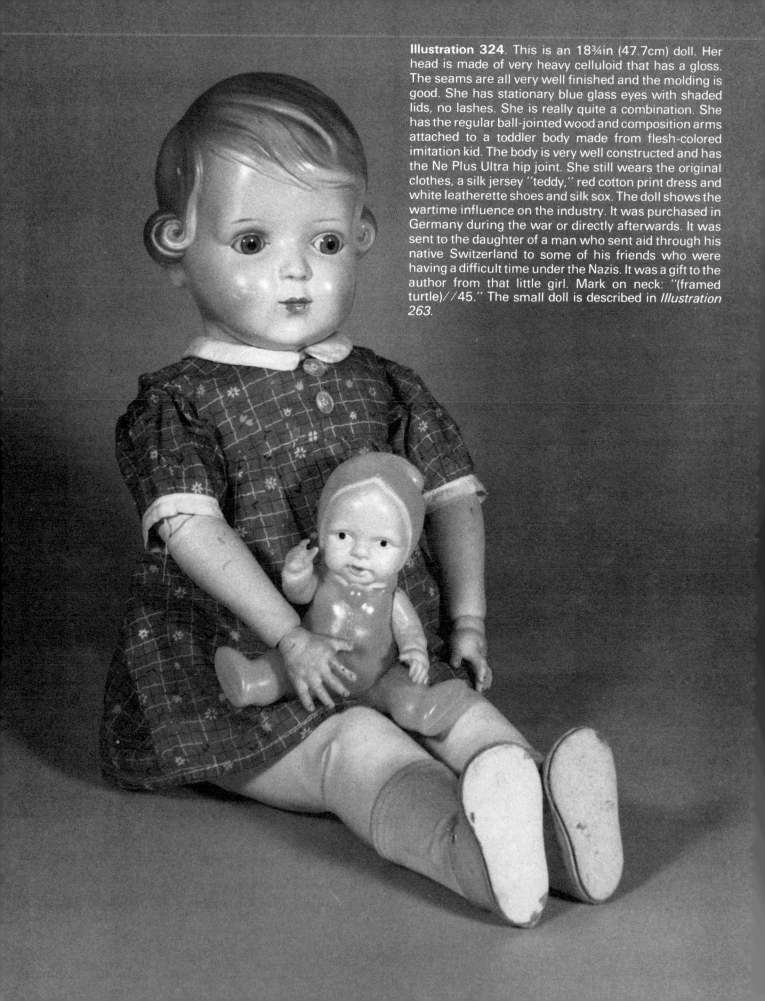

Illustration 324. This is an 18¾in (47.7cm) doll. Her head is made of very heavy celluloid that has a gloss. The seams are all very well finished and the molding is good. She has stationary blue glass eyes with shaded lids, no lashes. She is really quite a combination. She has the regular ball-jointed wood and composition arms attached to a toddler body made from flesh-colored imitation kid. The body is very well constructed and has the Ne Plus Ultra hip joint. She still wears the original clothes, a silk jersey "teddy," red cotton print dress and white leatherette shoes and silk sox. The doll shows the wartime influence on the industry. It was purchased in Germany during the war or directly afterwards. It was sent to the daughter of a man who sent aid through his native Switzerland to some of his friends who were having a difficult time under the Nazis. It was a gift to the author from that little girl. Mark on neck: "(framed turtle)//45." The small doll is described in *Illustration 263*.

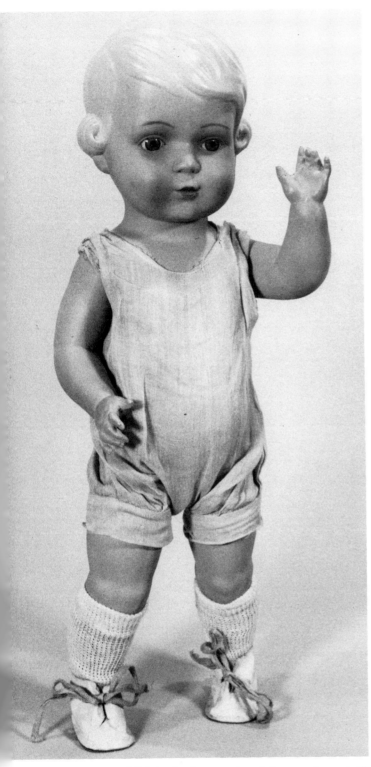

Illustration 325. Isn't she a twin of the previous doll? This one, 15¾in (40.1cm), is all-celluloid, jointed at hip and shoulder. She is made of a good quality and weight celluloid. Her blue glass eyes are stationary and her hair is painted blonde. She is definitely not of the material we refer to in this book as "transition," but is well-finished celluloid. She wears original blue cotton underwear, old shoes and sox. The most fascinating thing about this little girl is her mark on the back: "(figure of stork)//MADE IN//HOLLAND."

Illustration 326. Close-up of the doll made in Holland.

Illustration 327. Trademark found on the doll in *Illustrations 325 and 326.* Unidentified.

Illustration 328. Here are three more dolls of the same design with different marks. LEFT: The 16in (40.6cm) doll has molded brown hair, blue painted eyes and is marked with a turtle in a diamond//42. Her companion on the right is 15½in (39.4cm) tall, has brown painted eyes and is marked with the stork mark, but without country of origin or number. The tiny one is the same as the others, but only measures 6in (15.2cm) and is marked on the back like the largest doll, but with the numbers "16/16½." *Edward Wyffels Collection. Photograph by Berdine Wyffels.*

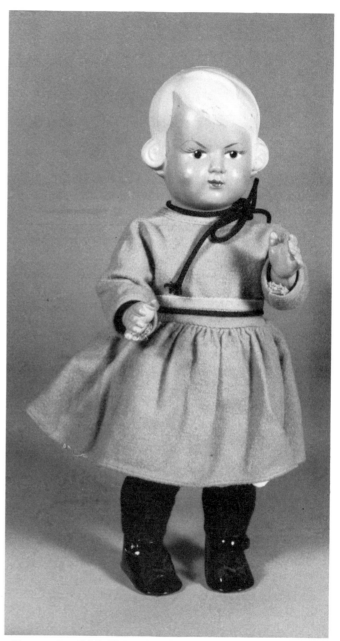

Illustration 329. This 11in (27.9cm) girl, made from the same mold, is heavy, dark-flesh color celluloid. It is really that transitional material that was called celluloid, but was the strong early plastic that came upon the scene just after World War II. She is jointed at hip and shoulder with molded pins across the holes in the limbs that hold the stringing elastic. This would not have been possible with the earlier technology. Her hair is painted a cream color and her eyes are blue. The painting of the brows and lashes definitely suggests that she was made in Japan. She is unmarked.

Illustration 330. Here she is again! This one measures 7in (17.8cm). Now her hair is back to the light brown color and her eyes are still blue. The modeling of this doll and the previous Japanese version are almost alike. The arms are bent in the same manner and the fingers are positioned the same, but the German doll has been cleaned between them better, leaving the fingers more separate. The little extra knob of hair just under the side curls is not so prominent on this doll, but the German girl in *Illustration 324* has them as does the Japanese version. The doll was purchased in Spain in 1980. She wears the Schildkröte tag and is marked: "(framed turtle)//18½/19." *John Axe Collection.*

Illustration 331. This vinyl version of the head has been in production for about 50 years. Her name is *Hilda*, as you can see on the box. She measures 11¼in (28.6cm). She is jointed at neck, hip and shoulder. Her molded hair is brown and her painted eyes are blue. She has molded brown one-strap shoes and white sox. She has white cotton panties and a pink cotton dress that has white collar and cuffs trimmed with brown braid. She is marked on the back with the trademark of the Sekiguchi firm in Japan. The box tells it all. It is a charming design, cream color with garlands of flowers and bluebirds both inside and out. The wonderfully German names, complete with umlaut, are on the ends and the name of the firm on the sides. The back is filled with Japanese characters. There is also a Sekiguchi label on the panties. She is a very good quality doll. She was purchased at F.A.O. Schwarz in 1980.

Illustration 332. The male doll, *Bühne*, is shown without the box. He wears a black felt suit with a print blouse. These dolls will fade if left in bright light. There was quite a variation in the ones that were on display and those that were brought out from stock. *John Axe Collection.*

Transition Dolls

The dolls that fall somewhere in between what we think of as celluloid and as plastic seem destined to forever float on a sea of indefinite terminology. For our purposes they will be called "Transition Dolls" since they bridge the gap between the two.

From the time the first patent was taken out, constant efforts were made to improve the product called celluloid. The changes were as varied as the uses to which it was put. Methods of coloring and finishing were developed for that part of the industry that made household items. The requirements of the doll making industry were similar but had their own unique specifications. One by one the problems were solved and as the years went by the evolution from one technology to another occurred. An analogy might be the textile industry. Today what looks like cotton is used in place of cotton and what is referred to by most consumers as cotton is a combination of fibers that include cotton, but meet the needs of the consumer in a more effective way.

The main difference between the early products and the late ones, if we exclude the methods used to make the material, is their physical properties. Since this book is about dolls, we will consider these differences as they relate to the subject, not write a scientific treatise.

There is no question about the early dolls. Regardless of how heavy the celluloid is, one always has the feeling it is fragile when it is handled. There is a feeling that too much pressure will result in a dent or crack, for these early dolls are not nearly so strong as the later ones. In most cases celluloid dolls were made of much thinner material than the transition dolls. There is a certain "give" to them if they are squeezed gently. When the test is applied to transition dolls it is done with much more ease, without the niggling fear that one's thumb is surely going to end up in the doll's interior.

Transition material is tough. The dolls feel tough. They give one the impression that a little tossing about would do minor damage, if any at all. The seams are smoother, sometimes almost invisible. This is the result of better methods of molding.

The transition dolls generally date from the 1940s and 1950s. Wartime technology had developed stronger materials that were not so flammable and that were able to be molded in a better manner than was available in the past.

Basically, the same companies made the dolls, but with different methods. Dolls from this period will be called "celluloid" by some and "early plastic" by others. Possibly the fact that the turtle mark appears on many of them and that the advertisements still called them "celluloid" leads to confusion among collectors.

Actually, the companies making the dolls and toys used whatever words they felt would sell their product. Their primary concern with terminology was its effect on sales. Celluloid is just as much a plastic as the materials used in the dolls we refer to as "hard plastic" and "vinyl." It is just the earlier form.

Inside the ends of the arms and legs where the joining takes place is where we find the most differences. Because of the strength of the transition materials, more advanced and easier methods of stringing are possible. The early dolls were not able to stand great pressure on these critical spots because of the weakness of the material when it was pierced. They usually had the entire socket solid with the exception of a small slit or hole only large enough for the elastic to be pushed through. The Parsons-Jackson dolls were outstanding exceptions to the rule. Collectors will probably always refer to them as celluloid because they were so early. They were, however, another variation of the material.

As the materials grew stronger, the holes were able to be molded open to insert various gadgets for securing the elastic. Finally, it became strong enough in the dolls we refer to as plastic that the arm and leg holes of the torso may be left completely open and hooks for attaching the stringing material (elastic, springs, huge rubber bands, and so forth) are able to be molded right onto the end of the limbs and are strong enough to withstand the pressure of holding the doll together.

The transition dolls have a little "give" in the bodies, but the heads and limbs are generally quite rigid.

Whatever they are called, in the final analysis, how important is it? The words we use are simply a method of communicating our thoughts to others. As long as we understand one another, the words should not be considered more important than the doll.

Illustration 333. This little 6in (15.2cm) doll is made of a heavier material, but is strung in the older manner, pushing the elastic through slits. Her whole appearance says "transition." The doll has a matte finish and the hair, which is a later style, has almost a silvery sheen to it. Even the painted features have a more modern look. Her provincial costume is very well made and removable. Many of these small dolls do not have snap closures on their costumes; this one does. Her skirt is bright red with a gay braid trim. She has a black fringed shawl and a little peaked cap that holds her secret. Years ago a little girl used the extra space in the doll's cap as a hiding place for very important information: the vital statistics about an 11-year-old boy who caught her eye. Mark: "(scallop shell)//16."

Illustration 334. This mark is found on the doll in *Illustration 333.* She is probably from the post World War II era in France or Germany. The mark is unidentified.

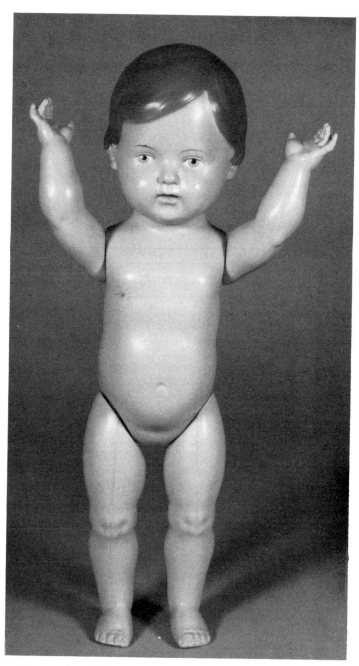

Illustration 335. This 13½in (34.3cm) boy is made from a heavy, dark flesh-colored material. He was probably advertised as "celluloid." He has painted features, brown hair and blue eyes. He is jointed at hip and shoulder. Inside the top of the limbs where the doll is strung there is a very innovative arrangement with a "ball-joint" that holds the elastic. One leg has a wire attached to the ball. The entire doll may have been originally spring-strung, but the elastic in the arms does seem to be original. Mark: "(turtle in diamond)//34."

Illustration 336. Mark found on the "transition" doll in *Illustration 335*. By the time this doll was made, the mark had been in use almost half a century.

SCHUTZ-MARKE

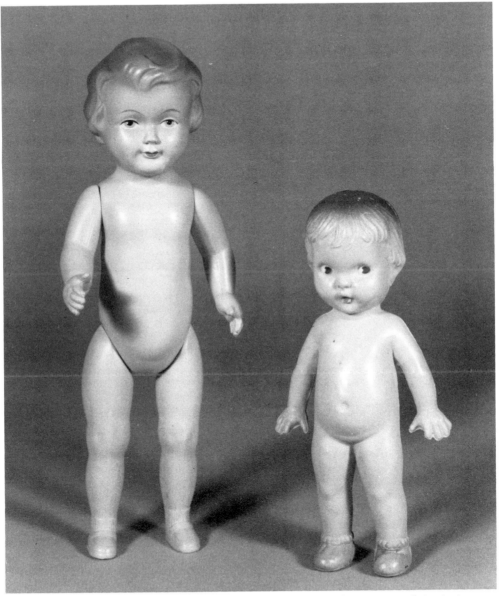

Illustration 337. The small 6in (15.2cm) unjointed doll is another model of the "Irwin" doll. It is the same heavy plastic that was seen in the baby in *Illustration 30*. The hair is painted a reddish brown and the molded booties are blue. The painted features are typical of the Irwin dolls, black dot eyes glancing to the side and a heart-shaped mouth. Mark: "NON FLAM//(Irwin symbol)." The larger 8½in (21.6cm) doll is one from the Cellba works in Germany. It is made of a strong, pink-flesh material. The modeling of the features is more like the little girl in *Illustration 333,* a more modern look. There is only a hint of sculpture of the hair except right around the face, but the doll is well made. The eyes are painted blue, but the molded shoes and sox are unpainted. This doll has another variation of the socket in the limbs. A molded socket with a metal insert for fastening the elastic has been placed in an opening in the end of the limb. It would be possible to do this by heating the opening area to a certain point and inserting the assembly. The plastic would return to its original form when it cooled. Mark: "(crowned mermaid)//22½."

Illustration 338. Mark found on transition doll on the left in *Illustration 337*. The crowned mermaid is the symbol of the Cellba works in Babenhausen, Germany.

Illustration 339. Mark found on the transition doll on the right in *Illustration 337*. This mark is unidentified.

Illustration 340. 15½in (39.4cm) This eager little boy is another that has the plastic ball inside the limbs holding the elastic in place. The head and legs are strung together and the arms are jointed to each other. The modeling is exceptionally nice. He has brown hair, an open/closed mouth with two painted teeth and what seems to be celluloid or plastic blue eyes. The costume is quite innovative. His pants and cap are made from a pair of men's gray wool ribbed sox, the kind that have a red edge at the top. The pants are basically a long "undershirt" type garment that has the legs made from the cuff of the sox that is split, sewn into legs and the bottom inch turned up. The neck and armholes and back opening have been blanket stitched with quite heavy red thread which is also used for button loops. The matching cap is made from the cuff of the other sock. It has been gathered at the top and turned up around the edge. His shirt, which opens completely in the back, is made of a white knitted material. Long red and blue uncut buttonholes (hand-sewn) on the front are outlined with running stitches and trimmed with pearl buttons. Red stitching outlines the edges of the shirt. A line of pearl buttons is sewn down the back, but it is fastened with snaps. The white sox are made from the same material and his little white "leather" shoes are marked on the bottom: "5/45//D.B.P."

Although the costume seems to be "homemade" in a sense, it really does seem to be the outfit he came in. Whoever did it was clever. Marked on both head and body: "(turtle in a diamond frame)//40" The limbs are marked: "40."

Illustration 341. This 14in (35.6cm) Käthe Kruse girl has a celluloid flange head on a cloth body. It was probably one of the first experiments of Frau Kruse with a head other than painted cloth. The doll has beautifully painted features and expressive blue eyes that have double white highlights and shaded upper lids. Her blonde human hair wig is made in the expensive manner of individually knotting small clumps of hair into a silk cap. Her original outfit consists of white ribbed cotton underwear, white silky lace-trimmed petticoat, pink rayon blouse and pale blue and white jumper. The white leather shoes are typical of the Kruse dolls. There are no visible markings on the head, but she is marked in the Kruse manner on both feet. Right foot: "(stamped signature of Käthe Kruse)." Left foot: "555478" and superimposed stamp "MADE IN GERMANY//U.S. ZONE." Since Germany surrendered May 7, 1945, and the war was officially ended between the United States and Germany October 19, 1951, the doll was made in that period of occupation. Unfortunately the tag which hangs around the doll's neck was under her hair when she was photographed. It is 1⅝in (4.1cm) square and is silver with red printing: "Original//(signature of Käthe Kruse)//STOFFPUPPE//handgeknupft." The wrist tag is a small yellow booklet of information. Her name, *Gabi,* is in the long space; above is the inked number: "IX H;" below is: "303." (See *Illustration 345*.)

The information inside translates (loosely):

"1. Body. If the body consists of calico, which is colorfast and water-repellant, it can be cleaned with water and soap using a soft brush, or with spot remover. The knit body should be cleaned only with spot remover or rub with dry bread. (No water!)

2. Head. Can be washed with water and soap. Dry softly, no rubbing, no chemicals!

3. Hair. (All Käthe Kruse dolls have real hair.) Use soft brush or comb softly. Hair can be curled using water and rollers. No curling iron, etc. (All hair had permanent treatment.)

4. Dresses. Are mostly washable. (Careful with wool trims.)

5. Repairs. Are done at Käthe Kruse Puppen factories. If repair for Christmas is desired, send no later than September. All repair items will be cleaned and disinfected to prevent child diseases."

Disregarding the painting, which is entirely different, this is not the same model head that is found on the dolls shown with the turtle mark, but one wonders if these heads were made by Schildkröte under contract to Kruse since they had later dealings. Records from a previous owner show that this doll was purchased from another collector in 1957 for $20.00.

Illustration 342. According to Louella Hart in her addendum to the Von Boehn book, *Dolls and Puppets*, because of the amount of handwork involved in making the dolls in her regular manner, not too many were available for export and so Frau Kruse sold 12 of her models to the Rheinische Gummi und Celluloid Fabrik Co. to be made in celluloid. They first appeared at the Nuremberg Toy Fair which Louella Hart dates as 1956 and were the sensation of the fair. Jurgen and Marianne Cieslick in their article "The Käthe Kruse Celluloid Doll," *Doll Reader*, November 1982, give the date for the fair as 1955.

These two dolls are listed in the Schildkröte pamphlet as 16in (40.6cm) but they measure 15¾in (40.1cm). The girl is *Gretchen* No. 5934/10 and the boy is *Karl* No. 5964/7. They are described as "New Process lightweight almost indestructible Plastic. Real human hair -- real leather shoes. New design lifelike sleeping eyes." They are two of the 12 models that Käthe Kruse sold to the Rheinische Gummi und Celluloid Fabrik Co. and which they introduced in 1955 or 1956. Collectors sometimes refer to them as celluloid since they bear the turtle mark. They are jointed at neck, hip and shoulder with heavy elastic that is held in place in the limbs with an inserted plastic plug. The "new

design" eyes are plastic that are covered by plastic lids with real hair lashes when the doll is laid down. The wigs are no longer individually knotted, but are strips of woven human hair that is sewn to silk caps. The mouths are much redder than that of the doll in *Illustration 341*, and the shading of the eyes is not nearly as artistic. Something of the charm of the earlier dolls is missing. These, instead of looking pouty, merely look like sulky children. The clothes, although bright and well made for a commercial doll, are not as high quality as the earlier doll. Hems are skimpier, materials are cheaper and less care seems to have been taken in the sewing. The heads are marked: "(turtle in diamond frame)//T 40." Bodies are marked on the back: "(turtle in diamond frame)//MODELL//(signature of Käthe Kruse)//T40." *Gretchen* wears panties of heavily sized white cotton, white muslin blouse with red and blue lace, a bright print skirt and a green apron. There is a wreath of cloth posies in her hair and blossoms in her pocket. Both dolls wear red leather shoes and white knitted sox. *Karl* has no underwear, only silky blue pants and a blue striped shirt. Records obtained from the previous owner show that *Karl* was purchased from another collector in 1956 for $16.95. *Gretchen* was a Christmas gift (purchased from a dealer) in 1961. She was valued at $10.00.

Illustration 344. The tag found on the girl in *Illustration 342* and the boy in *Illustration 343*. 1¾in (4.5cm) yellow paper printed with black. The tortoise is white on a blue field. Two identical tags are glued over the string. These dolls bear the trademark of the Rheinische Gummi und Celluloid Fabrik Co. or "Schildkrote."

Illustration 343. These dolls have the same plastic bodies as the ones in *Illustration 342*, but the heads are of vinyl with rooted synthetic hair and plastic sleep eyes with lashes. The lips are a softer pink and the movable eyelid has disappeared in favor of the regular individually sleeping eyes that are found in the modern dolls. The heads of soft vinyl have a slight flange that holds them in the opening of the bodies. They are movable. The limbs are strung in the same manner as the dolls in *Illustration 342*. The girl wears white knitted cotton panties and lace-trimmed organdy blouse and a red plaid skirt that is trimmed with black velvet ribbon. A red kerchief covers her braided blonde hair. The sandals are plastic. The boy wears the same outfit that *Hansel* wears in the pamphlet, except he wears black plastic climbing boots trimmed with red ties and straps and has gray plush lederhosen and a white muslin shirt. The Alpine hat is green felt. Neither doll is marked on the head, but the bodies are marked: "(turtle in diamond frame)//MODELL//(signature of Käthe Kruse)//40." Records from the previous owner show that they were both purchased from a store in 1961. *Hansel* was $12.95 and the girl was $11.95.

Illustration 345. Tags found on the Kathe Kruse girl in *Illustration 341*.

The dolls that were born of a child's dream . . .

346a.

Printed in Germany

346b.

Illustration 346. Pamphlet showing the 12 models of Käthe Kruse dolls that were manufactured and sold by Rheinische Gummi und Celluloid Fabrik Co. and which bear their trademark, the diamond-framed turtle, "Schildkröte." (Note the variations in spelling.)

"I WANT A NEW BABY JUST LIKE YOURS, MOMMY!"

That is the real reason children have wanted dolls as long as there have been children.

The creative mother who heard and responded to those words more than fifty years ago was Kaethe Kruse. Ex-actress, wife of a well-known sculptor, busy young mother, Kaethe Kruse had no idea of making dolls to sell.

But such was the attraction of the unique dolls she made *only to answer her children's wishes* that Kaethe Kruse one day found herself in the dolls business – and became world-famous almost overnight.

Kaethe Kruse Dolls have undergone many changes since her first one, made of a sand-filled towel. Every change has been designed to express more fully their first inspiration – to give them greater realism, greater durability, more magnetic appeal for children.

The original cloth-stuffed Kaethe Kruse dolls were made by process too slow and costly to meet the tremendous demand. So, the great German doll firm of

346c.

346d.

Schildkroet 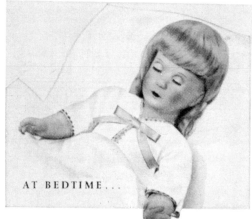 the first in the world to manufacture dolls on a large industrial scale was licensed to reproduce the Kaethe Kruse Dolls in a form that could be manufactured in adequate quantities – to the delight of thousands and thousands of children all over the world. Made of a new process, extremely light weight, skin-textured plastic, these new Kaethe Kruse Dolls are as close to indestructible as any doll can be. Kaethe Kruse believed that, to provide a real education in parenthood, a doll should last through all the formative years. In Europe, often the same Kaethe Kruse Doll has been the inseparable companion of two or three generations of little girls.

To-day's Kaethe Kruse dolls are life-like in nearly every detail. Each doll's face has its own special personality. Only Kaethe Kruse dolls have the new eyes with eyelids that open and close exactly like those of the human eye. Real human hair is knotted in strand by strand; it can be combed over and over again without coming loose. The clothes of Kaethe Kruse dolls are hand-sewn – the equal in quality of fine children's clothes. Shoes are of genuine leather.

To the fortunate child who receives one, a Kaethe Kruse Doll is more than an ordinary toy. It will serve as a beloved playmate for many, many years. It will be kept as a lifelong souvenir of a happy childhood experience.

AT BEDTIME...

Kaethe Kruse Dolls' eyes close with real eyelids. Unlike the ordinary sleeping eye dolls, Kaethe Kruse Dolls imitate the action of the human eye exactly and look real and lifelike asleep or awake.

346e.

346f.

GRETCHEN
5934/10 • 16 inch.

HANSEL
5964/1 • 16 inch.

New Process lightweight almost indestructible Plastic
Real human hair – real leather shoes · New design lifelike sleeping eyes

MODEL *Käthe Kruse* BY SCHILDKROET

346g.

HEIDI
5934/12 • 16 inch.

SUSI
5934/11 • 16 inch.

New Process lightweight almost indestructible Plastic
Real human hair – real leather shoes · New design lifelike sleeping eyes

MODEL *Käthe Kruse* BY SCHILDKROET

346h.

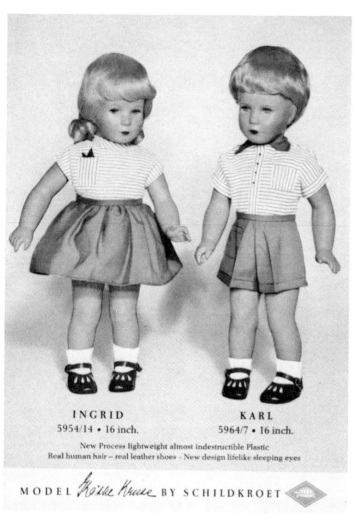

INGRID
5954/14 • 16 inch.

KARL
5964/7 • 16 inch.

New Process lightweight almost indestructible Plastic
Real human hair – real leather shoes · New design lifelike sleeping eyes

MODEL *Käthe Kruse* BY SCHILDKROET

346i.

BOBBY
5954/18 • 16 inch.

JUDY
5954/13 • 16 inch.

New Process lightweight almost indestructible Plastic
Real human hair – real leather shoes · New design lifelike sleeping eyes

MODEL *Käthe Kruse* BY SCHILDKROET

346j.

ALICE
5954/15 • 16 inch.

MARYLOU
5954/16 • 16 inch.

New Process lightweight almost indestructible Plastic
Real human hair – real leather shoes · New design lifelike sleeping eyes

MODEL *Käthe Kruse* BY SCHILDKROET

346k.

JANE
5954/6 • 16 inch.

LYNN
5934/17 • 16 inch.

New Process lightweight almost indestructible Plastic
Real human hair – real leather shoes · New design lifelike sleeping eyes

MODEL *Käthe Kruse* BY SCHILDKROET

346l.

Illustration 347. This 12in (30.5cm) young man in his lederhosen is an example of what the collector would call "hard plastic." He is here for comparison with the celluloid doll in *Illustration 150*. He is jointed at neck, hip and shoulder, has the blinky sleep eyes with lashes and shading above the eyes that one expects on a hard plastic doll. There are molded loops on the limbs to hold wire hooks. The doll is elastic strung. The quality of the synthetic wig is far below the quality of the clothing which is superb. His pants are brown suede and the little plastic suspenders have an Alpine design embossed on them. The costumes on the two examples are quite similar. Even the buttons are alike. He is marked on the head: "H.D."

The little celluloid chicken is far older, dating about the period following World War I. He has a molded, painted bow tie and a hat and comb of hot pink. He is white celluloid with jointed pink celluloid legs. He is marked: "(cross in circle)//MADE IN JAPAN." He also has the green inspection label.

OPPOSITE PAGE: Illustration 348. This 8½in (21.6cm) doll is interesting for several reasons, her Lenci label for one. The original thread that held it is still attached to the skirt, but the label is now attached by a staple (added to hold it when the paper tore loose). According to Dorothy Coleman, this label is the one used after World War II. This would be only a few years after Elena Scavini, known to the world as "Lenci," left the Lenci factory. Whether she had anything to do with the design of this particular doll is debatable, but her basic use of felt with appliqued designs in her costumes is carried out in the dressing of this provincial doll. The tangerine felt skirt is trimmed with gold braid and gold-striped gauze ribbon. Small posies of felt are sprayed across the front. The bodice is made of maroon felt with ecru lace sleeves and ruffles. The "jeweled" belt is woven gold metallic ribbon. At her throat is the gold cross on a black ribbon that is found so often on dolls in provincial dress. Her cap is lace with ribbon trim. She wears lavender rayon drawers! The overall effect has the touch of Madame Lenci, though. The wig is beautifully designed from fine light brown mohair, stitched at the part and braided into coils at the nape. The doll is made from a heavy ivory material (celluloid? plastic?). The most unusual feature is that the whole doll has been painted flesh color, not just the features. Usually the pigment is in the plastic before it is molded. In this case, only the torso is the unpainted ivory plastic. The features of the doll are not only a complete departure from the modeling generally found in a doll of this type, but the painting is exceptionally well done. The body has a molded bust and rigid legs with painted black shoes and white sox. The arms are attached by means of elastic held in place by a peg glued into a slash in the upper arm. When the doll was recently purchased, the head was rigid. Examination proved that at one time it was attached with a heavy, round rubber cord from somewhere in the head to a bar inside the body. It is not a socket head; it is simply sliced off at the neck. After the elastic hardened and broke, the head was glued to the body. It was not noticeable since the division is under the necklace. The doll is unmarked. The label is paper printed with varicolored rings around the border and a green shamrock. It has the following wording: "LENCI// TORINO//PIANA DEI GRECI//SICILIA//MADE IN ITALY."

Illustration 349. 16½in (41.9cm) This little charmer was made in the early 1950s. She is one of a series of "celluloid" dolls made by the Italian doll maker, Anili, daughter of Elena and Enrico Scavini, founders of the famous Lenci factory in Turin, Italy. According to Anili, this doll was sculpted under the supervision of Madame Lenci by the artist Borione. The molds were made by Madame's brother, Bubine. The doll was produced in the Mazzuchelli factory near Tragate.

According to her owner, she is made of light weight celluloid (the transition variety, I am sure). She has stationary gray-green glass eyes with painted brown upper lashes and brows. The wig is of brown mohair. She is jointed with wire springs held by metal discs in the limbs. The clothing is similar to that found on Lenci and Anili felt dolls. The underwear is white cotton with red felt trim and the navy blue felt dress is top-stitched in squares with circles of white felt at the corners. She wears white plastic shoes and cotton sox. Mark on center of back: "Anili//(heart)//Made in Italy" all within a circle. *Betty Grimes Collection. Photograph by John Schoonmaker.*

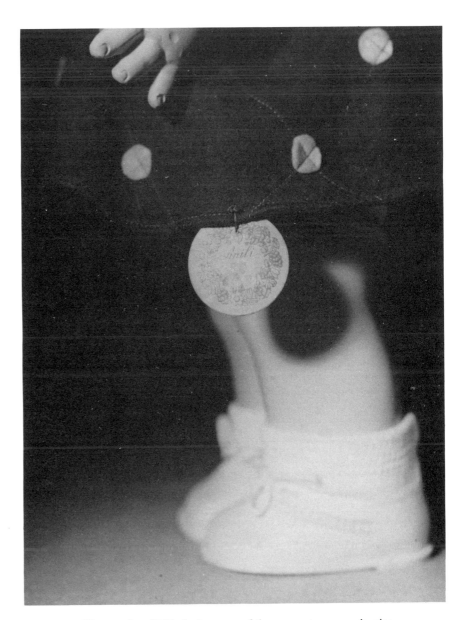

Illustration 350. A close-up of the paper tag worn by the doll in *Illustration 349*. It is a silver circle with a border of colorful flowers and fruit surrounding the name "Anili." Stamped on the tag are the words: "Made in Italy." *Betty Grimes Collection. Photograph by John Schoonmaker.*

Illustration 351. Mark found on the dolls made by Anili Scavini of Turin, Italy.

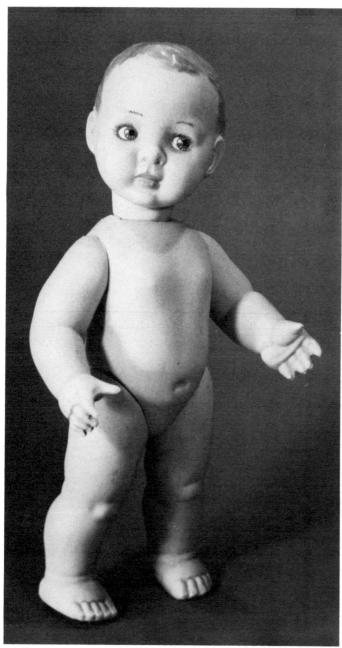

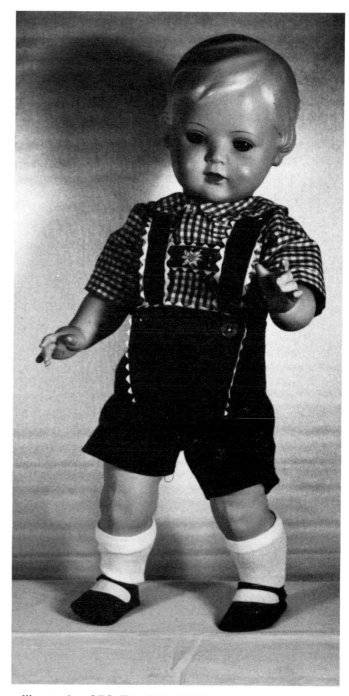

Illustration 352. 11¾in (29.9cm) A little boy also made by Anili. At the time these dolls were made, they were referred to as celluloid, although they are plastic. This one seems to be a rigid vinyl. He has elastic-strung arms and legs (the elastic is held by pieces of plastic inserted into the holes) and the head is attached to the legs by means of a spring. His features are painted in the same manner Anili paints her felt dolls, with oils. The eyes are blue with white highlights and his mouth is a soft pink with matching dots in the nostrils. His molded hair is oil-painted blonde with dark streaks, the way one would paint a portrait. The daughter of Anili told the author that she played with these "celluloid" dolls in the 1950s. This particular doll was sent to the author by Anili Scavini who found it among her old stock. Mark on back: "ANILI//(heart)//Made in Italy" all within a circle.

Illustration 353. This 21in (53.3cm) charming boy is of the later material used shortly after World War II. His arms and legs are attached with elastic that is threaded through plastic tubes in his torso. The head is attached by a spring to the lower tube that holds the legs. He is a well-sculpted doll with sleep glass eyes and the silvery blonde hair that is associated with the dolls of this period. The costume is all original. He wears a red and white checked cotton shirt, green felt lederhosen, white sox and black plastic shoes. Mark on head: "(turtle in a diamond frame)//5056." Mark on body: "(turtle in a diamond frame)//56." *Ursula Mertz Collection. Photograph courtesy of Ursula Mertz.*

Heads Only

As was previously mentioned, heads of celluloid could be purchased separately to either repair a broken doll or to put with other parts that were able to be bought to make a complete doll. Custom design in the toy world. Wouldn't that be a wonderful idea to revive today in our throw-away world?

These few photographs have been included to give the reader a closer look at the design of some of the celluloid heads.

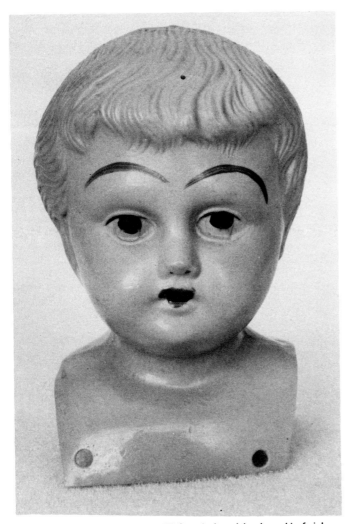

Illustration 354. This 3in (7.6cm) shoulder head is fairly thin celluloid. The modeling is good, but the painting is poor. The eyes are bright blue and the mouth is vivid red. It is, however, another example of the American doll. Mark: "AMERICAN//(symbol of Indian head)." *Photograph by Jane Buchholz.*

Illustration 355. Unidentified trademark found on celluloid dolls made in the United States.

Bisque

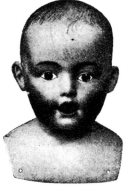

C71762 to C71768

Finest Tinted Character Bisque Heads; two assorted expressions of face; painted hair and eyes; bust with four holes.

	Shoulder Width, In.	Height, Inches	Dozen in Box	Dozen
C71762.	2⅝	3⅜	1	2.30
C71764.	2⅞	4	1	3.50
C71766.	3	4¼	½	4.00
C71768.	3¾	5¼	½	5.50

356a.

Celtid

C72420 to C72412

Celtid Smiling Baby Head, Showing Teeth, Painted Hair and Eyes

	Size	Shoulder width, inches	Height, inches	Dozen in box	Dozen
C72420.	5½	1⅜	2¼	1	.80
C72422.	8½	2⅜	3⅜	1	1.50
C72424.	10	3	4⅛	½	2.50
C72412.	12	3¼	4½	½	4.00

356b.

Bisque

C72193 to C72201

Superior quality bisque, the very best made. Full molded bust with four holes; finest side-parted sewed wigs, pure Angora; blondes and brunettes.

Moving Eyes with Hair Eyelashes

	Shoulder width, inches	Height, inches	Dozen in box	Dozen
C72193.	3⅜	4½	1/12	8.00
C72194.	3¾	4¾	1/12	10.00
A72196.	4⅜	5	1/12	12.00
C72197.	4¾	5¼	1/12	16.00
C72198.	5⅛	6	1/12	18.00
C72199.	5¾	7	1/12	24.00
C72200.	6	7½	1/12	30.00
C72201.	6¼	7¾	1/12	36.00

356c.

Celtid

C72310 to C72319

Beautiful, natural flesh color, dull finish. Handsome baby features and teeth; **full sewed Angora wig**, side-parted; silk ribbon bow; blondes and brunettes.

Moving Eyes with Hair Eyelashes

	Size	Shoulder width, inches	Height, inches	Dozen in box	Dozen
C72310.	8½	2⅜	3½	1/12	7.50
C72312.	10	2⅞	4	1/12	8.50
C72314.	12	3¼	5	1/12	12.00
C72316.	14	4	5½	1/12	17.00
C72318.	16½	4½	6⅛	1/12	24.00
C72319.	18	5¼	7⅛	1/12	36.00
C72320.	20	6	8	1/12	42.00

356d.

Metal

C72600 to C72609

Painted Hair and Eyes

Size	Shoulder width, inches	Height, inches	Dozen in box	Dozen
C72600.	0	1¾	2⅝	½	1.60
C72602.	1	2¼	3¼	½	2.40
C72604.	3	2⅝	4	¼	3.70
C72605.	4	2⅞	4¼	1/12	4.30
C72606.	5	3⅜	4¾	1/12	5.70
C72607.	6	3⅝	5⅛	1/12	7.50
C72608.	7	3⅞	5⅝	1/12	8.00
C72609.	8	4¼	6	1/12	9.00

356e.

Celtid

C72399 to C72407

Painted Hair and Eyes

Size	Shoulder width, inches	Height, inches	Dozen in box	Dozen
C72399.	7	1⅞	2⅝	1	.90
C72401.	8½	2¼	2½	1	1.50
C72403.	9½	2⅜	3⅛	1	2.30
C72406.	12	3½	4½	½	4.00
C72407.	15	3¾	5	½	6.00

356f.

Illustration 356. A through f. These doll heads were available in 1914. The heads and bodies could be bought separately. Instructions for ordering the bodies were to order by corresponding shoulder width. In order to make a comparison of the celluloid doll heads and other doll heads that could be purchased at the same time, we chose the dolls above since they were similar. 356a is a familiar bisque Heubach character. The 3" (7.6cm) size sold for $4.00 a dozen, or a bit more than 33¢ each. 365b is a similar head of Celtid. In the 3" (7.6cm) size the cost was $2.50 per dozen, or about 21¢ each. Surprisingly, the 4⅜" (11.1cm) bisque girl in 356c costs $1.00 each while her Celtid counterpart (356d) is twice as much, $2.00 for the 4½" (11.5cm) size. The metal head (356e) cost a bit more than 66¢ each, while the comparable size in Celtid was 50¢ each. It is an interesting note that even though the shoulder widths are approximately the same, there is quite a variance in height. *1914 Marshall Field & Company Doll Catalog,* reprinted by Hobby House Press, Inc.

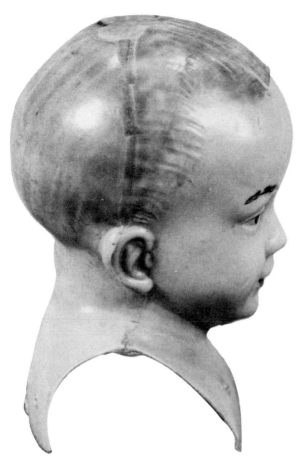

Illustration 357. Unfortunately, this tiny 2in (5.1cm) shoulder head was damaged before a photograph could be taken. He is a very small character boy with painted black eyes (mere dots) and lightly molded brown hair. He is well marked: "(unframed turtle)//SCHUTZ-MARKE// 14//GERMANY."

Illustration 358. Components of the trademark of the Rheinische Gummi und Celluloid Fabrik Co. found on the shoulder head in the *Illustration 357*.

Illustration 359. This 4in (10.2cm) celluloid head is of the *Dream Baby*-type. It was no doubt intended for a cloth body since it has a flange neck. The stationary eyes are blue glass and the hair only lightly painted brown. Mark around the flange: "(framed turtle) 103/14 GERMANY." He wears the cap to hide damage. These may have been advertised as hard to break, but as time goes on and they are exposed to temperature and humidity changes, they become brittle and will break easily.

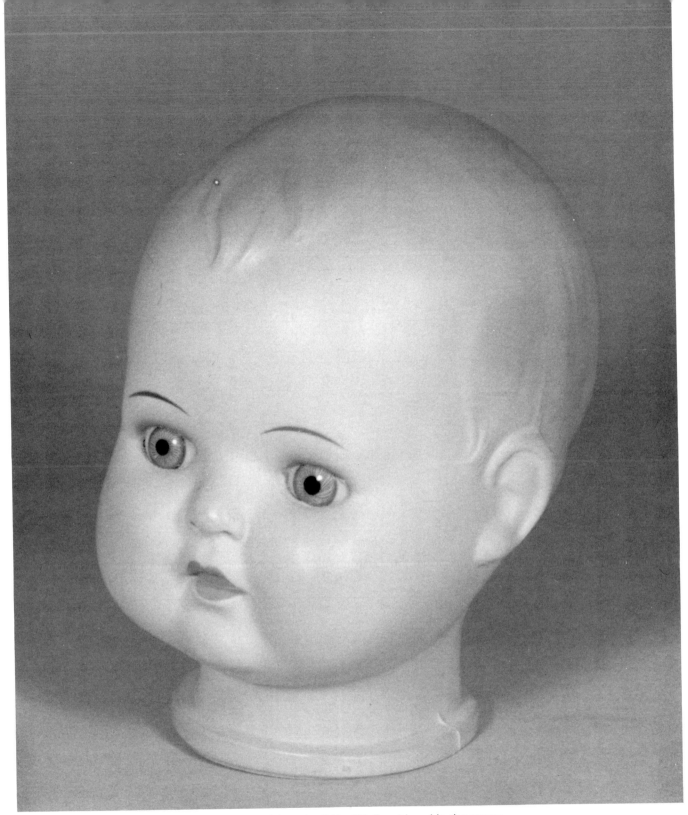

Illustration 360. This 4½in (11.5cm) head is the same type of material the later Käthe Kruse dolls are made of. Because it has the turtle mark, collectors persist in calling it celluloid. It is a strong, pink plastic with a matte finish. Notice how much better defined the flange is because of the new techniques in molding. This doll also has glass eyes, but they are the round type that are generally found on rockers for sleep eyes. The previous doll had oval eyes made for stationary setting. Mark on back of neck: "(framed turtle)//40."

Patents

The following United States Patents concerning celluloid and celluloid dolls are reproduced in this section.

No. 91,341 dated June 15, 1869 to John W. Hyatt.

No. 235,933 dated December 28, 1880, to W. B. Carpenter.

No. 237,559 dated February 8, 1881, to M. C. Lefferts & W. B. Carpenter.

No. 1,120,331 dated December 8, 1914, to F. W. Parsons.

No. 1,645,275 dated October 11, 1927, to Albert Beyler.

UNITED STATES PATENT OFFICE.

JOHN W. HYATT, JR., OF ALBANY, NEW YORK, AND ISAIAH S. HYATT, OF ROCKFORD, ILLINOIS.

IMPROVED METHOD OF MAKING SOLID COLLODION.

Specification forming part of Letters Patent No. 91,341, dated June 15, 1869.

To all whom it may concern:

Be it known that we, JOHN W. HYATT, Jr., of the city of Albany, in the State of New York, and ISAIAH S. HYATT, of the city of Rockford, in the State of Illinois, have invented a new and useful Method of Making Solid Collodion, or compounds of pyroxyline; and we do hereby declare the following specification to be a true and exact description of the nature of our invention.

Our convention consists of a new and improved method of manufacturing solid collodion and its compounds; its essential feature being the employment of a very small quantity of ether or other appropriate solvent, and dissolving pyroxyline therewith, under a heavy pressure, so that a comparatively hard and solid product is obtained, with great economy of solvents and saving of time.

The following description will enable others skilled in the art to use our process:

We place soluble cotton, pyroxyline, or prepared cellulose into a strong cylinder or suitably shaped mold. With the pyroxyline may be mixed ivory dust, bone dust, asbestus, flake white, or any other desirable substance, according to the nature of the product required.

This compound is then pressed into a tolerably compact mass by means of a plunger in the cylinder, or by a movable part of the mold. The plunger to said cylinder or part of the mold is then retracted to give room for the ether or other solvent. The proportion of solvent to the pyroxyline is as five to ten, seven to ten, or equal parts, by weight, according to the nature and proportions of the compound. When the pyroxyline is used alone, from one-half to three-fourths, by weight, of solvent will be sufficient; but when ivory dust or other material is added, a somewhat greater proportion of solvent will be required, which can readily be determined by trial. After the plunger to the cylinder or part of the mold has been retracted, as aforesaid, the solvent is poured or forced in through a hole which is then closed, and the plunger or movable part of the mold is immediately forced against the contents with great power—a pressure of from five to twenty tons per square inch being required to produce the best results. The pressure must be applied quickly, so that the solvent will be forced into contact with every particle of the pyroxyline before the dissolving process has time to commence. This, however, may be varied according to the degree of activity of the solvent employed. The cylinder or mold must be made or packed to work so closely that none of the solvent can escape the pressure. Other mechanical means may be employed equivalent to the foregoing, and we do not confine ourselves to the precise apparatus described.

The product is then taken out of the cylinder or mold, and will be found to be hard and solid, of uniform quality throughout, and liable to only a very slight degree of shrinkage, because of the very small proportion of volatile elements which it contains.

After the solid compound thus formed is taken out of the cylinder or mold, and before it thoroughly seasons, we subject it, in the manufacture of many articles, to additional pressure in molds, whereby it is caused to conform perfectly with all the configurations of the mold.

Having thus described our invention, what we claim, and desire to secure by Letters Patent, is—

1. Dissolving pyroxyline under pressure, substantially as described.

2. Dissolving pyroxyline under pressure, when mixed with ivory dust or other material, substantially as described.

JOHN W. HYATT, Jr.
ISAIAH S. HYATT.

Witnesses:
HENRY DEITZ,
C. M. HYATT.

(No Model.)

W. B. CARPENTER.
Method of Coloring the Eyebrows, &c., of
Celluloid Dolls.

No. 235,933.   **Patented Dec. 28, 1880.**

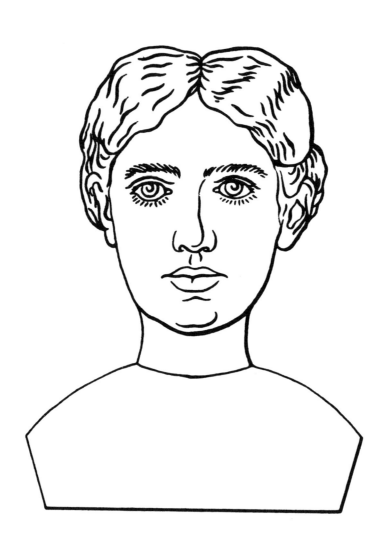

Attest:

Joseph W. H. Emis

Wm. L. Fish

Inventor.

William B. Carpenter

By Horace Harris

Atty

UNITED STATES PATENT OFFICE.

WILLIAM B. CARPENTER, OF NEWARK, NEW JERSEY, ASSIGNOR TO HIMSELF AND CELLULOID NOVELTY COMPANY, OF NEW YORK, N. Y.

METHOD OF COLORING THE EYEBROWS, &c., OF CELLULOID DOLLS.

SPECIFICATION forming part of Letters Patent No. 235,933, dated December 28, 1880.

Application filed May 28, 1880. (No model.)

To all whom it may concern:

Be it known that I, WILLIAM B. CARPENTER, of Newark, in the county of Essex and State of New Jersey, have invented a new and useful Improvement in the Method of Coloring the Eyebrows, &c., of Celluloid Dolls, of which the following is a specification.

My invention relates to the matter of finishing dolls' heads made from celluloid or other like plastic material; and it consists in the method of working in the eyebrows and other hair-lines, and in giving a natural flesh-like appearance to the face and neck.

The figure is of a doll's head, and shows the lines indicating the eyebrows, &c.

Dolls' heads made of celluloid, when molded, have a glazed or glossy look, making them resemble the crockery dolls. To remove this gloss I use a fine pumice-stone or some similar powder, and this powder rubbed over the face and neck takes off the polish and gives the features the most natural and flesh-like appearance, and the tinting on this surface has the natural bloom of health and beauty. But I have found that, if the eyebrows and other lines indicating hair have been put on, as they usually are, before the powder is used, these hair-lines will be rubbed off by the attrition of the powder; or if these lines are put on after the surface has been abraded, they will show rough and uneven, and be liable in handling the dolls to be worn off. I therefore take a sharp-pointed knife, and, holding it usually at an oblique angle from the face, make fine incisions in the surface in the places for these hair-lines, and into the incisions I work a coloring of the shade required, which becomes fixed in the incisions, so that no rubbing with pumice-stone in finishing or handling afterward will remove it; and the powder, applied after the coloring has been worked in for the eyebrows, &c., will smooth up and finish the surface, made a little rough by cutting the incisions. These hair-lines may be made much finer and more perfect by means of the incisions than they could be made with a brush or pen. These two steps together make a great improvement on the state of the art in the manufacture of dolls' heads, giving them the most beautiful and natural look, which no other known process will do.

I claim—

1. In finishing up dolls' heads made from celluloid or like plastic material, the use of pumice-stone or other similar powder, substantially as and for the purpose specified.

2. The eyebrows, &c., having the hair-lines worked into the surface by means of incisions and afterward finished up with pumice-stone, for the purpose set forth.

WILLIAM B. CARPENTER.

Witnesses:
HORACE HARRIS,
JOSEPH A. ENO.

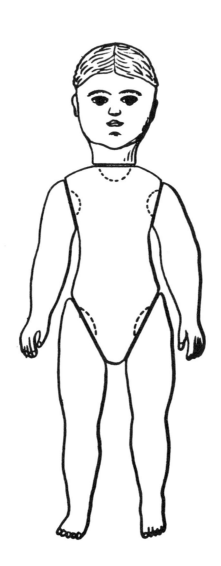

Attest: Inventor.

George B. Adams   Marshall C. Lefferts

Joseph McEwan   William B. Carpenter

                            By Horace Harris

UNITED STATES PATENT OFFICE.

MARSHALL C. LEFFERTS, OF NEW YORK, N. Y., AND WILLIAM B. CARPENTER, OF NEWARK, N. J., ASSIGNORS TO CELLULOID MANUFACTURING COMPANY, OF NEW YORK, N. Y.

CELLULOID DOLL.

SPECIFICATION forming part of Letters Patent No. 237,559, dated February 8, 1881.

Application filed January 7, 1881. (No model.)

To all whom it may concern:

Be it known that we, MARSHALL C. LEFFERTS, of New York city, county, and State, and WILLIAM B. CARPENTER, of Newark, in the county of Essex and State of New Jersey, have invented a new and useful Improvement in Celluloid Dolls, of which the following is a specification.

Our invention relates to the manufacture of dolls, either in whole or in part, from celluloid, or other compound of pyroxyline, wherein the whole structure is made of this material, or some part thereof, as that the outer surface may be of celluloid and the inner or an interlining of some other material.

The figure is of a whole doll articulated at various points.

In our manufacture of dolls or dolls' heads, we take the pyroxyline in any suitable form for molding into the desired shape, which may be done by any process that will put the material into the form required, so that the celluloid shall appear on the outer surface. This may be done by molding the dolls in sections, and then putting the parts together, making a whole; or by molding them from tubes by a process of pressing into complete form by devices and mechanism for which a patent was allowed July 26, 1880, to one of the present applicants, (Carpenter,) or by some other process accomplishing the same purpose.

The figure shows a complete form articulated, making a flexible doll; or we may make but a head, or head and breast in a fixed order to receive such additions as taste may dictate.

The dolls, when molded, will be finished by any suitable means, but preferably by a process set forth in the patent to the within-named Wm. B. Carpenter, No. 235,933, December 28, 1880.

We claim—

1. A head or other part of a doll made wholly or in part of celluloid or other compound of pyroxyline.

2. A doll consisting wholly or in part of celluloid or other compound of pyroxyline.

3. A head or other parts of a doll the surface of which is coated with celluloid or other compound of pyroxyline.

4. The doll or part of a doll made of material substantially as described, and molded into form in separate sections, substantially as set forth.

5. The doll or parts of a doll made of materials substantially as described, and molded whole, substantially as and for the purpose specified.

MARSHALL C. LEFFERTS.
WILLIAM B. CARPENTER.

Witnesses:
HORACE HARRIS,
GEORGE B. ADAMS.

F. W. PARSONS.

DOLL.

APPLICATION FILED FEB. 26, 1912.

1,120,331.

Patented Dec. 8, 1914.

2 SHEETS—SHEET 1.

Fig. 1

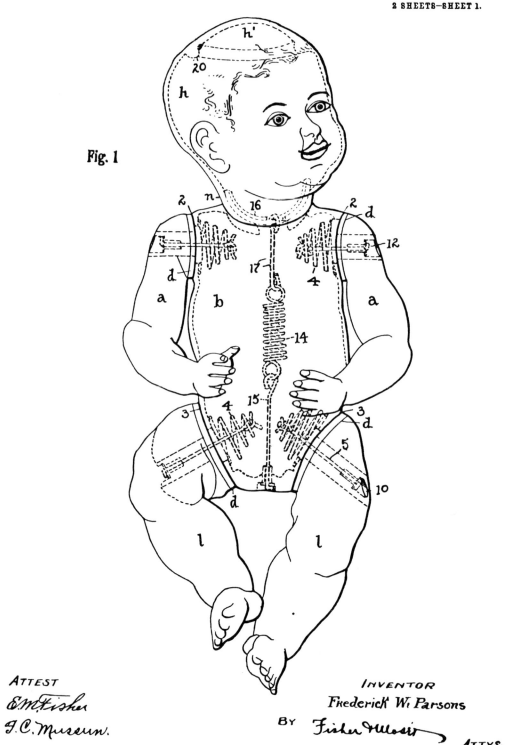

UNITED STATES PATENT OFFICE.

FREDERICK W. PARSONS, OF CLEVELAND, OHIO, ASSIGNOR TO THE PARSONS-JACKSON COMPANY, OF CLEVELAND, OHIO, A CORPORATION.

DOLL.

1,120,331. Specification of Letters Patent. **Patented Dec. 8, 1914.**

Application filed February 26, 1912. Serial No. 679,818.

To all whom it may concern:

Be it known that I, FREDERICK W. PARSONS, citizen of the United States, residing at Cleveland, in the county of Cuyahoga and
5 State of Ohio, have invented certain new and useful Improvements in Dolls, of which the following is a specification.

This invention relates to an improvement in dolls, and the invention consists in a
10 doll having the construction and combination of parts substantially as shown and described and particularly pointed out in the claims.

The object in view is to provide a doll of
15 exceptional durability, particularly in the places and parts heretofore found to be weak and defective.

In the accompanying drawings, Figure 1 is a front elevation of a complete doll em-
20 bodying the invention and showing the internal mechanism in dotted lines. Fig. 2 is a central sectional elevation thereof front to rear and showing the means for securing the several attached parts together and espe-
25 cially the connections for the head. Fig. 3 is an inside view of the top or crown on line *x—x*, Fig. 2, and Fig. 4 is a cross section on line *z—z*, Fig. 2. Fig. 5 is a sectional view centrally through one of the leg
30 joints and the portion of the body to which it is attached.

As thus shown the doll is represented as a hollow or shell-like embodiment, having thin walls for the most part except where
35 special reinforcement is required at the joints and elsewhere to give needed strength, and the said doll may be made of any material which combines lightness with strength and firmness and can be molded into the desired
40 shape. Assuming, however, that a suitable material is found for this use, and I would not fix an arbitrary limit to the material, the doll is made up with six distinct and independent parts or pieces comprising the
45 body *b*, the head *h*, the two arms *a* and the two legs *l*. These parts are made to be united with spring or yielding joints which enable each attached member to be independently mounted and also rotated into
50 different positions on the body and in respect to each other, and to this end the body *b* has flattened ring-shaped side facings or bearings 2 and 3 respectively, with central holes 6 for the attachment of the
55 arms and the legs, but with said bearings

at such different angles of inclination in respect to each other as the function of each may require. Thus, the flat ring-shaped bearings 2 on the body for the arms are in substantially parallel planes with 60 each other and slightly inclined toward the front, and the flat ring-shaped bearings 3 for the legs are set at an inward and forward inclination in like manner so as to bring the legs into a natural position and 65 relation substantially as seen in Fig. 1. The arms and legs likewise have flat disk-shaped facings *d* to correspond to those on the body, so that in these respects the limbs lie flat against the body, normally, whatever their 70 position of adjustment or rotation thereon may be. In other words all the legitimate adjustments are on the plane of these flat meeting surfaces and a great variety of positions and combinations are possible. 75 Other movements involving dislocation or tilting of the parts are possible but they are arbitrary and will not stay fixed, particularly in view of the novel means for supporting the said parts in jointed relation 80 with the body.

To illustrate, the arms and legs have each an attachment consisting of a helical wire spring 4 of conical form and a tension wire 5. The spring is seated at its base against 85 the inside of the body about the hole 6 and the wire 5 is hook-engaged with the inturned top or apex-end of the spring and passes transversely through the center of the spring to the outside of the doll where the wire 5 is 90 shown as having its end 12 bent at right angles to secure it against endwise pull or tension. However, other necessary details enter into the construction of these joints. Thus, the disk-shaped part *d* is made originally in a 95 separate piece and permanently cemented or secured to the leg, becoming a fixed and inseparate working portion thereof in the manufacture. The said disk has an annular cupped boss or projection 7 which fits snugly 100 in the circular hole 6 in the body and has a central aperture for the passage of wire 5, thus affording the equivalent of a ball and socket joint and by which even if the limb be drawn out far enough to withdraw the 105 boss 7 against the comparatively strong tension of spring 4 it will be guided back to place by the spring and wire and the boss when the pull is relaxed. The stock in body *b* about hole 6 is shown as somewhat heavier 110 than in other side portions of the body, and the limb itself is further reinforced by a heavy tube or sleeve 8 which is seated and cemented at its inner end in the cup-portion of the boss 6 and also cemented or otherwise secured to the wall of the limb at its outer end where it is cut to conform to the outer contour of the limb. This tube 8, like disk *d*, is built into the leg as a permanent portion and is the same as if it were originally molded therewith. Finally, I provide an elongated eyelet or a small metallic tube 9 with a flanged outer end and insert it in the outer portion of the sleeve 8 to serve as a rotatable bearing for the wire 5, or in which the said wire may turn when the limb is turned. The said tube is, however, set back from the face of the limb at the bottom of a counter-bored socket or cavity 10 at the end of sleeve 8 and within which the flanged end of eyelet 9 and the bent end 12 of the wire is retired and seated to turn and not contact with anything on the surface of the limb. The tension of the spring is thus distributed directly to the sleeve 8 and disk-plate *d* and only indirectly to the limb.

The construction shown in Fig. 5 clearly discloses all the parts and features just described, and these are characteristic of all the other joints for the legs and arms respectively.

The head *h* has a rounded and more or less tapered neck *n* of the ball pattern and shaped to conform to the round socket-shaped opening in the top of the body. That is, the said opening is adapted to receive the said neck in the relationship of a ball and socket joint and with such freedom of movement that the head can be turned or rotated to any desired inclination or position within limits and turned bodily around horizontally at pleasure. To these ends the head is placed under suitably strong spring tension corresponding to the legs and arms, but with this difference that a spiral spring 14 is used and which comes at about the middle of the body *b* and is hook-connected by a wire 15 with the bottom of said body and by wire 17 with the yoke 16 in head *h*. The eyelet 9' at the bottom of body *b* for wire 15 serves the same bearing purpose as in the legs and arms, and a cavity or recess 13 in the body forms a seat for the flange of the eyelet and retires the right-angled detaining end 12' of wire 15. Yoke 16 is made of fairly heavy wire and of semi-circular shape conforming to the size and shape of the interior of neck *n*, and wire 17 is secured centrally between the ends of this yoke and prevented from shifting thereon or separating therefrom by the back-turned ends 17'. The yoke is thereby also always centered and held upright within the neck and the strain on the neck

more equally distributed, the ends 17' doubling the seating surface or area of contact with the rounded neck. By this construction and connection of the parts the head is adapted to be rocked in its socket and will slide in respect to the said yoke, but if the head be horizontally rotated the rotation will carry the yoke with it and turning will take place through the wire 15 in rotatable bearing 9' below. Thus, in any event the head is irremovably fastened on the body and there is no way to release it but by straightening the right-angled end 12' of the detaining wire 15. This is so difficult for any one to do without tools that the head as well as the arms and legs are to be regarded as irremovably and permanently fastened in place, and a child can neither pull them nor get them out of working position.

The head *h* is made in one piece without seam or joint which makes it very durable and strong, and in Fig. 3 I show the crown *h'* of the head, as reinforced on the inside by thickening the stock, and as further reinforced around the crown by an internal annular bead 20. This gives additional strength where the strain of shocks and blows are centered. I also show opposite ribs 21 at the sides within the neck *n* which taper upward and serve to strengthen this part and which also provide stops to prevent yoke 16 from turning. The neck *n* is also gradually thickened from the head downward to take up the strain or pull of the spring 14 which is necessarily stiff, and the ribs 21 also aid in resisting this strain. The pull upward on the body *b* is also met by the inclined walls having the flat bearing faces 3, as seen in Fig. 5, and by thickening the rounded bottom, as indicated by 22. The neck portion 23 of body *b* is also gradually thickened to provide a strong and relatively large cup-shaped seat or socket for rounded neck *n*.

In assembling the parts, either originally or for repairs, the practice is to first engage the wire with the springs and then draw the wire out through the leg or arm so as to bring the spring under the desired tension. The wire is then bent to form the right angled stop 12, thus locking the parts together and holding the tension wanted. The crescent shape of yoke 16 permits the yoke to be easily inserted into head *h*, and the helical form of the springs 4 make it very convenient and practical to screw the same into openings 6 when entrance into body *b* at its top is debarred by head *h*.

What I claim is:

1. A hollow doll body having side facings at its ends at different angles to a vertical plane and inclined toward the front, arms and legs seated on said facings and having transverse bores with outer recesses, wires through the said bores terminating in said

F. W. PARSONS.
DOLL.
APPLICATION FILED FEB. 26, 1912.

1,120,331.

Patented Dec. 8, 1914.
2 SHEETS—SHEET 2.

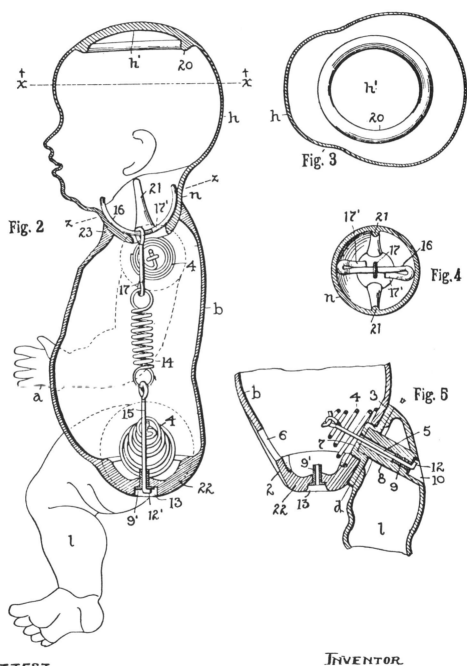

Fig. 3

Fig. 2

Fig. 4

Fig. 5

ATTEST
Em Fisher
F.C. Mussun

INVENTOR
Frederick W. Parsons
By Fisher & Moet
ATTYS.

-185-

recesses and helical springs in said body having said wires engaged therewith.

2. A doll body having a head provided with a substantially ball and socket connection therewith, a yoke adapted to confine the head rotatably on said body and fastening devices for said yoke comprising a spring having a wire rotatably engaged in the bottom of said body.

3. A doll having a body with holes in its sides and ends and members having substantially disk-shaped face portions with bosses at their center centered in said holes and tubes socketed in said bosses, and wire connections rotatably mounted in said tubes, and having spring connection inside said body.

4. A doll having a hollow body and hollow limb members, said members having tubes transversely through their upper ends and separate tubular bearings therein, and springs having wires provided with bent ends engaged with said bearings and serving as retaining means for the said limbs.

5. A doll having a head with a circular tapered neck having ribs inside tapering from base upward, in combination with a body having a socket seating said neck and means to fasten the head rotatably in place comprising a substantially semi-circular yoke fitting the inside of said neck and disposed between said ribs.

6. In a doll, a body having a separate head, and means to rotatably secure said head in rocking relation with said body, comprising spring tension connections and a curved yoke provided with stops to fix the working relations of the tension connections therewith.

7. A doll body having a hollow limb-member, a tension device to rotatably connect said parts, and said limb-member having a cupped bearing-plate and a reinforcing tube at the joint to relieve the main strain of the tension device from the limb-member.

8. A doll having a body with a seat at its side with a circular opening into said body, a member provided with a raised annular projection seated in said opening, a spiral spring surrounding said projection and means connecting the inner end of said spring through said projection with said member to hold the member in operating position.

9. In a doll, a hollow body having rotatable members and means securing the same in place comprising helical springs having their wider portion seated against the inside of the body, and wires anchored in the outside of said members and engaging the smaller end of said springs.

10. A doll body having flat annular facings at its outsides and ends and members faced to seat thereon, wires engaged transversely through the upper portions of said members and rotatably mounted therein, and helical springs on the inside of said body seated at their base against the same opposite said facings and the said wires extending through said springs and engaged with the smaller ends thereof, whereby said members are held in place under spring tension.

11. In a doll, a mechanism to secure the head and body of a doll together comprising a crescent shaped yoke made out of a strip of metal of wire shape having its ends lapped back upon the body thereof and forming curved and widened bearing portions, in combination with spring tension devices secured to said yoke between said ends, the said head and neck having ball and socket meeting surfaces overlapped by said yoke.

12. A doll having a neck of concavo-convex shape in its bottom seating portion, a body having a concave socket adapted to seat said neck and means securing said parts together comprising a tension spring anchored in said body, a free slidable yoke in said neck and a link connecting said spring with the said yoke.

13. A doll body having a concavo-convex neck and a head having a socket conforming to said neck, a crescent shaped wire yoke bearing upon the inside of said neck and spring tension connections with said yoke engaged with the bottom of said body.

In testimony whereof I affix my signature in presence of two witnesses.

FREDERICK W. PARSONS.

Witnesses:
F. C. Mussun,
H. T. Fisher.

UNITED STATES PATENT OFFICE.

ALBERT BEYLER, OF MANNHEIM-NECKARAU, GERMANY, ASSIGNOR TO RHEINISCHE
GUMMI- UND CELLULOID-FABRIK, OF MANNHEIM-NECKARAU, GERMANY.

MANUFACTURE OF DOLLS AND PARTS THEREOF FROM CELLULOSE DERIVATIVES.

No Drawing.   Application filed September 29, 1926, Serial No. 138,570, and in Germany October 19, 1925.

This invention relates to the manufacture of dolls and component parts from celluloid or other cellulose derivatives, and its object is to produce such articles in colours that really simulate the natural flesh tints of human beings, and more particularly of human beings whose skins are naturally white or whitish.

Dolls' heads, dolls' limbs and the like have hitherto suffered from a defect which could not be overcome even in the case of porcelain and other materials, namely, the shiny and wax-like appearance of the colour intended to imitate the tint of white or whitish human skin but quite unlike this latter.

Attempts have long been made in the ceramic industry to make porcelain resemble white or whitish human skin by the incorporation of suitable pigments, but without any great success, and the various endeavours to imitate nature by the aid of celluloid material may also be regarded as failures.

A great variety of methods have been proposed for accomplishing the ultimate result or effect accomplished by this invention by means of which the skin of the doll is made a somewhat transparent and cream-like white with a greenish tint that is somewhat accentuated but at the same time subdued by bloodish red coloring matter which unites with the green tint and produces a natural, healthful rosy effect that is distinctly new in the cellulosic doll head and member art. For example, transparent celluloid has been taken and painted on the outside or inside. White celluloid has been employed and attempts made to produce a flesh tint by lacquering, dipping, etc., but always with the same lack of success. Finally, the practice was adopted of simply incorporating the flesh tint colouring with the celluloid composition, a method which is still in general use but which nevertheless gives rise to the aforesaid defect.

My invention, however, produces a colouration that corresponds exactly to the tint of white or whitish human flesh or skin. It is based upon the discovery that blood-reddish colouring matter will produce the soft and delicate hue or bloom of white or whitish human skin when applied to a specially tinted background, namely, a cellulose derivative of cream-white colour having a greenish tinge. By using a semi-transparent celluloid having the required creamy colour and greenish tinge, an effect of reflection is produced which enables the flesh tint of a white or whitish human body to be truly reproduced in all its modifications.

In carrying the invention into practice, a white pigment and a small proportion of green colouring matter are first incorporated with the celluloid or cellulose derivative to produce a composition having a greenish tinted foundation which gives the foundation material the somewhat green color of a corpse of the white race, and then the blood-like colouring matter is applied thinly, preferably by spraying in order to effect a relatively dull or non-shiny, cream-like and rosy skin of the white or whitish race; the superposed, blood-like, reddish coloring matter, mentioned below, coacting with the underlying, greenish surface of the foundation material to produce the natural somewhat dull and non-shiny, healthy appearance of a natural creamy and rosy skin. The composition initially prepared as stated has the ashen greenish appearance of the flesh of a corpse of the white race, and it is a singular if unexpected fact that the application of the reddish colour thereto results in a most lifelike hue quite unlike the waxen appearance of dolls as heretofore manufactured, but substantially identical with the actual hue or bloom created by human blood flowing beneath human skin of the racial type above indicated.

The following is an example of the preparation of the greenish white composition now preferred:

About 100 parts of nitro cellulose, acetyl cellulose, or a suitable cellulose derivative, are mixed with about 30 parts of camphor, camphor substitute or other suitable gelatinizing agent, and there is added about 1.5 parts of white pigment (zinc white; white lead or the like) together with about 0.03 parts of greenish colour which may be either metal green, mineral green or aniline green examples of all of which are well known.

The blood-like substance to be applied consists of blood red colouring matter dissolved in alcohol, benzine, benzol, ether, acetic acid or other known solvent. It is sprayed on to the moulded composition with a fine spraying apparatus, an essential condition being that it penetrates completely into and adheres intimately to the composition. The thickness of the coating of red blood colouring matter applied may be varied in parts to imitate different aspects of flesh, such as rosy cheeks.

The blood-like or reddish coloring matter consists of red aniline color but may be made of cinnabar or native red sulphide mercury or red earth color and the like. The red aniline color or other coloring matter just referred to may be combined with small quantities of white pigment such as zinc white, for instance, together with a little yellow earth color; such, for examples, as yellow ochre, yellow aniline color, chrome color and the like.

The addition of the white coloring material and yellow coloring material to said foundation material, and of the blood-like coloring matter may be varied, according to the will of the manufacturer, to effect variations in the complexion of the particular skin to be formed on the doll's head or other member by penetration into and adherence of the superposed, reddish coloring matter on the greenish or ashen green basic foundation material of which the doll head or doll member is molded. The blood-red surface or red dye or red color may be made lighter or darker as preferred. The finished skin forming material is permanently colored and washable and free from the shiny or wax-like appearance which has heretofore characterized colored cellulosic material.

The impregnation of the base or foundation creamy-white and greenish tinted material by the blood-red material effects a permanently adhesive superficial surface giving the doll head and particularly the face, a novel physical, characteristic condition and appearance strikingly resembling that of a healthy, natural, creamy-white and rosy complexion, that is such a complexion as is frequently referred to as "a peaches and cream complexion."

In comparison with more or less analogous colored doll heads and faces heretofore made, in which the exposed surfaces are noticeably and positively shiny, the corresponding surfaces effected by this invention are relatively dull and very natural.

Nevertheless it is to be said that by this invention, when and if more of a yellowish or brownish coloring matter is added to the greenish tinted or tinged foundation material, doll heads and members of the positively brunette or dark skinned races may be obtained. In all instances, the bloodish red coloring matter modifies the greenish tinted or tinged foundation material and if more or less yellowish or brownish coloring matter be added to the greenish foundation material, the blood red coloring matter effects in the completed product a skin having the physical characteristic of a natural, healthy human skin having a human blood foundation.

The creamy white, greenish tinted foundation material has a waxy appearance and physical characteristic. This waxy physical characteristic of the foundation material is positively changed, molecularly in all probability, by its impregnation with the bloodish-red coloring matter with the result that the finished product, which is a hardened composition, is given the distinctly different and novel physical characteristic of natural healthy human skin. The quantity of said bloodish-red coloring matter which is either incorporated in or sprayed on the foundation material is in its nature variable but is in all cases small relatively to the mass of the finished composition.

The process of manufacture herein described can be applied both to finished dolls' heads, component parts etc., (which is preferable), and to the raw material which is afterwards formed into such articles. Modifications can be introduced in respect of combined colours by making the green-tinged cream-white colour of the composition a little less green and somewhat redder, browner, etc. at the same time, and by lightening the imitation blood colouring to a corresponding extent. In this way it is easily possible to imitate the flesh tint of humans of different races and types.

In conclusion, I desire to emphasize that the mixture and proportion of colours herein given is by way of example and that the invention is not limited to the same, as the proportion of the different colours and the colours themselves may be varied within wide limits without departing from the scope of the invention as defined by the following claims.

Having now fully described my invention what I claim and desire to secure by Letters Patent is:—

1. The herein described process of manufacturing dolls and component parts from cellulose derivatives in colors which simulate the natural flesh tints of human beings, said process comprising forming a creamy-white, greenish tinged, wax-like foundation of cellulose derivatives; and in coloring the outer surface of said foundation material with an impregnating blood-like coloring matter, thereby destroying the wax-like appearance of said foundation material and converting said wax-like material superficially into a relatively dull condition resembling that of natural, healthy human skin.

2. The herein described process of manufacturing dolls and component parts from cellulose material in colors which simulate the natural flesh tints of human beings, said process comprising forming a creamy-white, greenish tinged, wax-like foundation of cellulose derivatives; and spraying the

outer surface of said foundation material with an impregnating, blood-like coloring matter thereby destroying the wax-like appearance of the foundation material and converting said wax-like composition superficially into a relatively dull condition resembling that of natural, healthy human skin.

3. The herein described article of manufacture for use in the manufacture of dolls, component parts thereof and other articles in simulation of natural flesh tints, said article including a creamy-white, greenish tinged, wax-like foundation of cellulose derivatives modified by a reddish coloring matter effective to destroy such waxy characteristic and to give to a surface of the finished composition a relatively dull physical condition resembling that of natural healthy human skin.

4. The herein described article of manufacture which comprises a foundation made from about 100 parts of cellulosic derivatives; 30 parts of a gelatinizing agent; 1.5 parts of white pigment; 0.03 parts of green coloring material, substantially such as described; modified by a bloodish-red color, substantially such as described, in a relatively small quantity sufficient for converting the creamy-white, green tinged wax-like foundation into a non-waxen surface condition and to give to a surface of the foundation the physical characteristic of natural, healthy human skin.

In testimony whereof I affix my signature.

ALBERT BEYLER.

A Chronology of Celluloid

1832   Braconnot first prepared cellulose nitrate.

1835   Theophile-Jules Pelouze made Pyroxylin.

1845   C. F. Schoenbein invented guncotton.

1856   Alexander Parkes invented Parkesine.

1862   Parkes won medal for his product.

1869   June 15, Hyatt patent for celluloid.

1870s   Three important Eastern United States firms making celluloid: The Celluloid Manufacturing Company (Hyatt), The Celluloid Novelty Company and The Celluloid Fancy Goods Company.

1873   Rheinische Gummi und Celluloid Fabrik Co. founded.

1878   Compagnie Francaise du Celluloid awarded medal at International Exhibition in Paris, France.

1880   December 28, W. B. Carpenter patent.

1881   February 8, M. C. Lefferts/W. B. Carpenter patent.

1885   Rheinische Gummi und Celluloid Fabrik Co. making dolls of celluloid.

1887   Valmore Boitel patent for making dolls' heads of celluloid. (France.)

1888   Buschow & Beck were in business.

1889   Rheinische Gummi und Celluloid Fabrik Co. registered "Schildkrote" trademark, turtle.

1890   Casein plastic "Erinoid" developed in Germany.

1891   Hyatt absorbed his competitors. Reorganized as The Celluloid Company.

1895   Butler Brothers advertised "Zylonite" rattles. Zylonite was the name of the material used for dolls and heads that were distributed through this firm. They advertised that all-zylonite dolls would float.

1899   March 8. Rheinische Gummi und Celluloid Fabrik Co. registered the turtle in a diamond frame for dolls of pyrolin compounds.

1900   Buschow & Beck registered trademark "Minerva" with the helmet.

1900   Circa. Société Industrielle de Celluloid founded. Headed by Neumann and Marks. Used wyvern mark.

1900-1901   Dr. Paul Hunaeus obtained three German patents.

1902   Petitcolin in business. Paris, France, firm specialized in baby dolls.

1903   Kämmer & Reinhardt. German patent for inserting sleep eyes in celluloid heads.

1903   Advertisements for "bisque finish on celluloid dolls."

1904   Buschow & Beck obtained German patent for celluloid heads on ball-jointed bodies.

1905   Rheinische Gummi und Celluloid Fabric Co. patent for inserting eyes in celluloid heads.

1906   Butler Brothers advertised Zylonite dolls with painted hair and features.

1906   A new feature was cloth bodies with celluloid hands.

1906   Kestner advertised their celluloid heads would not fade.

1907   In Prussia, Matilde Sehm, who had been in the doll business since 1869, advertised celluloid dolls.

1907   A New Jersey firm patented fireproof celluloid.

1907   Buschow & Beck advertised Minerva celluloid heads. Minerva metal heads were coated with a combination of celluloid and washable enamel.

1907   *Playthings* reported an "elegant lady doll...her slim, bejewelled fingers have celluloid fingernails shaped like almonds and carefully manicured."

1909   Horsman advertised dolls with celluloid faces.

1909   Kämmer & Reinhardt character dolls introduced.

1909   Karl Standfuss (Juno) granted two patents for celluloid bathing dolls.

1909-1912   Franz Schmid and Hugo Braun used the patented material "cellulobrin" to make bodies.

1910   Bähr & Proschild registered a trademark for dolls made of celluloid.

1910   Butler Brothers advertised celluloid heads on kid bodies. They showed dolls made by Kestner.

1910   Parsons-Jackson starting to make dolls from celluloid scrap.

1911   Doll with five celluloid heads advertised in *Youth's Companion.*

1912   February 26. Parsons-Jackson applied for patent.

1912   February. Parsons-Jackson advertised "Stork Brand Dolls" in *Playthings.*

1912   Sears, Roebuck & Co. advertised all sorts of celluloid novelties and dolls.

1912   Joseph Kallus began his association with the Borgfeldt Company.

1913   Kley & Hahn used the trademark "Cellunova," registered in Germany.

1913   Karl Standfuss (near Dresden, Germany) made celluloid *Kewpies.*

1914   Butler Brothers advertised all kinds of celluloid novelties and dolls.

1914   Parsons-Jackson moved to New York, New York, and developed "Biskoline." They received their patent December 18. There was a disastrous fire at the factory.

1914   Kestner made celluloid character babies and heads of celluloid.

1914   Petitcolin had factories at Lilas, Seine, Etain, Meuse and a shop in Paris, all in France. Made celluloid dolls and bebes. "Head of eagle" trademark.

1915   Dupont purchased the Arlington Company in New Jersey. Made "Pyrolin."

1916   March. *Playthings* advertised a "New American Industry-Celluloid Toys." About this time celluloid eyes were developed and dolls were being imported from Japan.

1917   Haber Brothers (New York, New York,) advertised Japanese dolls and celluloid dolls.

1917   Bo Peep Brand celluloid and composition character dressed dolls made by the Baby Outfitters 1917 to 1918 in New York, New York.

1917   L'Oncle Hansi made character dolls with heads and arms of celluloid.

1918   Hyatt's company now called the American Cellulose and Chemical Co.

1918   Kestner advertised celluloid heads.

1918   Marks Bros. Co. of Boston, Massachusetts, made and imported celluloid heads.

1919   Louis Wolf and Co. advertised composition dolls with celluloid enamel.

1919   September 16, Patent No. 122,745 registered to Lester Clark Brintnall, Los Angeles, California, for the words "Sunny Twin."

1919   September. Morimura Bros. advertised celluloid dolls and character babies of all sizes.

1919   Sears, Roebuck & Company advertised floating swans and fish -- 6 for 67¢.

1919-1920. Sicoine. Trade name used by Société Industrielle de Celluloid for a non-flammable material for dolls and parts.

1920   John W. Hyatt died.

1920   Yano & Joko made celluloid dolls. New York, New York.

1920s   In Poland. P. R. Zast made celluloid dolls.

1920-1925. Charles N. Roose of Wilmette, Illinois, United States patent for a stuffed doll with hands and feet of rubber with celluloid fingernails.

1922   Minerva metal head had celluloid arms. Japanese celluloid dolls advertised.

1925   Karl Standfuss advertised he was the sole manufacturer of celluloid *Kewpies* and *Bye-Los.*

1925   Circa. Ignac Redo of Budapest manufactured celluloid dolls and toys.

1925   "La Cellulosine" trade name for celluloid dolls and toys distributed by J. Helft, Paris, France.

1926   September 29. Albert Beyler filed for patent. Granted October 11, 1927.

1926   *Baby Bo-Kaye* copyrighted.

1927   Hyatt's company now called Celanese Corporation of America.

1927   Introduction of first plastics based on organic ester of cellulose nitrate to be used for molding by injection.

1927-1935. Winged mermaid symbol. Celba -- Celluloidwarenfabrik. Babenhausen, Germany.

1928   Kämmer & Reinhardt catalog advertised full line of celluloid dolls of all types.

1929   Celluloid dolls by Madame Hendren advertised in a retail catalog.

1930   Dr. Paul Hunaeus factory merged with Rheinische Gummi und Celluloid Fabrik Co.

1930   French doll maker Le Minor in business. Used French celluloid dolls.

1930s   Schreyer & Co. ("Schuco") made celluloid toys.

1934   Rheinische Gummi und Celluloid Fabrik Co. advertised five "Schildkröte" children: *Hans, Cristel* (short hair), *Barbel* (snail braids), *Inge* (bobbed hair) and the baby *Strampelchen* (kicker).

1945-1951. Items from Japan marked "MADE IN OCCUPIED JAPAN."

1945-1951. Items from Germany marked "MADE IN US ZONE GERMANY"

1952   Crowned mermaid symbol used by Cellba, Babenhausen.

1955   Käthe Kruse Tortulon dolls introduced at the Nuremberg Toy Fair.

Thanks must go to the Colemans for many of these dates.

Original Trademarks

The trademarks that have been produced in this book were taken from the dolls. They were drawn by Joyce Kintner. All of them may be found in the book along with the doll from which they were taken. They are identified where possible. Some, like the Parsons-Jackson, need no further identification. These marks may be found in conjunction with other words or numbers.

American Trademarks

THE PARSONS-JACKSON CO.

CLEVELAND, OHIO.

The Parsons-Jackson Company, Cleveland, Ohio, 1910-1918.

Unidentified.

Unidentified.

Unidentified.

Unidentified.

Marks Brothers Co., Boston, Massachusetts, 1918-. Made and imported celluloid heads.

Unidentified.

German Trademarks

GERMANY

Minerva. Registered in Germany by Buschow & Beck, 1888-.

GESCHSCH

Juno. Karl Standfuss, 1904-.

Rheinische Gummi und Celluloid Fabrik Co., 1873-1950+. Mannheim-Neckrau now known as Schildkröte Puppen.

Mark first registered in 1889.

GERMANY

SCHUTZ-MARKE

Mark used after 1891.

SCHUTZ-MARKE

Mark with diamond frame first used in 1899.

Cellba. Celluloidwarenfabrik, Babenhausen, 1952-.

Dr. Paul Hunaeus, 1900-.

GERMANY

J. D. Kestner, Jr., Waltershausen, 1805-.

König & Wernicke, Waltershausen, 1912-.

Bruno Schmidt, Waltershausen, 1900-.

40

E. Maar & Sohn, Mönchroden (near Coburg, Thür), 1917-1925-.

GERMANY

Kämmer & Reinhardt, Waltershausen, 1886-.

Unidentified.

Unidentified.

Petitcolin, circa 1902-1925+.

French Trademarks

FRANCE

Societe Industrielle de Celluloid,
Neumann and Marx, 1902-.

Société Nobel Francaise. Mark
registered in 1939 and again in
1960.

Société Industrielle du Celluloid.

Unidentified.

Additional
Trademarks

Only the "land" was legible on this mark. Unidentified.

Anili Scavini, daughter of Elena and Enrico Scavini, founders of the Lenci factory, Turin, Italy.

Unidentified.

Unidentified.

P. R. Zast, 1920s.

Unidentified.

Japanese Trademarks/Stickers
(None of these marks/stickers have been identified.)

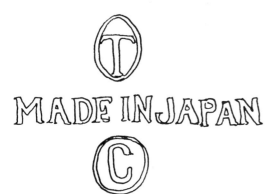

Japanese Trademarks/Stickers
(None of these marks/stickers have been identified.)

MADE IN JAPAN

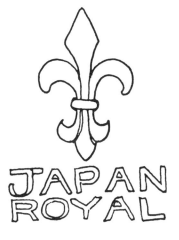

JAPAN ROYAL

MADE IN JAPAN

JAPAN

JAPAN

TRADE MARK

MADE IN JAPAN

MADE IN JAPAN
○ PAT NO 54317

Japanese Trademarks/Stickers
(None of these marks/stickers have been identified.)

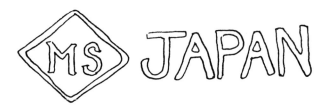

NIPPON

Earliest mark.

MADE IN JAPAN

MADE IN
OCCUPIED
JAPAN

JAPAN

MADE IN
OCCUPIED
JAPAN

Japanese Trademarks/Stickers
(None of these marks/stickers have been identified.)

MADE IN
OCCUPIED
JAPAN

Between 1945 and 1951.

MADE IN
OCCUPIED
JAPAN

MADE IN
OCCUPIED
JAPAN

Red and white paper inspection sticker.

Green and white paper inspection sticker.

Appendix

A book of this type is never completed; new information surfaces constantly. After we had written "finis" to this one, we learned from Dorothy Coleman of research being done in France at CERP, Centre D'Étude et de Recherche sur La Poupée. (Center of Study and Research on Dolls) under the direction of Madame Florence Poisson of the Musée de Roybefould, 178 Blvd. St. Denis, Courbevoie. Their Bulletin # 9, dated February 1983 is the first part of research on French celluloid dolls by Elisabeth Chaveau.

In this bulletin, Chaveau discusses celluloid manufacture in France from its beginning at a factory founded by the Schmerbeer Brothers in Stains, in 1875, to the slow demise of the industry from the 1930s to the 1950s. She lists various firms that made celluloid in the twentieth century and their evolution. We, however, are primarily interested in the celluloid dolls of France and so shall direct our attention to that portion of her work.

Her studies show that, in France, the greatest era for celluloid dolls was from about 1930 until about 1955, with their popularity reaching its peak in the last decade. She credits three major firms with making the finest, most expensive dolls. We have written of Nobel and Petitcolin; she adds another, G. Convert.

In tracing the history of celluloid dolls in France and elsewhere, the author agrees that we do not have precise knowledge of when the first dolls were made, but that W.B. Carpenter in the United States was the first person to patent one. She has an added bit of interesting information, namely that Carpenter applied for the first French patent concerning dolls' heads. It was Patent No. 140.905, dated February 1881, and was for a process for molding articles, including dolls' heads, from celluloid. There is no proof, however, that production commenced at this time.

In Elisabeth Chaveau's discussion of Valmore Boitel's patent of 1887, she reports that he considered himself a supplier of parts, not a dollmaker. It is her opinion, but without proof, that he probably was the first in France to make dolls' heads of celluloid. The same lack of proof of production is cited for other early French patents, namely those of:

Leon Jourlait, a bronze fitter who protected his process for molding dolls' heads from celluloid without any seams by applying for Patent No. 220.752 on April 7, 1892.

Orthon-Henri Kratz-Boussac did the same thing May 14, 1892, with his Patent No. 211.627 concerning a "new" process for making dolls' heads of celluloid in one piece by blow molding them with steam. The drawings attached to the patent are very vague. (There is no explanation as to why the patent number is lower than one applied for at a later date.)

March 11, 1893, the Société Valée and Schultz applied for a similar patent with a system for unmolding and removing the heads from the molds.

November 13, 1893, Mandel and Sichert applied for Patent No. 234.019 that seems to be mainly concerned with making toys of celluloid, but does include "dolls and dolls' heads."

The first trademark that is recorded in France for a celluloid doll would seem to be that of the Widow Chalory. June 10, 1893, she applied for a patent (No. 230.073) for a celluloid doll which she called "Bébé Leger sans Rival." ("Light Baby without Compare.") This was also the first time that anyone had specified in a patent application that the applicant was a maker of dolls. Madame Chalory was so listed in the Almanac of Commerce for the years 1893 through 1896. Her address was # 32 Rue Pastourelle in the heart of the doll making district, and on the same street as Maison Jumeau, listed at #38 Rue Pastourelle.

Madame Chalory claimed that dolls had become indispensable toys for children, but that the main shortcoming of dolls made of the usual materials, such as carton (cardboard), papier-mâché, leather, wood, rubber, stone, porcelain, etc., was their weight. She said they were too heavy for a small child to carry around without becoming tired. Therefore, she had utilized a new material, celluloid, to fabricate a doll that was two-thirds lighter than its counterparts and that small children would now be able to carry their dolls without becoming tired. She claimed the material was unalterable and unbreakable, that it was an ivory color, and that it had the elasticity of rubber and if a child dropped its celluloid doll or walked on it, it would return to its original form!!!

Unfortunately, no dolls have ever been found with this mark. Perhaps it was printed on the box or on a removable label.

Elisabeth Chaveau traced the origins of the company G. Convert that she lists as one of the three great firms producing celluloid dolls. According to references in the Almanac of Commerce, it had its beginnings in 1878 when Charles Bernadac showed celluloid combs at an exposition in Paris. In 1880 he moved to Paris and made combs and other bibelots. In 1895 his associate and successor, Charles Tissier, made combs, balls and toys of celluloid. In 1904 Anel and Fraisse, associates of Tissier and Sons, were active at the same address. In 1905 Anel and Fraisse, successors of Tissier, moved to another address. Anel was listed at the same address in 1920, and Anel and Sons of the same address had a factory at Oyonnaux in 1922.

It is definite that Anel or its predecessors were making toys in 1895 and that by 1913 they were making dolls, for there were advertisements stating this. They were the non-articulated "bathers" and articulated dolls with molded clothes.

In 1925 at the International Exposition of Decorative Arts, Anel showed a variety of dolls in the Village of The Toys. The theme of the Exposition, "Land of the Sun," may have influenced the display of many black dolls, "their expressions resembling the 'Kewpies' " and jungle animals. Chaveau considers Anel the best example of the first kind of celluloid dolls which were made in this period, but says Anel was not to know the great period of popularity of the celluloid doll in France, the years of the 1930s, for the company was purchased by G. Convert in 1933-34.

She declares that even though there were several great factories producing celluloid, there is no proof that they made dolls in the early years of the twentieth century. It is possible that Société Industrielle de Celluloid made them in 1902, and certain that they did in 1909. In fact, celluloid dolls were not terribly popular in France when they first appeared, and early dolls usually have German marks. Celluloid dolls do not appear in store catalogs until 1908-1910 and, naturally, these catalogs are not good research references because they seldom are dated and do not usually reveal the name of the manufacturer.

In seeking further information, the author asked some French women of various ages about their recollections of celluloid dolls. Interestingly, those born between 1895 and 1904 did not remember them, but those born between 1905 and 1910 did remember having celluloid dolls, but they were always of a small size. These statements coincide with that of M. Louis Convert, a retired director of G. Convert, that their firm began making celluloid dolls in 1911, and Petitcolin in 1907, and Société Industrielle de Celluloid about 1909.

The first celluloid dolls to appear in the catalogs of department stores in France around 1908-1910 were celluloid masks on plush bodies. They seemed to be for small children and were called "Eskimo Babies," or "North Pole Babies." They were unbreakable and washable.

The regular type of doll in this period usually had a celluloid shoulder head and a body of composition, wood, kid, or stuffed cloth. They were made in the same manner as the popular porcelain dolls, but, she says, they were usually of German manufacture.

Celluloid toys did not seem to be too successful before 1914. Perhaps this was because many of the factories making celluloid were called into production for the war effort, although in France, SIC was the only firm requisitioned to make explosives.

Advertisements show that in 1932 celluloid dolls were cheaper than those of porcelain.

The greatest period of popularity of celluloid dolls in France was just before World War II, until about 1955, but in the latter part of this period the material became too highly colored and the bodies were not gracefully articulated. Plastic dolls were advertised in the department store catalogs in 1951, and some of them were the same models that were used for celluloid dolls.

I must express my appreciation to Mr. Raymond Mouly for his assistance in translating the material onto tape for me in order for the information from the CERP bulletin to be made available in time to be published here.

SHB

Bibliography

General Reference Books

Angione, Genevieve, and Whorton, Judith. *All Dolls are Collectible*. New York: Crown Publishers, Inc., 1977.

Cadbury, Betty. *Playthings Past*. England: David and Charles, 1976.

Chemical Technology. Vol. 5. New York: John Wiley & Sons, 1972. "Ivory / Imitations of Natural Materials."

_____ . *Vol. 6*. New York: John Wiley & Sons, 1973. "Synthetic Resins & Plastics."

Coleman, Elizabeth A. *Dolls - Makers and Marks*. Washington, D.C.: Dorothy S. Coleman, 1963.

_____ . Addenda to *Dolls - Makers and Marks*. Washington, D.C.: Dorothy S. Coleman, 1966.

Coleman, Evelyn, Elizabeth, and Dorothy. *The Age of Dolls*. Washington, D.C.: Dorothy S. Coleman, 1965.

Coleman, Dorothy S., Elizabeth A., and Evelyn J. *The Collector's Encyclopedia of Dolls*. New York: Crown Publishers Inc., 1968.

Eaton, Faith. *Dolls in Color*. New York: MacMillan Publishing Co., Inc., 1975.

Encyclopedia of Chemical Technology, Third Edition, Vol. 5. New York: John Wiley & Sons, 1979. "Cellulose Derivatives -- Inorganic Esters."

Encyclopedia of Polymer Science & Technology, Vol. 3. New York: John Wiley & Sons, 1965. "Cellulose Esters, Inorganic Plastics."

_____ . *Vol. 6*. New York: John Wiley & Sons, 1967. "Plastics."

Fawcett, Clara Hallard. *Dolls, A New Guide for Collectors*. Boston: Charles T. Branford Company, 1964.

Fraser, Antonia. *Dolls, Pleasures and Treasures*. New York: G. P. Putnam's Sons, 1963.

Freeman, Ruth. *American Dolls*. Watkins Glen, NY: Century House, 1952.

Gordon, Lesley. *A Pageant of Dolls*. New York: A. A. Wyn, Inc., 1949.

Hart, Luella. *Directory of British Dolls*. USA: Publisher unknown, 1964.

Hillier, Mary. *Dolls and Doll Makers*. New York: G. P. Putnam's Sons, 1968.

Johl, Janet Pagter. *The Fascinating Story of Dolls*. Watkins Glen, NY: Century House, 1941.

King, Constance Eileen. *The Collector's History of Dolls*. New York: St. Martin's Press, Inc., 1978.

_____ . *Dolls and Dolls' Houses*. London: The Hamlyn Publishing Group, Limited, 1977.

Lewis, Mary E. *The Marriage of Diamonds and Dolls*. New York: H.L. Lindquist, 1947.

Long, Luman H., Editor. *The World Almanac*. Cleveland: Newspaper Enterprise Association, Inc., 1968.

Merrill, Madeline, and Perkins, Nellie. *Handbook of Collectible Dolls*. USA: Woodward and Miller, Inc., 1969.

Revi, Albert Christian, Editor. *Spinning Wheel's Complete Book of Dolls*. Hanover, PA: Everybody's Press, 1975.

Schoonmaker, Patricia N. *Research on Kämmer & Reinhardt Dolls*. USA: Patricia N. Schoonmaker, 1965.

____ . *Further Research on Kämmer & Reinhardt Dolls*. USA: Patricia N. Schoonmaker, 1969.

Schroeder, Joseph J. Jr., Editor. *The Wonderful World of Toys, Games, and Dolls*. Chicago: Follett Publishing Co., 1971.

Von Boehn, Max. *Dolls and Puppets,* Revised Edition. Boston: Charles T. Branford Company, 1956.

(Continued on next page)

Articles of Special Interest (Listed by author)

Abbott, Jennie L. "Celluloid Dolls," *Dolls,* The Doll Collectors of America, Inc. (1946).

Hart, Luella. "Celluloid Turtle Marked Käethe (sic) Kruse Dolls," *Doll News,* Vol. IV, No. 2, United Federation of Doll Clubs, Inc. (February, 1956).

Hart, Luella. "Directory of United States Doll Trademarks, 1888-1968," *Spinning Wheel's Complete Book of Dolls* (1968).

Hillier, Mary. "Don't Despise Those Celluloid Dolls," *Doll Reader,* Vol. VIII, No. 6, Hobby House Press, Inc. (October/November, 1980).

Luckey, Pauline. "Celluloid Dolls of Europe, Part I," *Doll News,* Vol. XXX, No. 3, United Federation of Doll Clubs, Inc. (Summer 1981).

_____ . "Celluloid Dolls of Europe, Part II," *Doll News,* Vol. XXX, No. 4, United Federation of Doll Clubs, Inc. (Fall 1981).

McFadden, Sybill. "Celluloid Dolls with Character Faces," *Doll Castle News* (July/August 1980).

Merrill, Madeline. "Baby Dolls," *Doll Collectors Manual 1967,* Doll Collectors of America, Inc.

_____ . Section of "Interesting Dolls," *Doll Collectors Manual 1956-57,* Doll Collectors of America, Inc.

Metzger, Beverly Ann. "Hyatt's 'Celluloid', 1868 to 1920," *The Antique Trader,* Vol. 24, Issue 17 (April 23, 1980).

"New American Industries, Celluloid Toys," *Playthings* (March 1916).

Painter, Paul C. "From Guncotton to Bakelite -- The Early History of Polymer Science," *Earth & Mineral Sciences,* Vol. 49, #6 (July/August 1980).

Pickup, Marion W. "Beyond the Rainbow," *Doll Collectors Manual 1964,* Doll Collectors of America, Inc.

Polley, Jennie. "Ohio Dolls and Doll Makers, Part II," *UFDC Region 12 Souvenir Book* (1972).

Shorrock, Eugenia S. "Celluloid Dolls," *Doll Collectors Manual 1973,* Doll Collectors of America, Inc.

Tomkins, Dorothy. "The American Heritage of Dolls," *UFDC Region 12 Souvenir Book* (1976).

Pamphlet

180 Years of Sewing. Switzerland: Bernica Sewing Machine Co.

Catalog Reprints

Kämmer & Reinhardt -- 1928. California: Doll Research Projects.

"My Darling" Dolls. Kämmer & Reinhardt, 1927. (Introduction by Dorothy S. Coleman.) Princeton: The Pyne Press.

1914 Marshall Field & Company Doll Catalog. Cumberland, MD: Hobby House Press, Inc.

1902 Sears & Roebuck Co. Catalog. New York: Crown Publishers, Inc.

Index